Islam in Israel

Islam is the religion of the majority of Arab citizens in Israel and since the late 1970s has become an important factor in their political and socio-cultural identity. This leads to an increasing number of Muslims in Israel who define their identity first and foremost in relation to their religious affiliation. By examining this evolving religious identity during the past four decades and its impact on the religious and socio-cultural aspects of Muslim life in Israel, Muhammad al-Atawneh and Nohad 'Ali explore the local nature of Islam. They find that Muslims in Israel seem to rely heavily on the prominent Islamic authorities in the region, perhaps more so than minority Muslims elsewhere. This stems, *inter alia*, from the fact that Muslims in Israel are the only minority that lives in a land they consider to be holy and see themselves as a natural extension of the Middle Eastern Arab Islamic community.

MUHAMMAD AL-ATAWNEH is an associate professor in the Department of Middle East Studies at Ben-Gurion University of the Negev, Israel. He has published extensively on Islamic law and society in contemporary Arab and Islamic worlds. Research interests focus on the study of Islam in modern times, mainly in three concurrent areas: (1) Islamic law and modernity; (2) state and governance in contemporary Islamic thought and practice; and (3) Islam in Israel which cover significant issues regarding Muslim daily life, attitudes, beliefs, levels of (dis)satisfaction, and attitudes towards the Israeli establishment and Israeli society.

NOHAD ALI is a senior lecturer in the Department of Sociology and Anthropology at the Western Galilee College and senior researcher at the Jewish–Arab Center at the University of Haifa. He is the Head of the Arab-Jewish-State Unit at the Samuel Neaman Institute, Technion. He is an expert on religious fundamentalism (Jewish and Islamic in Israel), political Islam, Jewish–Arab relations in Israel, Arab women, and violence.

Advance Praise for *Islam in Israel*

"The case of a non-dominant Muslim minority in a highly secular, Jewish and Zionist state, in an Islam-endowed land, is historically unprecedented and unparalleled. *Islam in Israel* is the first book that tells us how Muslim Arabs conduct themselves under these inhospitable and unique circumstances."

Professor Sammy Smooha, University of Haifa

"Israel's 1.2 million Muslims are a unique population in the Middle East. In this exciting and timely book, Al-Atawneh and Ali provide the scholarly community with its first comprehensive look at the Muslim religious identity in Israel. Through richly detailed survey data, interviews and narrative insight, they show how Israeli Muslims have developed in relation to broader regional trends in Islam as well as to the experience of living in the Jewish state."

Professor Rameez Abbas, The National Defense University, Washington DC

"Al-Atawneh and Ali present us with a sterling and erudite analysis of a unique Muslim minority trapped in a complex political situation. This is a must-read for scholars and laymen who are grappling to understand contemporary Islam as politics and identity in non-Muslim states. A tour de force!"

Professor Nimrod Luz, Western Galilee College

"This book is a significant contribution to the study of three areas of theoretical interest: Muslims and Islam in general, and in Israel as a Jewish state in particular; minorities in general, and the Palestinian minority in Israel in particular; and interactions between religious groups in a religiously divided reality, such as that among Palestinians in Israel. Questions of coping with the challenges of modernity, attitudes towards others, processes of return to religion, and the development of a unique heritage that fits the political/social context are discussed at length, in a manner that has not been discussed so far. The authors systematically use a variety of quantitative, qualitative methodologies, anthropological observations and their own involvement in the field in order to provide us with a diverse and real account of the lives of Muslims in Israel. There is no doubt that the contribution of the authors and the book is absolutely vital to any student who has an interest in the aforementioned fields of interest."

Professor As'ad Ghanem, University of Haifa

Islam in Israel

Muslim Communities in Non-Muslim States

Muhammad Al-Atawneh

Ben-Gurion University of the Negev

Nohad Ali

Western Galilee College and University of Haifa

CAMBRIDGE
UNIVERSITY PRESS

CAMBRIDGE
UNIVERSITY PRESS

University Printing House, Cambridge CB2 8BS, United Kingdom

One Liberty Plaza, 20th Floor, New York, NY 10006, USA

477 Williamstown Road, Port Melbourne, VIC 3207, Australia

314–321, 3rd Floor, Plot 3, Splendor Forum, Jasola District Centre, New Delhi - 110025, India

79 Anson Road, #06-04/06, Singapore 079906

Cambridge University Press is part of the University of Cambridge.

It furthers the University's mission by disseminating knowledge in the pursuit of education, learning and research at the highest international levels of excellence.

www.cambridge.org
Information on this title: www.cambridge.org/9781108423267
DOI: 10.1017/9781108525671

First published 2018

Printed in the United Kingdom by Clays, St Ives plc

A catalogue record for this publication is available from the British Library.

Library of Congress Cataloging-in-Publication data
Names: Al-Atawneh, Muhammad K., author. | Ali, Nohad, author.
Title: Islam in Israel : Muslim communities in non-Muslim states / Muhammad Al-Atawneh, Nohad Ali.
Description: New York : Cambridge University Press, 2018. | Includes bibliographical references and index.
Identifiers: LCCN 2017034614 | ISBN 9781108423267 (hardback)
Subjects: LCSH: Islam   Israel. | Muslims   Israel.
Classification: LCC BP63.I8 A43   2018 | DDC 305.6/97095694 – dc23
LC record available at https://lccn.loc.gov/2017034614

ISBN 978-1-108-42326-7 Hardback

To Nimrod Hurvitz, a scholar of depth and
a man of style.

Contents

Figures

Tables

Acknowledgments

The work on this book began a few years ago. Throughout this process we were supported by a number of individuals, institutions, and research centers that helped us make it a reality. Its publication was possible thanks to the support of the Israel Science Foundation (ISF). We are also indebted to the following institutions for their assistance: the Herzog Center, the Center for Islamic Studies (CIS) at al-Qasemi College, and the Department of Middle East Studies at the Ben-Gurion University of the Negev.

We are very grateful to our entire research staff, who provided intensive field work, proofreading, and book-design concepts. Special thanks go to Ethelea Katzenell, our English editor, a constructive sounding-board and apt critic throughout the long book-preparation process. We also offer our thanks to Rimma' Da'as, our statistician, for her expertise, insightful comments, and suggestions. We applaud all the members of the field staff for the intensive efforts they made to collect the relevant materials: Afnan Hajj 'Ali, Nariman Diab, Mona Rabiaa, Rana Da'abess, Maisoon Hajj, Adi Ali, Mohammed Faour, Amir Ali, Maher Hushan, Rifa'at Bakria, and Mariam al-Aoubra.

Thanks are also due to Qadi 'Abd al-Hakeem Samarah, Qadi Eyad Zahalka, Rida Jaber, Shaykh Eyad 'Amer, Shaykh Ziad Abu Mukh, Shaykh Kamel Rayan, Shaykh Mofeed Abu Mukh, Shaykh Husein Muhammadi, Shaykh Muhammad Shehadeh, and Naief Sharkiya. Next, we offer our gratitude to the following colleagues for their valuable comments and advice: Asa'd Ghanem, Galit Gordoni, Ido Liberman, Ido Shahar, Khalid Ghanaiem, Khalid Mahmoud, Meir Hatina, Musa Abou Ramadan, Rassem Khamaisi, Sammy Smooha, Sarhan al-Atawneh, Yitzhak Reiter, and Yuval Feinshtein. Needless to say, any mistakes remain our own.

Finally, we would like to thank our families for their ongoing support and for their patience with our absences from home and preoccupation with this study. We are indebted also to the editorial staff at Cambridge University Press, especially Maria Marsh, the editor-in-chief, and the anonymous readers of the early draft of this book.

Notes on Transliteration and Translation

This book follows the transliteration standards of the *International Journal of Middle East Studies*. Arabic terms are italicized, except for those that recur often, such as Shari'a, 'ulama', qadi, and fatwa; ' is used for 'ayn and ' for the hamza. No subscript or superscript diacritics are used. Definitions of the Arabic terms are provided when they are first used, either in the text or in a bibliographical footnote.

Direct translations from the Arabic were initially made by the authors and then rendered into better English by the English editor. All the English translations of Qur'anic verses were done by 'Abdullah Yusuf 'Ali.*

---

* The English translations of Qur'anic verses are taken from 'Abdullah Yusuf 'Ali, *The Holy Qur'an* (Brentwood, Md.: Amana Corporation, 1989).

Notes on Transliteration and Translation

Introduction

This book examines the evolution of Islamic religious identity over the past four decades and its impact on the socio-cultural aspects of Muslim life in Israel. It focuses on the evolving role of Islam in the construction of an Islamic minority identity in Israel and on the impact of that newly developed Islamic identity as it has become integrated into religious and socio-cultural spheres since the 1970s. It investigates the means by which the Muslim minority relates to the challenges imposed by modernity within the non-Islamic context.[1] In addition, the present research draws on a public-opinion survey, to expand our understanding of popular Islam and of how Islam is perceived by the general public. This book is also based on analyses of religio-legal texts published by local and foreign religious scholars, who interpret Islam for the Muslim minority in Israel.

Islam is the religion of the majority of the Arab citizens in Israel. According to the latest Israeli Central Bureau of Statistics reports, there are 1.3 million Muslims in Israel, comprising about 83 percent of the Arab population residing across the country.[2] During this period Islam has become an important factor in the political and socio-cultural identity of the Arab minority in Israel; the number of Muslims in Israel who define their identity, first and foremost, in relation to their religious affiliation has steadily grown.[3] Muhammad Amara noted, for example, that today "the Arab minority in Israel places great emphasis on Islam as

---

[1] See John Voll, *Islam: Continuity and Change in the Modern World* (Boulder: Westview Press, 1982).

[2] According to the recent reports by the Israeli Bureau of Statistics, the Israeli population comprises 75.5 percent Jews, 20.3 percent Arabs, and 4.1 percent other: Central Bureau of Statistics, *Statistical Abstract of Israel*, no. 61, 2010; more on the Arab community in Israel in Amal Jamal, "The political ethos of Palestinian citizens of Israel: critical reading in the future vision documents," *Israeli Studies Forum* 23 (2) (2008): 3–28.

[3] As'ad Ghanem, *The Palestinian-Arab Minority in Israel, 1948–2000: A Political Study* (New York: State University of New York Press, 2001), 124; Gershon Shafir and Yoav Peled, *Being Israeli: The Dynamics of Multiple Citizenship* (Cambridge: Cambridge University Press, 2002), 111.

a factor in their identity, more than during any other period."[4] This is manifested by a sharp increase in the number of Islamic associations, mosques, cultural centers, schools, and academic religious institutions in Israel, such as al-Qasemi Academic College of Education in Baqa al-Gharbiyya and the Da'wa College for Islamic Studies in Umm al-Fahm. Students may even travel abroad to study Islam, mainly in the West Bank, Egypt, Jordan, and Turkey.

Islamic movements have been active in Israel since the late 1970s.[5] Today, political Islam is considered one of the major political forces of the Arab Muslim minority in Israel, with representatives in the Knesset (the Israeli parliament).[6] Since the early 1980s these movements have taken power in several Arab localities and succeeded in raising the standard of their local services.[7] Abbas Zakkur, a Knesset Member (KM) on behalf of the Islamic Movement (IM) in Israel, maintains that the movement aims to introduce Islam to the Muslims in Israel – to teach them about their religion in an attempt to re-create an Islamic ethos, an Islamic social order.[8] In the same vein, Shaykh Kamal Khatib, the vice-president of the northern branch of the Islamic Movement (NIM), added:

The Islamic Movement initially functions as a service to our people, through associations that we have established all over the country... We have clinics, ambulances and sports clubs for karate and soccer... in many Arab villages... We seek, by means of the abilities of our people, to build our own institutions and to maintain our own identity.[9]

Given the current momentum of religious trends, this study will elaborate on the various aspects of the religious life and practices of the Muslim minority in Israel. Emphasis will be placed on popular Islam

---

[4] Muhammad Amara, "The collective identity of the Arabs in Israel in an era of peace," *Israel Affairs* 9 (2003): 249–262, at 249.

[5] See Ibrahim Malik, *The Islamic Movement in Israel: Between Fundamentalism and Pragmatism* (Givat Haviva: Institute for Arabic Studies, 1990) [Hebrew]; Mahmoud Mi'ari, "al-Haraka al-islamiyya fi Isra'il," *Shu'un Filistiniya* 215–216 (1991): 3–15 [Arabic]; for more on the emergence of contemporary social movements see Alberto Melucci, "The symbolic challenge of contemporary movements," *Social Research* 52 (1985): 790–816.

[6] See Tilde Rosmer, "The Islamic movement in the Jewish state," in Khaled Hroub (ed.), *Political Islam: Context versus Ideology* (London: Saqi Books/London Middle East Institute, 2010), 182–209; Elie Rekhess, "The Islamic movement in Israel: the internal debate over representation in the Knesset," *Data and Analysis* 2 (Tel Aviv: Moshe Dayan Center, 1996): 1–5; Elie Rekhess, "The politicization of Israel's Arabs," in Alouph Hareven (ed.), *Every Sixth Israeli: Relations between the Jewish Majority and the Arab Minority in Israel* (Jerusalem: Van Leer Jerusalem Foundation, 1983), 135–142.

[7] Dan Rabinowitz, "Umm-al-Fahm: dilemmas of change," *ha-Mizrah he-Hadash* 37 (1995): 169–179 [Hebrew]. On the Arab local authorities in Israel see Maha al-Taji, "Arab Local Authorities in Israel: Hamulas, Nationalism and Dilemmas of Social Change," Ph. D. thesis (Seattle: University of Washington, 2008).

[8] Rosmer, "The Islamic Movement."   [9] Ibid.

and how ordinary Muslims perceive their religion, their Islamic identity, and their relationship with the Jewish Israeli majority. Several research questions are at the hub of our investigation: What is the legal and theological nature of Islam in Israel? What is the primary religious authority for Muslims in Israel? To what extent has Islam shaped the identity of the Arab minority in the state of Israel? How does all this affect the socio-cultural aspects of Muslim life in Israel?

The State of the Art

A quick glance at Islamic scholarship in Israel indicates that Muslim scholars have placed great emphasis on political Islam and on the role of the Islamic Movement in local politics, while much less attention has been paid to the evolution of Islamic religio-legal identity and its impact on the socio-cultural aspects of the Muslim minority in Israel.[10] Scholars' explanations of the Islamic revival (*sahwa*) in Israel may be divided into two major approaches. The first relies heavily on the global Islamic

---

[10] Important works in these fields include Elie Rekhess and Arik Rudnitzky (eds.), *Muslim Minorities in Non-Muslim Majority Countries: The Islamic Movement in Israel as a Test Case* (Tel Aviv: Moshe Dayan Center, 2013); Laurence Louër, *To Be an Arab in Israel* (London: Hurst, 2007); Shafir and Peled, *Being Israeli;* Alisa Rubin-Peled, *Debating Islam in the Jewish State: The Development of Policy toward Islamic Institutions in Israel* (Albany: State University of New York Press, 2001); Sammy Smooha and As'ad Ghanem, *Ethnic, Religious and Political Islam among the Arabs in Israel* (Haifa: University of Haifa Press, 1998); Elie Rekhess (ed.), *The Arabs in Israeli Politics: Dilemmas of Identity* (Tel Aviv: Moshe Dayan Center, 1998) [Hebrew]; Nadim Rouhana, *Palestinian Citizens in an Ethnic Jewish State: Identities in Conflict* (New Haven: Yale University Press, 1997); Michael Dumper, *Islam and Israel: Muslim Religious Endowments and the Jewish State* (Washington, D.C.: Institute for Palestine Studies, 1994); Raphael Israeli, *Muslim Fundamentalism in Israel* (London: Brassey's, 1993); Raphael Israeli, "Muslim fundamentalists as social revolutionaries: the case of Israel," *Terrorism and Political Violence* 6 (4) (1994): 462–475; Ian Lustick, *Arabs in the Jewish State: Israel's Control of a National Minority* (Austin: University of Texas Press, 1980).
A subject that drew less attention from the scholars is that of the Shari'a courts in Israel. Important works in this field include Aharon Layish, *Legal Documents from the Judean Desert: The Impact of Shari'a on Bedouin Customary Law* (Leiden and Boston: Brill, 2011); Aharon Layish, "The adaptation of religious law to modern times in a strange ambiance: *Shari'a* in Israel," *Divre ha-Akademiyah ha-Le'umit ha-Yisre'elit le-Mada'im* 9 (2) (2005): 13–51 [Hebrew]; Ido Shahar, *Legal Pluralism in the Holy City: Competing Courts, Forum Shopping, and Institutional Dynamics in Jerusalem* (Farnham: Ashgate, 2015); Raphael Israeli, "The impact of Islamic fundamentalism on the Arab–Israeli conflict," *Jerusalem Viewpoints* (Jerusalem Center for Public Affairs 1988): 1–6; Sammy Smooha, "The Arab minority in Israel: radicalization or politicization?" *Studies in Contemporary Jewry* 5 (1989): 1–21; Sammy Smooha and As'ad Ghanem, "Political Islam among the Arabs in Israel," in Theodor Hanf (ed.), *Dealing with Difference: Religion, Ethnicity and Politics – Comparing Cases and Concepts* (Baden-Baden: Nomos Verlagsgesellschaft, 1999), 143–173; Muhammad Amara, "The nature of Islamic fundamentalism in Israel," *Terrorism and Political Violence* 8 (2) (1996): 155–170.

revival of the past four decades.[11] Bernard Lewis argues, for example, that the Islamic movements activated during the second half of the twentieth century were rooted in the universal belief in the unity of 'church and state' and that Islam formed the central element in Muslim identity. According to Lewis, Islamic movements in the modern period, including the pan-Islamism of the Ottoman sultan ʿAbd al-ʿAziz I in the 1870s, the rise of the Egyptian Muslim Brotherhood in the 1930s, and the Iranian Revolution of 1977–1979, were manifestations of this universality and centrality.[12] Elie Rekhess asserts that there are strong ties between different Islamic movements, including those that are active among the Arab Muslims in Israel and their Palestinian counterparts in the West Bank and Gaza Strip. He states that political Islam in Israel is merely a branch of general Palestinian Islamic fundamentalism – that is, these Islamic movements share the same characteristics.[13] In the same vein, David Bukay adds that there is only one Islamic culture and that there is no difference between various groups of Islamic activists, even in their interpretations of religious texts.[14]

The second approach is that of a group of scholars who acknowledge the uniqueness of Islam and of the Islamic Movement in Israel. According to them, although political Islam in Israel is part of the general revival of Islamic fundamentalism (which began in the 1970s), it still has special characteristics rooted in the Israeli experience of the Arab minority, including the development of the Islamic Movement in the Jewish state, with its clear Jewish political and cultural hegemony.[15] For Sammy Smooha and Asʿad Ghanem, "political Islam varies from one place to another and its exact nature is determined by specific and historical circumstances. In Israel, it is strongly restrained by political democracy and the ultimate Jewish control of the state and society."[16]

---

[11] See Mazen Hashem, "Contemporary Islamic activism: the shades of praxis," *Sociology of Religion* 67 (1) (2006): 23–41.

[12] Bernard Lewis, *Islam and the West* (Oxford: Oxford University Press, 1993), 133–154.

[13] Elie Rekhess, "Political Islam in Israel and its connection to the Islamic Movement in the territories," in Elie Rekhess (ed.), *The Arabs in Israeli Politics: Dilemmas of Identity* (Tel Aviv: Tel Aviv University, 1998), 73–84 [Hebrew].

[14] David Bukay (ed.), *Muhammad's Monsters: A Comprehensive Guide to Radical Islam for Western Audiences* (Green Forest, Ark.: Balfour Books, 2004), 7–24; see also Gilles Kepel, *Allah in the West: Islamic Movements in America and Europe* (Cambridge: Polity Press, 1997).

[15] Nohad ʿAli, "Political Islam in an ethnic Jewish state: its historical evolution, contemporary challenges and future prospects," *Holy Land Studies* 3 (1) (2004): 69–92; on political Islam in general see Bernard Lewis, *The Political Language of Islam* (Chicago: University of Chicago Press, 1988).

[16] Smooha and Ghanem, "Political Islam," 144.

Nohad 'Ali, a native sociologist, and co-author of this book, argues that although the shared and universal ideology of the Islamic revival movements was adopted by the Islamic Movement in Israel, the movement has been trying to express itself in diverse and distinctive ways. In principle, there is a conflict between the commitment to the principle of Islamic revivalism, on the one hand, and to the secular laws of the ethnic Jewish state, on the other.[17] Furthermore, 'Ali claims that the Jewish context of the state of Israel continues to bedevil the development of the Islamic Movement in Israel. He adds that, since the 1930s, Islamic revivalism in Palestine has undergone five phases of development: Egyptian, Israeli, Palestinian, and two phases of 'adaptation' and 'post-adaptation'. These phases reflect ideological developments, rather than simple historical evolution. They are also the outcome of three sets of constraints: structural, ideological, and domestic.[18]

Alisa Rubin-Peled outlined the Israeli government's approach to Islamic activism, arguing that Israeli officials implement a system of strict centralized control on Islam and the Muslim minority in Israel, effectively preventing the emergence of a national Muslim leadership or an independent religious educational system.[19]

On the socio-cultural, ideological, and religio-legal aspects of Islam, one finds a few studies that focus mainly on ideological discrepancies within the Islamic Movement in Israel – issues of identity, Islamic law vis-à-vis Israeli secular law and the Shari'a courts. 'Issam Aburaiya, for example, sheds important light on the ideological motives behind the Islamic Movement's split in 1996.[20] Muhammad Amara and Izhak Schnell describe the religious aspect of identity in the Arab minority in Israel. Taking an approach that considers identity to be a multi-dimensional phenomenon, they argue that religion is an important factor for Arab Muslim minority in Israel.[21] Nadim Ruhana elaborates on the complexities and conflicts regarding identity amid the Muslim

---

[17] See Ziyad Asaliyya, "Athar al-qawanin al-isra'iliyya fi al-qada' al-shar'i fi Isra'il," MA thesis (Hebron: Hebron University, 2003) [Arabic]; on the implementation of Islamic law in Israel see Yitzhak Reiter, "Qadis and the implementation of Islamic law in present-day Israel," in R. Gleave and E. Kermeli (eds.), *Islamic Law: Theory and Practice* (London: I. B. Tauris, 1997), 205–231.

[18] Smooha and Ghanem, "Political Islam," 144.

[19] Rubin-Peled, *Debating Islam in the Jewish State*, 3.

[20] 'Issam Aburaiya, "The 1996 split of the Islamic Movement in Israel: between the holy text and Israeli–Palestinian context," *International Journal of Politics, Culture, and Society* 17 (3) (2004): 439–455, at 450–451.

[21] Muhammad Amara and Izhak Schnell, "Identity repertoire among Arabs in Israel," *Journal of Ethnic and Migration Studies* 30 (2003): 175–194.

minority in Israel.[22] Sammy Smooha and As'ad Ghanem provide a valuable account of the influence of political Islam on ethnic and religious Islam.[23] Aharon Layish, Musa Abou Ramadan, Ido Shahar, and other scholars focus on Islamic law and its implementation in the Shari'a courts in Israel.[24]

Methodology

Note the application of sociological, anthropological, and cultural methods, such as those anchored in the groundbreaking papers of Clifford Geertz (1968, 1993), Peter Brown (1981, 1995) and Victor Turner (1995) regarding religious culture and ritual sites,[25] and of Mary Douglas (1966) and, in her wake, of Emmanuel Sivan (1995) about "enclave culture."[26] The various theories suggested by these studies have significantly enriched the study of Islam and Islamic societies, yet they have barely touched upon Islamic research in Israel. Studies applying social history, or quantitative methods, or providing anthropological fieldwork, are scarce.[27]

---

[22] Rouhana, *Palestinian Citizens in an Ethnic Jewish State*; Nadim Rouhana, "Accentuated identities in protracted conflicts: the collective identity of the Palestinian citizens in Israel," *Asian and African Studies* 27 (1993): 97–12; Nadim Rouhana and As'ad Ghanem, "The crisis of minorities in an ethnic state: the case of the Palestinian citizens in Israel," *International Journal of Middle East Studies* 30 (3) (1998): 321–346.

[23] More on today's political Islam in Olivier Roy, *The Failure of Political Islam* (Cambridge, Mass.: Harvard University Press, 1994); Michael Salla, "Political Islam and the West: a new 'cold war' or convergence?" *Third World Quarterly* 18 (4) (1997): 729–742; Emad Eldin Shahin, *Political Ascent: Contemporary Islamic Movements in North Africa* (Boulder: Westview Press, 1997).

[24] See Musa Abou Ramadan, "Notes on the anomaly of the Shari'a field in Israel," *Islamic Law and Society* 15 (2008): 84–111; Musa Abou Ramadan, "Judicial activism of the Shari'a an Appeals Court in Israel (1994–2001): rise and crisis," *Fordham International Law Journal* 27 (1) (2003): 254–298.

[25] Clifford Geertz, *Islam Observed: Religious Development in Morocco and Indonesia* (Chicago: University of Chicago Press, 1968); Clifford Geertz, *The Interpretation of Cultures* (New York: Basic Books, 1973); Peter Brown, *The Cult of the Saints: Its Rise and Function in Latin Christianity* (Chicago: University of Chicago Press, 1981); Peter Brown, *Authority and the Sacred Aspects of the Christianisation of the Roman World* (Cambridge: Cambridge University Press, 1995); Victor Turner, *The Ritual Process: Structure and Anti-Structure* (Piscataway, NJ: Transaction, 1995).

[26] Mary Douglas, *Purity and Danger: An Analysis of the Concepts of Pollution and Taboo* (London: Routledge, 1966); Emmanuel Sivan, "The enclave culture," in Martin E. Marty and R. Scott Appleby (eds.), *Fundamentalisms Comprehended* (Chicago: University of Chicago Press, 1995), 11–63.

[27] For more on this see Inbal Tal, "Women's Activism in the Islamic Movement in Israel, 1983–2007: Influences, Characteristics and Implications," Ph.D. thesis (Haifa: Haifa University, 2011) [Hebrew]; Inbal Tal, *Spreading the Movement's Message: Women's Activism in the Islamic Movement in Israel* (Tel Aviv: Moshe Dayan Center, 2015)

Meanwhile, by focusing on the Islamic Movement, the existing research has adopted a very narrow approach, taking a 'top-down' political view, starting with the elites and their institutions and dealing much less with the middle and lower classes. These researchers present sociocultural observations and investigate minor ideological trends, internal tensions, intergenerational struggles, and the social networks created by Islamic activism. All the aforementioned are meant to provide a more dynamic and complex picture of dogmatism and renewal, conformity and opposition.

Moreover, the Arab Muslim public in Israel has undergone a number of acculturation processes, according to the studies published by Aziz Haidar, Henry Rosenfeld, and Reuven Kahane.[28] This acculturation is manifested in the increased adoption of modern lifestyles influenced by ongoing contact with the Jewish environment in the realms of: education, culture, economics, and politics. As such, it is possible to assume that, despite the attempts of the Islamic Movement to bolster the religious identity of the Arabs in Israel, it was not able to unite all the Muslims under its auspices, nor to gain seniority for itself. A good explanation of this is found in the consistent behavior of the opposing factions, particularly secular groups, such as Rakah (the Israeli communist party), which have expressed their aversion to the Islamic agenda. These are all very significant subjects worthy of in-depth study, but the methods for gathering the relevant data must first be determined.

It is generally accepted that there is no single complete and comprehensive research methodology that is suited to and correct for all types of research. Therefore, deciding which method to use requires a deep understanding and knowledge of targeted subject matter and a full justification for its use. Both scientists and scholars have long been involved in an epistemological argument, debating the best and most effective practical method(s) for carrying out research. According to Amaratunga et al., this ongoing debate stems from two quite divergent approaches to research: logical positivism and phenomenology.[29] Logical positivism applies quantitative and experimental methods to investigate and support both hypothetical and deductive generalizations. This approach is most suited for use by an objective observer or an independent researcher

[Hebrew]; Nohad 'Ali, *Between 'Ovadia and 'Abdallah: Muslim Fundamentalism and Jewish Fundamentalism in Israel* (Tel Aviv: Resling Press, 2013) [Hebrew].

28 Aziz Haidar, Henry Rosenfeld, and Reuven Kahane (eds.), *Arab Society in Israel: A Reader* (Jerusalem: Hebrew University of Jerusalem, 2003) [Hebrew].

29 D. Amaratunga, D. Baldry, M. Sarshar, and R. Newton, "Quantitative and qualitative research in the built environment: application of mixed research approach," *Work Study* 51 (2002): 17–31.

able to posit hypotheses for testing.[30] Information acquired in this manner is examined by means of suitable tools and measures, rather than being subjectively inferred from personal reflections, intuitions, or sensations. In short, logical positivism seeks causal effects and primary laws, and generally simplifies certain factors in order to facilitate outcomes.[31] Positivists often explain that the objects of a specific experience are 'atomic' and are thus described as 'independent events' (atomism).

Unlike the positivist approach, the phenomenological approach (interpretive science) adopts qualitative methods to inductively and holistically understand and identify human experiences within context-specific settings and in relation to the aims of the conducted research. This approach involves the understanding and explanation of various events and cases by determining their causes, as does the positivist approach. The phenomenological approach shares the subjective experiential perspective of the subjects/participants in the cases being tested. According to Amaratunga et al., this refutes positivist beliefs regarding atomism. The phenomenological approach supports the idea of deductivism, which shows that generalizations may be explained from a specific set of past events and experiences that can predict future outcomes.[32]

Acknowledging the strengths and weaknesses of these different methodologies, questionnaires (quantitative) have some advantages over interviews and textual analyses (both qualitative), because they are cost effective, easy to use, and maintain the uniformity of the questions. The disadvantages of questionnaires are that they do not guarantee participant motivation and require prior random sampling to control for biases. The advantage of interviews is their ability to uncover deeper and more specific details of a problem, though they are often time-consuming and inconvenient.

Taking all the above into consideration, it was decided that this research would avail itself of a mixed methodology – using interviews, textual analyses, and questionnaires (qualitative and quantitative methods) – to maximize the inherent advantages. As such, this study differs from other contemporary studies of Islam in Israel, both in its approach and in its methodology. Methodologically speaking, it presents a multidisciplinary analysis of various sources, textual and empirical, in an attempt to deepen understanding of the natures of Islam and

---

[30] Norman Denzin and Yvonna Lincoln (eds.), *Handbook of Qualitative Research*, 2nd edition (Thousand Oaks, Calif.: Sage, 2000), 1–29.
[31] John T. Cacioppo, G. R. Semin, and G. G. Berntson, "Realism, instrumentalism, and scientific symbiosis: psychological theory as a search for truth and the discovery of solutions," *American Psychologist* 59 (2004): 214–223.
[32] Amaratunga et al., "Quantitative and qualitative research in the built environment."

of the Muslim minority in Israel on both the theoretical and practical levels.

Because Islam is a religious code affecting all aspects of daily life, devout Muslims in Israel may seek religious guidance not only in spiritual matters but also in matters relating to temporal, social conduct. For example, observant Muslims in Israel shun monetary transactions, such as deposits/investments, loans, and mortgages with interest (*riba*), and so avoid Israeli commercial banks. According to Islamic law, *riba* is one of the capital sins; they therefore often use alternative Islamic banks in the West Bank, the Gaza Strip, and in other neighboring Arab countries. Devout Muslims are conflicted about mixed marriages; the mixed education of Jews and Muslims; the celebration of Jewish holidays; the observance of national memorial days, etc. Many refuse to serve in the national or civil services, such as in hospitals or the policing of schools or traffic, considering them to be at odds with Islamic doctrines of loyalty and enmity (*al-wala' wa 'l-bara'*).

The current study will elaborate on these and other related issues on both the theoretical and practical levels by adopting the aforementioned mixed, quantitative and qualitative, methodology. Three methods of enquiry are used: interviews, textual analyses (both qualitative) and questionnaires (quantitative). A semi-structured interview (a set of questions linked to the overall research aims and objectives) are posed to the selected interviewees, including people in senior positions (such as Muslim religious leaders, Arab Knesset members (KMs), and researchers in the field), approached at schools and universities, and in public places. This type of interview is flexible, and new questions may be raised during the interview as appropriate.

Various texts are chosen and analyzed: published fatwas, empirical studies, and other writings on Islam in Israel. Content analysis was applied to the texts and to the transcribed interviews, pointing out the recurring themes relevant to the present research and forming a basis for reaching certain conclusions.

In order to properly survey public opinion, a specially tailored questionnaire was designed to extract specific information with regard to the main research questions in an objective manner. However, prior to its actual use, a pilot study was done to familiarize the researchers with the survey and interview processes, to uncover any potential problems with the questionnaire or the interview questions, and to allow for appropriate adjustments to be made. This pilot study included five interviewees and fifty participants who filled in the questionnaire.

The revised questionnaire was also evaluated to ensure the consistency and reliability of the various items, and was validated by experts in the field. The random sample for the actual survey consisted of approximately 500 participants (Arab Muslims), citizens of Israel above the age of eighteen, residing in four geographical regions (in uncontested areas): Galilee (56 percent), the Triangle (23 percent), the Negev (12 percent), and the 'mixed cities' (9 percent). The term 'mixed cities' refers to Tel Aviv–Jaffa, Haifa, Acre, Ramlah, and Lod. The survey was conducted in 2015.

All the participants were asked to fill in the questionnaires; the data culled from the survey, after several analyses, were compared to other research findings. The responses in the questionnaires were coded into Statistical Package for Social Science (SPSS), and appropriate statistical analyses were performed to test previous hypotheses.[33]

The Structure of the Book

This book has six chapters. Chapter 1 provides a brief background for Islam in Israel, by tracing the history of Islam in pre-state Palestine, with emphases on the three major players who contributed to shaping Islam in Israel: the Ottomans, the British, and finally the Egyptians. Then, the discussion proceeds to examine various developments occurring in Islam and changes affecting the Muslim minority under the newborn Israeli state; at this point, the emphasis shifts to Islam under the Israeli military regime (1948–1966). The next chronological stage in Israel is that of the post-military regime, characterized by the restoration of religious life amid the Muslim minority in Israel. The Islamic awakening, manifested in the reestablishment of Islamic religious institutions and the creation of Islamic movements, restored Islam as a fundamental factor in shaping the socio-cultural and political landscape of the Muslim minority in Israel.

Chapter 2 focuses on Islamic religious authority and interpretation in Israel. The current study hypothesizes that devout Muslims in non-Muslim countries seek new religio-legal/theological interpretations, ones that will allow them to remain part of their societies without compromising their adherence to the Islamic codes (considered binding and comprehensive guides to life). Thus, new Islamic institutions have emerged in the West during the past four decades, such as the Islamic Society of North America (ISNA) and the European Council for Fatwa and

---

[33] In view of the vast range of subjects and issues undertaken herein, and for the sake of clarity, section VI of the questionnaire, dealing with Muslim Israeli women, was not included in this study analysis. Those findings will be presented separately in a future publication.

Research (ECFR), founded in 1982 and 1997, respectively.[34] These institutions have contributed to the creation of a new category of Islamic law – 'the religious law of minorities' (fiqh al-aqalliyyat), aimed at balancing traditional interpretations of Islamic law with the demands of everyday life in non-Muslim countries.[35] In Israel three agencies for issuing fatwas were created over the last few decades, intended to interpret Islam for the Muslim minority in Israel: (1) the Islamic Council for Issuing Fatwas (Bayt al-Maqdis) in Nazareth; (2) the Center for Islamic Studies (CIS) at al-Qasemi College in Baqa al-Gharbiyya; and (3) the ad hoc committees for ifta' of the southern branch of the Islamic Movement (SIM). This chapter will elaborate on these agencies, stressing their structures, actions, and methodologies of interpreting Islam. In addition, analyses are presented of religio-legal texts (fatwas) issued by local and foreign religious scholars, who interpret Islam for the Muslim minority in Israel.

The next four chapters are dedicated to the study of various aspects and different perspectives regarding Islam and the public. Chapter 3 examines affiliation, religiosity and observance, and their impacts on socio-cultural and political identities, as well as the impact of Islam on

---

[34] See the websites of these institutions, at www.isna.net and www.e-cfr.org/ar; also Alexandre Caeiro, "The power of European fatwas: the minority fiqh project and the making of an Islamic counterpublic," International Journal of Middle East Studies 42 (3) (2010): 435–449; al-Majlis al-'Urubbi li'l-Ifta' wa'l-Buhuth, Qararat wa-fatawa al-majlis al-'urubbi li'l-ifta' wa'l-buhuth (Cairo: Dar al-Tawjih wa'l-Nashr al-Islamiyya, 2002) [Arabic].

[35] On fiqh al-aqalliyyat see Shammai Fishman, Fiqh al-Aqalliyyat: A Legal Theory for Muslim Minorities (Washington, D.C.: Hudson Institute, 2006); Uria Shavit, "Should Muslims integrate into the West?" Middle East Quarterly 17 (4) (2007): 13–21; Khalid 'Abd al-Qadir, Fiqh al-qalliyyat al-muslima (Tripoli [Lebanon]: Dar al-Iman, 1998) [Arabic]; 'Abd al-'Ati Ashraf, Fiqh al-aqalliyat al-muslima bayna al-nazariyya wa'l-tatbiq (Bethlehem: Dar al-Kalima, 2008) [Arabic]; Khaled Abou El Fadl, "Islamic law and Muslim minorities: the juristic discourse on Muslim minorities from the second/eighth to the eleventh/seventeenth centuries," Islamic Law and Society 1 (2) (1994): 141–187; Khaled Abou El Fadl, "Legal debates on Muslim minorities: between rejection and accommodation," Journal of Religious Ethics 22 (1) (1994): 127–162; Taha Jaber 'Alwani, Towards a Fiqh of Minorities: Some Basic Reflections (Herndon, Va.: International Institute of Islamic Thought, 2003); Muhammad Jamal al-Din 'Atiyya, Nahwa fiqh jadid li'l-aqalliyyat (Cairo: Dar al-Salam, 2003) [Arabic]; 'Abd Allah Ibn Bayyah, Sina'at al-fatwa wa-fiqh al-aqalliyyat (Jeddah/Beirut: Dar al-Minhaj, 2007) [Arabic]; Andrew March, "Sources of moral obligation to non-Muslims in the 'jurisprudence of Muslim minorities' (fiqh al-aqalliyyat) discourse," Islamic Law and Society 16 (2009): 34–94; 'Abd al-Majid al-Najjar, Ma'alat al-af'al wa-atharaha fi fiqh al-aqalliyyat (Paris: al-Majlis al-'Urubbi li'l-Ifta' wa'l-Buhuth, 2002) [Arabic]; Yusuf al-Qaradawi, Fi fiqh al-aqalliyyat al-muslima (Cairo: Dar al-Shuruq, 2007) [Arabic]; A. Ibn Baz and S. Ibn Uthaymeen, Muslim Minorities: Fatawa Regarding Muslims Living as Minorities (Hounslow: Message of Islam, 1998); Sulayman Muhammad Tubulyak, al-Ahkam al-siyasiyya li'l-aqalliyyat al-muslima fi'l fiqh al-Islami (Beirut: Dar al-Nafa'is, 1997) [Arabic].

the daily life of Muslims in Israel and on their degrees of personal observance. Here, the 'Islamic awakening' in Israel is viewed from yet another angle – that of the public itself – focusing on attitudes held by Israeli Muslims toward their religion and on the extent to which they abide by Islamic laws, norms, and values. The symbiotic relationship between religiosity and identity is studied. How does Islam affect the normative behavior of Muslim Israelis? To what extent has Islam shaped the socio-cultural and political identities of the Muslim minority in Israel? To this end, many interviews were held and a random statistical sample of the Muslim population in Israel was asked to complete specially crafted research questionnaires about the relevant subject matter.

Recognizing the increasing influence of Islam on public attitudes, ideologies, social norms, and the formation of personal and collective identities,[36] chapter 4 explores the tensions stemming from encounters and conflicts between Shari'a law, local customs, and the modern social context. This discussion elaborates the means by which the Muslim minority in Israel deals with the challenges imposed by modernity within the non-Islamic context. Because Islam is a religious code covering all aspects of life, devout Muslims in Israel seek religious guidance not only in spiritual matters, but also in matters relating to temporal, social conduct. This study draws on the results of the public opinion survey to expand the understanding of popular Islam and to ascertain how Islam is perceived by the Muslim public in Israel. For the purposes of this survey, the random population sample was taken from three uncontested regions within the state of Israel: the Galilee, 'the Triangle,'[37] and the Negev. Jerusalem was not included due to the fact that the status of the Muslim population in the eastern section of the city remains indeterminate.

Chapter 5 presents the viable relationships currently existing between the Muslim minority in Israel and the Israeli Jewish majority. This discussion draws on case studies to make salient points regarding the relationships between Muslims and Jews in various spheres of life: social, economic, cultural, and political. It also elaborates on these interfaith interfaces, examining the theoretical and practical aspects by adopting both quantitative and qualitative methods. Here, emphasis is placed on the complex and difficult dilemmas experienced by the Muslims in Israel regarding their participation in the modern Israeli public sphere, while

---

[36] On the formation and politics of identities see Rogers Brubacker, *Grounds for Difference* (Cambridge, Mass.: Harvard University Press, 2015).

[37] A concentration of Arab villages and towns near the 'Green Line' in the Samarian foothills. The Green Line represents the demarcation lines following the 1949 Armistice Agreements between Israel, Egypt, Jordan, Lebanon, and Syria.

maintaining their Islamic socio-cultural norms and values. Such dilemmas are common mainly among Muslims living in non-Muslim or Western environments.[38]

Chapter 6, the concluding chapter, discusses the relations between the Muslim minority in Israel and the Israeli establishment. Emphasis is placed on some key questions, such as: How do Muslims relate to the Israeli institutions and authorities? What are the means that Muslims use to accommodate the contradictions between Islamic law and Israeli law and governance?

---

[38] See Philip Lewis, "The Bradford Council for Mosques and the search for Muslim unity," in S. Vertovec and C. Peach (eds.), *Islam in Europe: The Politics of Religion and Community* (London: Macmillan, 1997), 103–128.

1 Islam in Israel
Background

Islam, during the first half of the twentieth century in Palestine and on the eve of the creation of the state of Israel in 1948, was largely shaped by three major regional and colonial players: the Ottomans, the British, and finally the Egyptians. After all, Palestine had been one of the provinces of the Ottoman Empire for more than four centuries and had special importance, since it contained Jerusalem, one of Islam's holy cities (along with Mecca and Medina). The *mutasarrifate* of Jerusalem (Ottoman Turkish: *kudüs-i şerif mutasarrıflığı*), also known as the *sanjak* of Jerusalem, served as the capital and governmental headquarters, and had a special administrative status.[1] The governing authority, which derived its power directly from the Ottoman sultan, was extended to include the management of religious affairs, such as asset endowments (*waqf*s), education, Shari'a courts, mosques, and more. The Ottoman *millet* system is still in place for all recognized communities in Israel, including the Muslims and their Shari'a courts.[2]

The British Mandate (1920–48), which replaced Ottoman rule in the region after World War I, acknowledged the importance of the religious aspects of Muslim society in an attempt to maintain political stability.[3] Moreover, the British high commissioner, Herbert Samuel, established the Supreme Muslim Council (al-Majlis al-Shar'ī al-Islāmī al-A'lā; hereafter the Council) in December 1921. He served as one of the important actors in molding Islamic religious life prior to the establishment of

---

[1] Johann Büssow, *Hamidian Palestine Politics and Society in the District of Jerusalem, 1872–1908* (Leiden: E. J. Brill, 2011), 5.

[2] Aharon Layish, "The heritage of Ottoman rule in the Israeli legal system: the concept of *umma* and *millet*," in Peri Bearman, Wolfhart Heinrichs, and Bernard Weiss (eds.), *The Law Applied: Contextualizing the Islamic Shari'a* (London: I. B. Tauris, 2007), 128–148. Ottoman rule in Palestine has already received vast attention from scholars and other writers. See, for example, David Kushner, "The district of Jerusalem in the eyes of three Ottoman governors at the end of the Hamidian period," *Middle Eastern Studies* 35 (2) (1999): 61–82; Farid al-Salim, *Palestine and the Decline of the Ottoman Empire: Modernization and the Path to Palestinian Statehood* (London: I. B. Tauris, 2015).

[3] Robert Eisenman, *Islamic Law in Palestine and Israel* (Leiden: E. J. Brill, 1978), 50.

the state of Israel. Headed by the grand mufti of Jerusalem, Haj Amin al-Husayni (d. 1974), it represented the Muslim religious establishment and was empowered to conduct religious life and Islamic institutions, including *waqf*, the Shariʿa courts, educational institutions, religious schools, orphanages, and the appointment of Muslim officials to various Islamic institutions.[4]

In the political arena, the grand mufti focused his efforts on the struggle against Zionist aspirations, such as by forbidding the sale of land to Jews, by improving the state of the al-Aqsa Mosque, and by elevating the status of Jerusalem in the Arab and Muslim world. Prominent in this context were the Islamic Congress, held in Jerusalem in 1930, and the attempt to establish an Islamic university in the capital city.[5] Toward this end, holidays and important rituals, such as Nebi Musa, Nebi Salah, the Muslim New Year, Laylat al-Miʿraj (celebrating the nighttime journey by the Prophet in 620 from Mecca to the al-Aqsa Mosque and his ascent to heaven, *al-isra waʾl-miʿraj*) were also intertwined in this effort.[6]

Yet, while the Ottomans and the British seemed to play significant roles in shaping the politics in pre-state Palestine, the Egyptians, particularly the Muslim Brotherhood (al-Ikhwan al-Muslimun; hereafter the Brotherhood) seemed to play a central role in consolidating the ideologies of Islam in Palestine – part of the subject matter of this book. Note that Palestine became exposed to the religio-cultural and ideological influences of certain Islamic movements due to regional development in the Middle East and to various colonial power-plays. These movements, enmeshed in the political and nationalist developments in the region, aimed at promoting national and religious goals within and outside

---

[4] Uri M. Kupferschmidt, *The Supreme Muslim Council: Islam under the British Mandate for Palestine* (Leiden: E. J. Brill, 1987), 78; more on the British Mandate in Palestine in ibid.; Bernard Wasserstein, *The British in Palestine: The Mandatory Government and the Arab–Jewish Conflict, 1917–1929* (Oxford: Blackwell, 1991); Naomi Shepherd, *Ploughing Sand: British Rule in Palestine, 1917–1948* (London: John Murray 1999); Rosemary Sayigh, *Palestinians: From Peasants to Revolutionaries* (London: Zed Press, 1979); Eugene Rogan, *Frontiers of the Late Ottoman Empire: Transjordan, 1850–1921* (Cambridge: Cambridge University Press, 1999); Sami Hadawi, *Bitter Harvest: A Modern History of Palestine* (London: Scorpion Publishing, 1989).

[5] Bayan al-Hut, *al-Qiyadat waʾl-muʾassasat al-siyasiyya fi filistin, 1917–1948* (Beirut: Muʾassasat al-Dirasat al-Filistiniyya, 1986), 134–137 [Arabic].

[6] For more on pan-Islamic activism under al-Husayni, see Kupferschmidt, *The Supreme Muslim Council*, 187–220; Martin Kramer, *Islam Assembled: The Advent of the Muslim Congresses* (New York: Columbia University Press, 1986), 1–9, 123–141; Erik Freas, "Hajj Amin al-Husayni and the Haram al-Sharif: a pan-Islamic or Palestinian nationalist cause?"*British Journal of Middle Eastern Studies* 39 (1) (April 2012): 19–51; Butrus Abu-Manneh, "The Husaynis: the rise of a notable family in 18th century Palestine," in David Kushner (ed.), *Palestine in the Late Ottoman Period: Political, Social and Economic Transformation* (Leiden: E. J. Brill, 1986), 93–108.

their countries of origin.[7] Among the most prominent and significant movements was the Brotherhood, founded in 1928 by Hasan al-Banna (d. 1949), which greatly influenced and shaped Islam in pre-state Palestine.

In the 1930s, only a few years after its inception, the Brotherhood spoke about Palestine, emphasizing its historical religious status in Islam.[8] For example, three years after the establishment of the Brotherhood, in December 1931, a position paper was sent by the founder, al-Banna, to the Islamic Congress, where Mufti Haj Amin al-Husayni presented the Brotherhood's position on the 'Palestinian problem'. This paper addressed some relevant issues, such as the acquisition of Palestinian land by Jews, economic aid to the Palestinians, religious education, and protection of the holy places.[9]

The Brotherhood's concern regarding Palestine became even stronger after the second and third Council conferences (held in 1933 and 1935, respectively), in which the 'Palestinian problem' was identified as a fundamental Islamic problem. The 1936–1939 Arab Revolt, instigated by Palestinian Arabs in Mandatory Palestine against British colonial rule and demanding independence and opposition to mass Jewish immigration, only increased the support given by the Brotherhood toward alleviating the Palestinian problem. This was evident in the various measures taken, including an Egyptian daily newspaper regularly delivered to Palestine, economic aid for political activity, and, later, participation in the 1948 war. For example, in May 1936 the Brotherhood established an association called Jam'iyyat al-Qirsh li-Ighathat Mankubi Falastin (al-Qirsh Relief Association for Palestinian Victims), led by al-Banna. The major objective of this association was to provide financial assistance to the Palestinians to facilitate their inclusion in the armed struggle of the 'Izz al-Din al-Qassam Brigades in 1935 and in the Arab Revolt.[10]

The Brotherhood was also actively involved with Palestinian leadership; it attended their meetings, helped organize demonstrations and conduct conferences, and it also established branches in Palestine. Following the third conference of the Council, held in March 1935, a delegation consisting of al-Banna's brother, 'Abd al-Rahman (al-Sa'ati), Muhammad Asad al-Hakim, and the Tunisian 'Abd al-'Aziz al-Tha'alibi met first with the Palestinian leadership, headed by Haj al-Husayni, to promote their cause, with a view toward strengthening the relations

---

[7] More on national and religious identities in Brubacker, *Grounds for Difference*, ch. 4.
[8] See Hasan al-Banna, *Mudhakkarat al-da'wa wa'l-da'iya* (Kuwait: Maktabat Afaq, 2012), 337–338 [Arabic].
[9] Kramer, *Islam Assembled*, 123–141.   [10] Al-Hut, *al-Qiyadat*, 502.

between the two parties and to express solidarity with the Palestinians. These visits became more frequent during World War II. These meetings were led by two prominent leaders, 'Abd al-Mu'iz 'Abd al-Sattar and Sa'id Ramadan, who sought to increase the Brotherhood's impact in Palestine primarily by recruiting new Palestinian members.[11] In March 1948 al-Banna himself visited Gaza, where he met with representatives from different areas of Palestine, including Haj Hussein Abu Sitta from Beersheba (Heb. Be'er-Sheva').[12]

The Brotherhood's political activity was also manifested at conferences held in Palestine. The Haifa Conference, in October 1946, provided a significant example of this. It was attended by representatives from Lebanon and Jordan. A number of important decisions were adopted at this conference: (1) to place the responsibility for the situation of the Palestinians on the British; (2) to support any project or initiative that might 'save' the land of Palestine; (3) to vote for the non-recognition of Jewish rights to Palestine; (4) to open more branches of the Brotherhood across Palestine.[13]

Indeed, following the Haifa Conference, over twenty additional branches were established in various places throughout pre-state Palestine, located in Gaza, Jaffa, Haifa, Jerusalem, Qalqilya, Lod, Nablus (Heb. Shekhem), Tulkarem, Majdal (Heb. Ashkelon), Silwad, and elsewhere. Through these branches, the Brotherhood sought to spread its principles by different means and methods – especially via the mosques, which served as bases of activities such as lectures, sermons, rallies, religio-cultural and educational events, and where the Brotherhood's membership was able to participate and/or manage the religious activities, some of which were conducted secretly and included the distribution of leaflets against the British Mandate.[14]

Note that the Brotherhood demonstrated a pragmatic approach when cooperating with non-Muslim groups and political activists in Palestine, as with the communist and Christian populations. This cooperation was evident in the nomination of representatives from these groups to the national committees of the Brotherhood, demonstrating that the Muslim Brotherhood saw no problem in the inclusion and support of non-Islamic entities sharing the same nationalist goals.[15]

---

[11] Ibid.   [12] Ibid.   [13] Ibid., 503.

[14] Avraham Sela, "Palestinian society and institutions during the Mandate: changes, lack of mobility and downfall," in Avi Bareli and Nahum Karlinsky (eds.), *Economy and Society in Mandatory Palestine, 1918–1948* (Beersheba: Merkaz le-Moreshet Ben-Guryon, 2003), 291–348.

[15] 'Ali, "Political Islam."

Islam under Siege, 1948–1966

The military regime (1948–66) that the state of Israel imposed on the Muslim Arab minority led to an immediate and physical disconnection of this community from the international Arab and Muslim worlds. This was a traumatic stage for the Muslim Arab population in Israel, which had far-reaching implications on socio-economics, culture, politics, and religious life.

In the religious sphere, Israeli Muslims found themselves without any real religious leadership, since the majority of the former Palestinian religious leaders ('ulama') had either fled or had been forced to leave their homes. At that time, religious practices were also restricted by the military governor of Israel, who limited the number of religious service positions to a few essential, traditional functions, such as clerics for leading prayers (imams), judges (qadis) and those who call to prayers (mu'azins) – all of whom became government-appointed employees, paid by the Ministries of Religion and the Interior. The roles and duties of the religious leaders were curtailed, leaving only basic, traditional religious tasks. Even the properties of waqf were confiscated by the state of Israel and, in some cases, were reassigned to certain Muslim committees under Israeli government supervision.[16] For example, the state, based on the Law of Absentees (1950), established boards with appointed trustees in mixed cities to be in charge of the Waqf 'released properties.'

Furthermore, Islamic religious education of the Israeli Muslim minority was not encouraged by the formal Israeli education system. In fact, only a limited number of hours were dedicated to the study of religion in the schools – a subject that had been very popular before the 1948 war. The dominant ideologies existing in the Arab countries surrounding Israel at that time were nationalist. It is therefore no surprise that the Arab movements established in the 1960s in Israel, for example, al-Ard (the Land Movement), were nationalist movements that dealt with issues such as the identity of the Palestinian Arabs, secularism, and Arab unity – and completely ignored the religious aspect.[17] Among other things, this change of focus was also evidenced by the absence of any new religious movements under this military regime. Thus, the combination of the military rule and the general, secular environment in Israel between the 1950s and early 1960s led to the stagnation of religious life in the Israeli Muslim community. The Israeli military regime ended in 1966, marking

---

[16] Ibid.; more on Islamic institutional decline under the military regime in Rubin-Peled, *Debating Islam in the Jewish State*, ch. 7.

[17] 'Ali, "Political Islam."

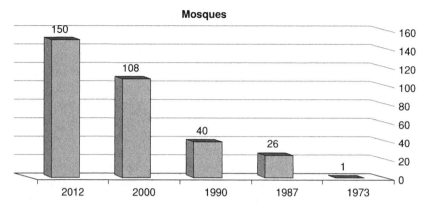

Mosques

Figure 1.1 The growing number of mosques in Muslim communities in the Negev, 1973–2012.[18]

a turning point in the history of Islam in Israel. The next stage, from the early 1970s, was characterized by an Islamic awakening (*sahwa*).

The Islamic Awakening (*Sahwa*) in Israel

The termination of the military regime marked the end of the most traumatic stage in the religious and political development of the Muslim Arab minority in Israel. The research literature tends to cite both the end of military rule and the 1967 war (the 'Six Day War') as two historic watersheds that signified turning points in the religious awakening of the Muslim minority in Israel. This became apparent in various aspects of Muslim daily life: religious dress; women's use of veils; bearded young men; compliance with Islamic dietary law (*halal*); and a greater and still growing presence of young men at prayers in the mosques (see Figure 1.1).

This Islamic awakening has attracted the attention of scholars from different disciplines, who suggest two main theories in explanation of the phenomenon.[19] The first theory is based on local factors related to

---

[18] Farraj Abu Freih, "Islam in the Negev: Conflict and Agreement between the ʿUrf and the Shariʿa in the Muslim Arab Population in the Negev," MA thesis (Beʾer-Shevaʾ: Ben-Gurion University of the Negev, 2014) [Hebrew], 24.

[19] See, for example, Yvonne Haddad, "Islamists and the 'problem of Israel': the 1967 awakening," *Middle East Journal* 46 (2) (Spring 1992): 266–285. More on the Islamic awakening in Ali E. Hillal Dessouki, "The Islamic resurgence: sources, dynamics, and implications," in A. E. H. Dessouki (ed.), *Islamic Resurgence in the Arab World* (New York: Praeger Publishers, 1982), 3–31; Thomas Mayer, *Islamic Resurgence among the Arabs in Israel* (Givat Haviva: Arab Studies Institute, 1986); Thomas Mayer, *The*

the socio-economic crisis experienced by the local Muslim minority. It highlights the traditional nature of the local Muslim community, which underwent rapid modernization and integration into the modern state of Israel.[20] These radical changes are reflected by the facts that agriculture was no longer their main source of income, as more and more Muslims were employed in businesses and services (mainly in Jewish localities) and that they experienced a rise in living standards, as more Arabs received Israeli schooling at various academic levels. All this relatively rapid change, the researchers claim, undermined the traditional, patriarchal structure of Muslim Arab society.

Moreover, although these many changes led to higher living standards and higher levels of education (though undermining the traditional structure of Arab society), they also contributed to the strengthening of religious identity, due to many factors, the most significant of which were the frequent political and economic crises, along with the rift created between the Arab and Jewish communities. The combination of the common economic/political uncertainty and stress, along with growing alienation between the Muslim Arab minority and the Jewish majority, increased the importance of religion as part of an emerging national identity.[21] However, this modernization process did not answer some very profound existential questions; as such, Israeli Muslims became

Awakening of the Muslims in Israel (Givat Haviva: Institute for Arabic Studies, 1988) [Hebrew]; Thomas Mayer, "The 'Muslim youth' in Israel," *ha-Mizrah he-Hadash* 32 (1989): 10–21 [Hebrew]; Elie Rekhess, "Resurgent Islam in Israel," *Asian and African Studies* 27 (1–2) (1993): 189–206. For more on religious resurgence see Shmuel Eisenstadt, "The resurgence of religious movements in processes of globalisation: beyond end of history or clash of civilisations," *International Journal on Multicultural Societies* 2 (1) (2000): 4–15; James Beckford, "Religious movements and globalization," in R. Cohen and S. Rai (eds.), *Global Social Movements* (London: Athlone Press, 2000), 165–183; Muhammad Hourani, "The *tawba*: repentance among Israeli Muslim Arabs," *Bamikhlala* 2 (1991): 102–110 [Hebrew]; Robert Wuthnow, "World order and religious movements," in A. Bergson (ed.), *Studies of the Modern World System* (New York: Academic Press, 1980), 57–75.

20 Majid al-Haj, "The Arab internal refugees in Israel: the emergence of a minority within the minority," *Immigration and Minorities* 7 (2) (1988): 149–165; Majid al-Haj, "The sociopolitical structure of the Arabs in Israel: external vs. internal orientation," in John E. Hofman (ed.), *Arab–Jewish Relations in Israel: A Quest of Human Understanding* (Bristol, Ind.: Wyndham Hall, 1988), 92–123; Sammy Smooha, "The implication of transition to peace for Israeli society," *Annals of the American Academy of Political and Social Science* 555 (1988): 23–45; Sammy Smooha, "Minority responses in a plural society: a typology of the Arabs in Israel," *Sociology and Social Research* 67 (4) (1983): 436–456.

21 Y. Peres and N. Yuval-Davis, "Some observations on the national identity of the Israeli Arabs," *Human Relations* 22 (3) (1969): 219–233; D. Waxman and I. Peleg, "Neither ethnocracy nor bi-nationalism: in search of the middle ground," *Israel Studies Forum* 23 (2) (2008): 55–73.

disillusioned with and disappointed by the false promises of positive returns.[22]

Often, this dissatisfaction caused many Arabs in Israel to (re)turn to their religion, Islam, as the source of a new (or renewed) lifestyle. Many young Muslims, for example, left their homes to work in the modern Israeli cities, such as Tel Aviv, and would spend their weekends there, away from their villages, friends, and families. This would often lead to a search for another way to handle their loneliness, some rediscovering their religion and adopting a religious Islamic lifestyle. Muslim leaders across Israel found these groups of young Muslims to be their best audiences. The power of religion became even more evident as political leaders failed to deliver satisfactory answers to various mundane and spiritual problems.[23]

In contrast, the second theory emphasizes external factors, particularly the impact of the renewed encounter of the Muslim minority in Israel with regional and global Muslim Arab societies after the end of the military regime. The Israeli occupation of the West Bank and Gaza Strip opened the gates, enabling the Muslim minority to visit some important Islamic religious sites, especially in Jerusalem and Hebron (prior to 1967 they had been forbidden to visit such sites). In addition, in 1978 the Israeli Muslim population was granted permission to make holy pilgrimages to Mecca (*hajj*), by passing through Jordan.[24]

There are also other external factors associated with the global 'Islamic awakening' of the 1970s. The year 1979, for example, was particularly important in that many religious revolutions and political rebellions occurred across the Middle East. In Iran, for instance, a revolution, spurred on by radical Shi'ite ideology, occurred, overthrowing the government of Iran. In addition, that same year, Egypt witnessed the rising power of various radical Islamic movements that called for a 'holy war' (*jihad*) against the national regimes and their supporters. Syria also experienced a powerful, clandestine Islamic movement that declared a *jihad* against the oppressive 'Alawite regime. Such an ideological struggle, between religious and national movements in the Middle East post-1967, led to the strengthening of pan-Islamism, to a large extent, at the expense of pan-Arabism.[25]

---

[22] Yochanan Peres, "Modernization and nationalism in the identity of the Israeli Arabs," *Middle East Journal* 24 (4) (Autumn 1970): 479–492.

[23] Ibid.

[24] Elie Rekhess, "Israeli Arabs and the Arabs of the West Bank and Gaza: political affinity and national solidarity," *Asian and African Studies* 23 (2–3) (November 1989): 119–154.

[25] More on pan-Arab nationalism versus pan-Islamism in Bassam Tibi, *Arab Nationalism: A Critical Enquiry* (New York: St. Martin's Press, 1990), ch. 9.

These newly formulated Islamic ideologies, introduced by Muslim rebels in the above-mentioned countries, served the Muslim minority in Israel by addressing their local needs.[26] As such, regional and global geopolitical factors from the early 1970s inspired and catalyzed the formation of new Islamic movements and ideologies that, in turn, played central roles in the 'Islamic awakening' in Israel.[27] Among the most important Islamic movements that arose at that time was the one established in 1971 by Shaykh 'Abd Allah Nimr Darwish, the Islamic Movement (hereafter IM), which has since gained much public attention.[28] The IM is often described by scholars as being a religious–nationalist movement.[29] Indeed, its nationalist tendencies were manifested in its anti-Israeli actions, such as the creation in 1979 of a paramilitary, underground organization, 'Usrat al-Jihad (Family of the Jihad), that was involved in a number of violent incidents. This led to the imprisonment (until 1983) of its leaders, including Shaykh Darwish, for their association with the organization.

However, after the release of the IM's leaders from jail, the late 1980s witnessed its transformation to emphasizing religious, social, and cultural rather than nationalist aspects, and denouncing violence as an illegitimate means of resistance. In this way, the IM's leaders distanced the movement from various militant Islamic movements, such as that of Shaykh 'Izz al-Din al-Qassam.

Since the 1980s the IM has engaged in religious community building within the Muslim minority in Israel by means of religious preaching (da'wa) and socio-political activism. Abbas Zakkur, a KM and also a member of the IM, said that the IM aims at instructing Muslims in Israel about their religion in an attempt to recreate the Islamic ethos, Muslim social and cultural life, and to restore the Islamic social order.[30]

Indeed, since its establishment, the IM has founded dozens of religious, social, cultural, and economic associations, organizations, and institutions that have played fundamental roles in the 'awakening' of the

---

[26] Rekhess, "Resurgent Islam in Israel," 189–193.

[27] Alisa Rubin-Peled, "Towards autonomy? The Islamist Movement's quest for control of Islamic institutions in Israel," *Middle East Journal* 55 (3) (2001): 378–398.

[28] The Arab minority in Israel, political Islam, and the Islamic Movement have attracted the attention of many scholars from various disciplines. See, for example, Rekhess and Rudnitzky (eds.), *Muslim Minorities*; Louër, *To Be an Arab in Israel*; Shafir and Peled, *Being Israeli*; Rubin-Peled, *Debating Islam in the Jewish State*; Smooha and Ghanem, *Ethnic, Religious and Political Islam*; Rekhess (ed.), *The Arabs in Israeli Politics*; Rouhana, *Palestinian Citizens in an Ethnic Jewish State*; Dumper, *Islam and Israel*; Israeli, *Muslim Fundamentalism in Israel*; Lustick, *Arabs in the Jewish State*.

[29] Amara, "The nature of Islamic fundamentalism."

[30] Rosmer, "The Islamic Movement"; Rubin-Peled, *Debating Islam in the Jewish State*, 121–146.

Muslim community in Israel.[31] Kamal Khatib, deputy head of the NIM, describes services provided to the Muslim community via non-profit organizations established throughout the country. According to him, the IM seeks to support clinics, emergency medical services, karate and soccer clubs, etc. in many Arab villages.[32] Yet, these IM actions strive not only to bolster Muslim religion, by returning people to their faith and practice, but also to involve them in the many activities of the IM itself.[33] This is clearly manifested in the *da'wa* strategies.

Da'wa Strategies

A look at the behavioral patterns and action mechanisms adopted by the IM in Israel indicates the sense of self-empowerment derived from the Islamic principles of mutual responsibility (*takaful*), alms-giving (*zakat*), and charity (*sadaqa*) – three major sources of funding for its activities in Israel. In fact, the IM sought to replace the social mechanisms of the 'welfare state' by providing community social services, especially to vulnerable populations.

It is also individual Muslims who provide an effective mechanism for promoting and spreading religious messages – directly, when they serve as preachers/teachers in the mosques or organize public events; and indirectly, when they teach in the schools or become involved in the economic system or the political arena. The IM has a personalized recruitment process that begins with a personal visit to a potential recruit, especially someone non-religious, such as many of the academics, professionals, educators, and university students (including college graduates in Islamic studies).[34]

Recruiters are chosen according to stringent criteria: the recruiter must have a sturdy moral fiber; be fully conversant in Islamic religious law; be knowledgeable in Muslim history; present a proper appearance; be able to speak fluently; have a good reputation; and be characterized by reliability and integrity. This personal recruitment process is very important, since it also generates some funding for the IM. Therefore, personal recruiting is generally kept under the close supervision and is done with the active involvement of the local religious leaders; that is to say, the IM is an ideological movement, which takes an active part in the training of its membership and takes responsibility for their actions. The mission of each recruiter is to speak to the hearts of the recruits,

---

[31] 'Ali, "Political Islam."
[32] Rosmer, "The Islamic Movement." [33] 'Ali, "Political Islam."
[34] Ibid. Also see Tilde Rosmer, "Raising the green banner: Islamist student politics in Israel," *Journal of Palestine Studies* 45 (1) (2015): 24–42.

while extolling the glorious history of Islamic civilization and contrasting it with underdeveloped modern-day Arab societies. Nonetheless, some of these personal visits are unofficial and casual, spontaneously initiated by individual members of the IM and, as such, not subject to the control and guidance of IM leaders.

With regard to the preaching done in the mosques, the IM invites guest preachers, commentators, known local legal scholars, and Muslim scholars from important and renowned institutions across the Arab/Muslim world, such as al-Azhar University in Cairo. In such cases the community of believers is invited, notified by means of enormous billboards posted at the entrances to the mosques and in other public places. These guest speakers stay for days, even weeks, offering their teachings to all who attend the mosques. The invitation of significant religious sages from all corners of the Muslim world provides another mechanism for drawing potential believers into Islam and, perhaps, also into the IM.[35]

As for preaching to the broadest possible audience, this is also done at public events and is not limited to the confines of the mosques. These events, such as 'preaching week' (*usbu' al-da'wa*), the al-Aqsa festival, and massive fund-raising dinners (*al-'asha' al-khayri*), are meant to serve two main purposes: to disseminate religious ideas and to bolster the status of the IM within the Arab minority in Israel. Thus, for instance, 'preaching week' is designed to highlight the importance of *da'wa* as a religious commandment and to promote stronger piety in Arab Israeli society. These events are held in predetermined locations and the task of hosting is delegated to local IM members and associates. Invitations to such events are open to the general public, especially to the secular populace, who are meant to meet with preachers (*wu'az*), often members of the IM's senior leadership. At these events, among other things, free packs are distributed containing instructional materials and tape recordings about illustrious proselytizers from the Muslim world.

The event organizers determine how the instruction will be given, specifically choosing the right preacher for each audience, so that an educated audience will enjoy an academic speaker; an audience of women is provided with a woman speaker. After each event, the participants are invited to a summary evening at a mosque or at one of the IM's centers, where they are evaluated by the IM member responsible for that group regarding their likelihood of returning to the observance of Islam. Among the criteria taken into consideration when determining each individual's potential for joining the Muslim community are the attendance

---

[35] Ibid.

rate of each invitee and his/her apparent interest in the messages being relayed. Those invitees showing the highest potential are granted further, frequent follow-up visits by IM members.[36]

An important contribution of the IM to the revival of religiosity is reflected in the areas of education and culture. In fact, the IM is trying to create an alternative heritage education, parallel to the Israeli state education system, but based on Islamic values (somewhat resembling the separate Israeli Orthodox school system). Such education begins in the kindergartens, continues throughout the public and high schools, and ends with academic studies. Within this framework, the IM recruits women kindergarten aids and women educators, taking care to train them in accordance with the values and ethos of the IM. Seminars, lectures, and instructional sessions that are held are given primarily by the IM's leadership.[37]

Most important in this regard are the activities teaching the oral recitation of the Qur'an. To this end, the IM has established a number of classes and clubs, available to students of all ages, from kindergarten through academia. One of the many schools that teaches Qur'anic recitation is called the Furqan Institute for the Recitation of the Holy Qur'an (Mu'assasat al-Furqan li-Tahfiz al-Qur'an al-Karim), which belongs to the SIM. One of the declared goals of this school is to train new religious leadership, including Muslim preachers and teachers for the Islamic education system.[38]

As part of the Islamic higher education system, the IM established al-Da'wa College for Islamic Studies (Kulliyyat al-Da'wa) in Umm al-Fahm in 1989, whose graduates also serve as recruiters for the IM and as activists among the Arab youth and high-school and college students. This college was officially recognized by varous Arab and Muslim institutions, such as the Union of Arab Universities, the Union of Muslim Universities, the Union of Arab-European Universities, and the Palestine Commission for Higher Education. However, it has not been recognized by the Israeli Commission for Higher Education or by Israel's Ministry of Education. According to IM leaders, this lack of recognition stems from political motives, since the college is very important for the

---

[36] Ibid.

[37] Ayman K. Agbaria and Muhanad Mustafa, "The case of Palestinian civil society in Israel: Islam, civil society and educational activism," *Critical Studies in Education* 55 (1) (2014): 44–57. More on Islamic education in Israel in Rubin-Peled, *Debating Islam in the Jewish State*, ch. 6; Mordechai Kedar, "Our children are in danger: education as seen by the Islamic Movement in Israel," in Ami Ayalon and David J. Wasserstein (eds.), *Madrasa Education: Religion and State in the Middle East: Studies in Honor of Michael Winter* (Tel Aviv: Tel Aviv University, 2004), 353–381 [Hebrew].

[38] More on this institution may be found at its homepage: www.alforkan.org.

'Islamic awakening' in Israel. An investigation of the goals of al-Da'wa College indicates its desire to promote religious training in various areas, including the preparation of teaching staff, *imams*, *murafi' shar'i* (lawyers within the Shari'a courts), and preachers. The intent is to establish a professional, well-educated cadre that can handle the religious and legal demands of the Muslim population in Israel and help to expand the IM by means of returning the Arab multitude to its faith.[39]

The involvement of the IM in higher education appears in the form of various campus activities, mostly organized by student cells, such as Iqra (lit., read!) and al-Qalam (lit., the pen), that hold events at Israeli universities and colleges. These cells help Arab students (both men and women) with many things, even offering financial support. For example, Iqra has two special projects: a student loan/scholarship project; and the *da'wa* camp project that deals with the dissemination of Islam amongst the secular student populace. These student cells function within the purview of certain associations that grant unlimited scholarships to members of the IM; it is possible to learn about this from the grant/loan forms circulated by IM activists on campuses and at various mosques. For the past few years this process of bestowing grants has even occurred at parties – an occasion also used as a recruitment opportunity.[40]

Approaching Politics and the Jewish Public Sphere

Islamic political involvement began at the end of the 1980s, when the IM ran, somewhat successfully, in the local elections in the Arab sector in Israel. The municipal elections of 1989 officially placed the Islamists in the Israeli political landscape, when they gained many seats in every community in which they ran.[41] The IM had managed to establish numerous new associations and institutions for mobilizing voters and religious preaching, while using election campaign slogans such as 'Islam is the solution'; 'Islam is justice'; and 'Islam is the alternative.' The main political platform suggested finding new ways for the Arab community to deal with its social and economic problems. Note that the Arabs in Israel, who had been excluded from influencing foreign policy, security matters, and national economics, now perceived the local municipality

---

[39] Nohad 'Ali, "Religious Fundamentalism as an Ideology and a Practice: A Comparative Study of Jews' Shas [political party] and the Islamic Movement in Israel," Ph.D. thesis (Haifa: Haifa University, 2006) [Hebrew], 110–120.

[40] Ibid.

[41] Muhanad Mustafa, "Political participation of the Islamic Movement in Israel," in Rekhess and Rudnitzky (eds.), *Muslim Minorities*, 95–113; Binyamin Neuberger, "The Arab minority in Israeli politics, 1948–1992: from marginality to influence," *Asian and African Studies* 27 (1–2) (1993): 149–170.

as the arena in which they might become an integral part of the decision-making process and, thus, fulfill their aspirations.

While the focus on local municipal powers was growing, there were additional attempts by the Arab community leadership to create a national lobby that might influence Israeli national politics. One such effort was the establishment of the Committee of Mayors of Arab Munic-ipalities, whose goal was to represent the general Arab public in Israel. Even though this committee was not officially recognized by the Israeli authorities, it enjoyed broad public legitimacy. Another body formed was the Committee of Arab Municipalities. Following the 1989 municipal elections, the IM proceeded to become a significant participant in these two committees.[42]

Having obtained a foothold in local government by the mid-1990s, the IM was motivated to contend in the national political arena by running for seats in the Knesset, the Israeli parliament. The leaders of the IM saw their electoral success as an encouraging sign, and also as a symbol of Arab voters' disappointment with the existing Arab parties and their elected representatives. These leaders further sought to capitalize on the IM's growing support at the national level, and wanted to demonstrate that the Knesset can be used to serve the Arab public in a more effi-cient way. However, the resulting national exposure only highlighted the IM's need to address its tangled interpretation of religious, national, and secular guidelines.

Meanwhile, the act of running for the Knesset had caused a fracture within the Islamist community. This was manifested mainly on the eve of the elections for the fourteenth Knesset in 1996, causing a deep rift within the IM that led to a split and the creation of two ideological camps within the Muslim community in Israel – one dogmatic and hardline, led by Shaykhs Raed Salah, Kamal Khatib, and others (NIM), and the other, pragmatic, led by Shaykh Darwish, Shaykh Muhammad Dahamshe, KM Abed al-Malik Dahamshe, and others (SIM).[43] The basis of the dis-pute between these two factions was the extent to which Islamic ideals might accommodate the limitations dictated by Israeli political and legal realities.[44] The IM thus faced internal tensions between its national, civil, and religious proponents over the principal question of how to approach the Israeli political and public spheres.[45]

---

[42] Reuven Paz, "The Islamic Movement in Israel and the municipal elections of 1989," *Jerusalem Quarterly* 53 (Winter 1990): 3–26, at 4.

[43] More on the 1996 IM split in Aburaiya, "The 1996 split of the Islamic Movement."

[44] Dakwar Jamil, "The Islamic Movement inside Israel," *Journal of Palestine Studies* 36 (2) (2007): 66–76.

[45] Ibid.

While the SIM, headed by Shaykh 'Abd Allah Nimr Darwish and his followers, considered the Knesset to be a legitimate arena in which to seek an improved status for Muslim citizens, the NIM, headed by Raed Salah, rejected such participation, explaining that the Knesset represents Israeli sovereignty and secular legislation. This tension also affected the Israeli–Palestinian conflict, when the SIM accepted the Oslo Agreements (1993), while the NIM rejected them, claiming that they do not safeguard Palestinian interests, nor do they support the establishment of an independent state or the Arab refugees' right of return (*haqq al-'awda*).[46]

Shaykh Darwish and his supporters advocated for participation in the elections as a means to strengthen the legitimacy of the IM and its public establishments in Israeli society. This participation, they claimed, would also enable the assessment of the electoral power of the IM, and might help it to better serve the Arab population in Israel from within the Israeli parliament. Ibrahim Sarsur, former head of the SIM, noted in this regard that:

Religious preaching is the main thing, and politics is part of it . . . Political activity is part of a range of activities to bring people to religion, to build the human and the community, and maintain identity and land. Therefore, there is no contradiction between our participation in the *Knesset* and our other activities.[47]

Indeed, at the end of the twentieth century the IM resumed its social, welfare, and educational programs in various Arab communities, now under a political umbrella. Illustrating the efforts made to maintain Israeli law-and-order guidelines, grassroots charities sought to register with the Ministry of Internal Affairs, as well as with the local Arab municipalities. Furthermore, the leaders of these charities emphasized, time and again, that they would work within the Israeli legal system.[48]

The opposite camp, led by Shaykh Salah, did not accept these arguments. Shaykh Salah dismissed the claim that his camp's opposition to participation in the elections was due to ideological motives, such as the non-recognition of the state of Israel and its institutions. He claimed to accept the fact that he is an Israeli citizen, though he does not feel the need to prove his loyalty to the state of Israel every day and in every prayer. Salah noted, however, that his objection to the IM's participation in the elections stemmed from tactical, not strategic, reasons – that it was still "too early" for them to participate in Knesset elections.[49]

---

[46] More on the NIM in 'Issam Aburaiya, "Developmental Leadership: The Case of the Islamic Movement in Umm al-Fahm, Israel," MA thesis (Worcester, Mass.: Clark University, 1989).

[47] *Al-Mithaq*, 21 January 2008, 2–3.   [48] 'Ali, "Political Islam."   [49] Ibid.

This question, regarding the effectiveness of participation in the elections, was repeated in various arguments between the two camps. Shaykh Salah's supporters demanded a response from their competitors concerning the achievements of the IM as a result of participating in the local and national elections. Some had suggested that participation in the municipal elections was unnecessary, and had asked their supporters not to participate.

Though disagreements on these basic issues undermined internal relations, neither side stopped the momentum acquired by the IM on the whole. Today, the Muslim minority in Israel considers the IM to be among the central political forces in the country, alongside the secular and nationalist Arab parties. Furthermore, it appears that the IM has succeeded in raising the level of educational, medical, cultural, religious, and other services to the Arab minority, in addition to the establishment of new associations and institutions that also serve to recruit the voting public and provide religious preaching.

In the same vein, one observes the NIM's course of action in Israel – attempting to provide a new alternative to Arabs in Israel, based on creating a social infrastructure for a self-sufficient and self-sustaining community. The ultimate goal is to develop an autonomous community that can exist on its own merits, providing its members with all that the state of Israel does not provide, whether due to social or budgetary priorities. The IM's range of activity is vast, and includes a widespread system of kindergartens at nominal fee; almost fully subsidized clinics; ambulances; mosques (which function as community centers, libraries, and lecture halls); an independent soccer league (with thirty-eight teams); karate training dojos; dozens of bookstores; voluntary activities for the welfare of the citizenry (including house-building and home restoration for needy families); maintenance and restoration of Islamic sites and abandoned mosques (work done by the al-Aqsa Organization since 1948); the development of the Islamic Palestinian heritage; organizing national and religious activities; various festivals; religious 'pirate' cable television; the funding of weddings for the needy; and organizing various community activities, such as trips and other social, cultural, educational, and sporting events.[50] There are also dozens of organized charities and local and international non-profit organizations following the mandate of *zakat*. International support is often rendered under the auspices of the Islamic Relief Organization (Hay'at al-Ighatha al-Islamiyya)

---

[50] Ayman Agbaria and Muhanad Mustafa, "Two states for three peoples: The 'Palestinian Israeli' in the future vision documents of the Palestinians in Israel," *Ethnic and Racial Studies* 35 (4) (2005): 718–736.

in the spirit of cooperation with external Muslim communities: Palestinians in the Gaza Strip and the West Bank; Muslims in Kosovo, Chechnya, Kashmir, and Afghanistan.[51] Together with the increase in religious tendencies amid the Muslim minority in Israel came an avalanche of criticism – from the outside. For example, some Israeli right-wing political parties sought to reverse this trend. They claimed that the IM is a clearly anti-Israeli element that is likely to harm the already fragile and delicate relationship between Jews and Arabs in the country.[52] The debate over this issue made it to an official public hearing in the Knesset, in which some of the speakers referred to the IM as "a cancer inside the nation" and requested that it be outlawed.[53] The IM's growing strength was also a source of concern within the Arab minority in Israel, namely in the Christian and Druze communities. The strongest criticism from within the Israeli Arab population appeared in Hadash and Rakah political party pamphlets and newspapers.[54]

The pragmatic SIM made an effort to calm the internal and external critics. Explaining the IM's victories in the 1989 municipal elections, Shaykh Darwish claimed:

It was not a statement against the communists, rather it was a vote of confidence in the Islamic Movement and its ways...The Movement frightens the Jews, because they do not know what is written in our policy paper. Our platform does not speak of an Islamic state from the river to the sea. 'Greater Israel,' like all of Palestine – these approaches will only bring the two peoples back to the battlefield. Those who desire peace must throw dreams aside and compromise.[55]

Similarly, Shaykh Khatib, during an interview on Israeli television, declared in his name and in the name of the IM, an unconditional recognition of the state of Israel and a willingness to respect its laws.[56]

On other occasions, Shaykh Darwish turned to various elements in the Arab public to calm their fears regarding the growing strength of his

---

[51] More on the Islamic Relief Organization on its homepage at www.egatha.org/eportal.
[52] Ha'aretz, 12 February 1995.   [53] Ma'ariv, 8 February 1995.
[54] Smooha and Ghanem, "Political Islam."
[55] 'Abd Allah Nimr Darwish, "al-Hall al-muqtarah wa'l-salam al-manshud," al-Mithaq (24 August 2001) [Arabic]; 'Abd Allah Nimr Darwish, Akhi al-'aqil ijlis bina nufakkir sa'a (Kufr Qasim: Mitba'at Kufr Qasim, 1994) [Arabic]; 'Abd Allah Nimr Darwish, "Mashru'ana al-hadari bayna al-intilaq wa'l-inghilaq," unpublished book (1999) [Arabic]; 'Abd Allah Nimr Darwish, "al-Islam huwa al-hall," unpublished booklet (2005) [Arabic]; see also As'ad Ghanem, "The perception by the Islamic Movement in Israel of the regional peace process," in Ilan Pappe (ed.), Islam and Peace: Islamic Attitudes toward Peace in the Contemporary Arab World (Givat Haviva: Institute for Peace Research, 1992) [Hebrew], 83–99.
[56] 'Ali, "Religious Fundamentalism," 48–97.

movement. In an 'op-ed', the shaykh wrote that the IM has opened its gate to non-Muslim Arabs, also arguing that anyone who believes that Muslim adherence to their religion and that the ongoing growth in the strength of the IM pose a threat to non-Muslims is wrong.[57] A similar attitude has also been expressed by other IM leaders.

These sentiments illustrate the pragmatic attitude of the SIM, when approaching the Israeli public sphere. IM leaders stress their commitment to Israeli law and to maintaining transparency during their activities (focused on social and religious issues), and they also publicly reject the aggressive attitudes formally represented by militant Islamic groups.[58] That is, the IM in Israel distinguished itself from the militant Islamic movements in the Arab and Muslim worlds, and in the West Bank and the Gaza Strip.

This pragmatic approach may also be seen in the perception of the SIM regarding the Israeli–Palestinian conflict. In a conference held in Givat Haviva, Shaykh Darwish stressed that a Palestinian state, alongside the state of Israel, is an optimal solution for the Palestinian–Israeli conflict. Based on Islamic theological principles, the shaykh stated: "according to Islam, it is permitted to be satisfied with only parts of the land, in order that the Palestinian People might establish its own independent country alongside the state of Israel."[59] Still, the religious–political combination is not so simple – the shaykh added that he understands the feelings of the extreme Islamic elements within his own movement that claim sovereignty over all of Palestine and deny Israel's right to exist altogether. However, extremism in the Palestinian camp, according to Darwish, is more legitimate than Israeli extremism, in which the political right demands sovereignty over all of pre-state Palestine. He claimed that the Palestinians are the disadvantaged in the Arab–Israeli conflict, while the Israelis have already received much more than they deserve.[60]

The complexity of the religious–political view is further exemplified by the shaykh's analysis of the relationship between the Arab community in Israel and the state of Israel. While addressing the Israeli authorities, he commented: "Every place in which the Islamic Movement acts in an oppressing environment, it becomes violent. The more the secular authority implements a liberal policy, the more the Movement maintains moderation."[61] At the same time, Darwish maintained his commitment to the democratic 'rules of the game', stating that his movement would "in due time respect the opinion of the majority of the Palestinian

---

[57] Ibid.   [58] Mayer, *Islamic Resurgence*, 42–53.
[59] See Darwish, "al-Hall al-muqtarah wa'l-salam al-manshud."
[60] Ibid.   [61] Ibid.

population regarding the solution of the Palestinian–Israeli conflict. The Movement would stand firm against those elements that would try to harm a solution that is accepted by the majority."[62]

To summarize, the above discussion suggests three major chronological stages of Islamic history in Israel: (1) Islam under the Israeli military regime (1948–66), during which the socio-cultural and religious life of the Arab Muslim minority was significantly restricted and Muslim Arabs also suffered a sudden disconnection from the global Arab and Muslim worlds; (2) the 'Islamic awakening' that began in the late 1970s, during which a new religious community emerged, mainly due to the creation of various Islamic movements; and (3) entrance into the public and political arena by the late 1980s, while attempting to further religious community building by the establishment of Islamic religious authority and institutions, the subject matter of the next chapter.

[62] *Davar*, 10 November, 1992.

2   Islamic Religious Authority and Interpretation in Israel

The issue of 'religious authority'[1] in contemporary Islam has drawn the attention of scholars from various disciplines in modern Islamic studies.[2] These authors concluded that there is no single locus of religious authority within Islam today, while multiple groups in a variety of states are simultaneously claiming to speak on Islam's behalf.[3] A quick look at these studies indicates one of the major problems in this respect – that of God's vis-à-vis human sovereignty, an age-old issue that emerged during the very early stages of Islam and is still being debated today.[4] In his book

---

[1] The notion of 'authority' is one of the most diverse and controversial concepts found in legal and political philosophy literature and in different disciplines that suggest various definitions. For our purposes, I found R. B. Friedman's observation of "being in authority" versus "being an authority" very useful. According to Friedman, being "in authority" relates to a person who holds a structural position that empowers him/her to issue commands or directives. There is no "surrender of private judgment" in this case, because a person may disagree with the person in authority and yet feel that there is no choice but to comply. That is, the private conscience is rendered irrelevant due to the recognition that those 'in authority' ought to be obeyed. Obeying 'an authority', on the other hand, involves different dynamics. Here, a person surrenders private judgment in deference to the perceived superior knowledge, wisdom, or insight of 'an authority'. In Friedman's words "It is this special knowledge that constitutes the vindication of the layman's deferential acceptance of the authority's utterances, even though he does not or even cannot comprehend the grounds on which those utterances rest." See Richard Friedman, "On the concept of authority in political philosophy," in Richard Flathman (ed.), *Concepts in Social and Political Philosophy* (New York: Macmillan, 1973), 121–145.

[2] See Wael Hallaq, *Authority, Continuity, and Change in Islamic Law* (Cambridge: Cambridge University Press, 2001), 24–85; Wael Hallaq, "*Takhrij* and the construction of juristic authority," in Bernard Weiss (ed.), *Studies in Islamic Legal Theory* (Leiden: E. J. Brill, 2002), 317–335; Khaled Abou El Fadl, *Speaking in God's Name* (Oxford: Oneworld Press, 2001), 23–85; Khaled Abou El Fadl, *And God Knows the Soldiers: The Authoritative and Authoritarian in Islamic Discourses* (Lanham, Md.: University Press of America, 2001), ch. 2.

[3] John Esposito and Dalia Mugahid, *Who Speaks for Islam? What a Billion Muslims Really Think* (New York: Gallup Press, 2007). See also Gunder Krämer and Sabine Schmidtke (eds.), *Speaking for Islam: Religious Authorities in Muslim Societies* (Leiden: E. J. Brill, 2006).

[4] See Richard Tuck, "Why is authority such a problem?" in P. Laslett, W. Runciman, and Q. Skinner (eds.), *Philosophy, Politics and Society*, 4th series (Oxford: Blackwell, 1972), 194–207; Friedman, "On the concept of authority."

33

Speaking in God's Name, Khaled Abou El Fadl dated the Muslim dispute over sovereignty to as early as the reign of ʿAli Ibn Abi Talib, the fourth Rightly Guided Caliph (656–661), when a group in his camp, called the Khawarij, opposed the resolution of a political dispute with a competing political faction (led by Muʿawiya, the founder of the Umayyad dynasty, 661–750) by means of arbitration.[5] According to the Khawarij, this act of arbitration represented the acceptance of human dominion, rather than God's alone, following the Islamic saying *la hukm illa li-Allah* (judgment is God's alone) – meaning that all political decisions must be based solely on the words of God. ʿAli responded by calling upon the people to gather around him, and brought a copy of the Qurʾan, instructing it to speak to the people and inform them regarding God's law. The people were shocked and exclaimed: "What are you doing? The Qurʾan cannot speak, for it is not a human being!" ʿAli then explained that this was exactly his point – that the Qurʾan is merely paper and ink and does not speak for itself. Instead, it is human beings who enact it, according to their limited judgments and opinions.[6]

In principle, jurists from all generations stress that sovereignty ultimately rests with God, the supreme lawmaker, who has defined good and evil, the legal and the illicit (*al-halal waʾl-haram*). For example, al-Ghazali (d. 1111) stressed that the ultimate sovereignty of God is even more important than God's unity.[7] For Abu al-Aʿla Mawdudi (d. 1979), later supported by Sayyid Qutb (d. 1966), God is the sole sovereign over all creatures.[8] Qutb insists that there is "no sovereignty except God's, no law except from Allah, and no authority of one man over another."[9] That is, members of the Muslim community (*umma*) are God's subjects; the community's laws are divine; all its property belongs to God; its army is His and its enemies are also His.[10]

This omnipotent sovereignty is manifested in divine legislature, which seeks to regulate all human actions.[11] Thus, worship (*ʿibada*) must include all human actions, both explicit and implicit; one must

---

[5] Abou El Fadl, *Speaking in God's Name*, 23–25.

[6] Ibid.; see also Muhammad al-Shawkani, *Nayl al-awtar sharh muntaqa al-akhbar* (Cairo: Dar al-Hadith, n.d. [1938]), VII: 166 [Arabic]; Ibn Hajar al-ʿAsqalani, *Fath al-bari bi sharh sahih al-Bukhari* (Beirut: Dar al-Fikr, 1993), XIV: 303 [Arabic]; Montgomery Watt, *Islamic Political Thought: The Basic Concepts* (Edinburgh: Edinburgh University Press, 1968), 54.

[7] Ann Lambton, *State and Government in Medieval Islam: An Introduction to the Study of Islamic Political Theory* (Oxford: Oxford University Press, 1981), 109.

[8] Abu al-Aʿla Mawdudi, *The Islamic Law and Constitution* (Lahore: Islamic Publications, 1969), 204.

[9] Sayyid Qutb, *Milestones* (New Delhi: Islamic Book Service, 2008), 26.   [10] Ibid.

[11] Khaled Abou El Fadl, "Islam and the challenge of democratic commitment," *Fordham International Law Journal* 27 (1) (2003): 4–71, at 68.

completely submit to God's will as it manifests itself particularly in the Qur'an and the Sunna. The Qur'an is much more than just the highest source of the Islamic *corpus juris*; it is a constant source of inspiration. It constitutes an eternal constitution, appropriate for any time and place, and, as such, it contains all the basic principles of Islamic law and provides the platform for the development of political, legal, and moral norms. Therefore, any ruler or government that does not implement the strictures revealed in the Qur'an and the Sunna does not merit obedience.[12]

However, God does not seek to regulate all mundane human affairs, since human beings are taken to be vice-regents of God, with abilities approaching the divine (i.e. the miracle of the human intellect). Humanity has been given considerable latitude in regulating its own affairs, as long as it observes certain standards of moral conduct, including the preservation and promotion of human dignity and well-being. This is primarily based on the Qur'anic verses (2:30) that state:

> Behold, thy Lord said to the angels: I will create a vice-regent on Earth. They said: Wilt Thou place therein one who will make mischief therein and shed blood? Whilst we do celebrate Thy praise and glorify Thy holy [name]? He said: I know what ye know not.

Based on this and other related sources, jurists and commentators authorized a measure of human authority, arguing that God's sovereignty has, from the beginning of Creation, taken the form of human agency. This begs the questions: Who exactly should fulfill this human agency? To whom may authority be granted? And lastly, what form of domination shall human agency take?

Most jurists from various generations and schools of thought associate human agency with authority-holders (*wulat al-umur* or *ahl al-hall wa'l-'aqd*) – religious scholars and rulers. For example, Ibn Taymiyya (d. 1328) divided the ruling hegemony of the state between the 'ulama', the authorities in matters of jurisprudence, and the *umara'* (political rulers), who presumably consult the 'ulama'. Accordingly, the Shari'a needs the ruler's commitment and enforcement, while the state needs the Shari'a for its legitimacy.[13] He based himself on the premise that the purpose of government in Islam is to preserve the Shari'a and to enforce its dictates. In order to maintain and enforce the Shari'a, a temporal ruler is needed, making obedience to him a religious obligation. However, this

---

[12] Ibid.; Bernard Lewis, "Politics and war," in Joseph Schacht and C. E. Bosworth (eds.), *The Legacy of Islam* (Oxford: Clarendon Press, 1974), 156–209, at 159.

[13] 'Abd Allah al-'Uthaymin, *Ibn 'Abd al-Wahhab hayatuhu wa-fikruhu* (Riyadh: Dar al-'Ulum, 1987), 136 [Arabic].

ruler must consult the religious scholars, who are designated as those most authorized to clarify the instructions of the Shari'a.[14]

It must be noted, however, that 'human agency' still evokes disputes among modern Muslim scholars and jurists. For example, Hasan al-Turabi, a leading Sudanese activist and thinker, differentiates between God's sovereignty (*hakimiyya*) and humanity's vice-regency (*istikhlaf*). According to him, the proper political and social structures may be established on the basis of mutual contracts; since the Qur'an speaks to the individual consciousness, individuality should be maintained against any power of the state.[15]

Applying Friedman's notion of authority to the Islamic context in Israel, it is possible to claim that, while temporal rulers are principally recognized as being 'in authority', the religious scholars are expected to function as 'the authorities'.[16] In the following pages, I will try to describe the search for religious authority in Israel by discussing the various means of Islamic interpretation and the practice of issuing fatwas.

Islamic Interpretation in Israel

The previous chapter suggested a political and ideological fragmentation process within the Muslim community in Israel that reached its peak in the 1996 split, leading to the creation of three major ideological communities, differing in religious perceptions and tendencies: two branches of the Islamic Movement (IM, north and south) and the Sufis. These communities seem to act independently in terms of interpreting Islam by practicing *ifta'* (issuing fatwas) written by their own religious authorities. In addition to the permanent fatwa agencies: (1) Bayt al-Maqdis, the Islamic Council for Issuing Fatwas (ICIF), in Nazareth; (2) the Center for Islamic Studies, Manuscripts, and Issuing Religious Opinions (CIS) or the Ifta' Center ('Markiz al-Dirasat al-Islamiyya wa'l-Makhtutat wa'l-Ifta'), at al-Qasemi College in Baqa al-Gharbiyya; and (3) ad-hoc *ifta'* committees of the SIM, which also engage in independent fatwa practice.

---

[14] Ibid.

[15] See Ahmad Moussalli, "Hasan al-Turabi's Islamist discourse on democracy and *shura*," *International Journal of Middle East Studies* 30 (1994): 52–63, at 61.

[16] It must be noted, however, that these two notions of authority are not necessarily dichotomous in some parts of Islamic world. That is, a religious scholar may be politically empowered, as in the Shi'i case of religious–political theory (*wilayat al-faqih*), by which the supreme religious leader is simultaneously both 'in' and 'an' authority. Moreover, official religious authorities in the modern nation-state are acting as integral parts of their governments, often making these notions of authority inseparable.

Note that twentieth-century *ifta'* was characterized by the emergence of the *hay'a*, or 'fatwa committee', where more than one mufti ratifies the same fatwa.[17] One of the earliest official *ifta'* bodies was the Hay'at Kibar al-'Ulama' (Board of Senior 'Ulama') at al-Azhar in Egypt, founded in 1911. This board consisted of thirty leading 'ulama', from among whom Shaykh al-Azhar was selected.[18] In Indonesia, the first such organization, called Nahdatul 'Ulama', was founded in 1926 by traditionalist 'ulama'.[19] Other fatwa boards included: the World Muslim League in Mecca; the Fatwa Committee of the Organization of Islamic Countries; the Council of Islamic Ideology in Pakistan; Majlis Agama Islam in Malaysia; al-Majlis al-Aurubbi li'l-Ifta' (European Council of Ifta') of the International Union of Muslim Scholars (al-Ittihad al-'Alami li-'Ulama' al-Muslimin – hereafter IUMS),[20] and others.[21]

Various Muslim scholars stressed the essential nature of collective *ifta'*, due to the magnitude of the challenges facing modern Islamic societies. Shaykh Yusuf al-Qaradawi argues, for example, that dealing with important legal problems, especially those related to public affairs, requires collective scholarly efforts. According to him, an opinion issued by a group of muftis is much better than the opinion of an individual mufti, since a group has the advantage of mutual consultation, thereby preventing the inadvertent neglect of certain aspects of the problem under discussion and ensuring that all the relevant issues are properly addressed. Therefore, collective decisions are to be considered much more solid than those of individual muftis, regardless of those individuals' intellectual capacities. Al-Qaradawi draws on specific traditions, such as the Prophet's answer to 'Ali Ibn Abi Talib (the fourth caliph, d. 661), when

[17] Muhammad K. Masud, Brinkley Messick, and David. S. Powers (eds.), *Islamic Legal Interpretation: Muftis and their Fatwas* (Cambridge, Mass.: Harvard University Press, 1996), 28.

[18] Ibid., 147; More on the movement to reform al-Azhar in Daniel Crecelius, "Al-Azhar in the revolution," *Middle East Journal* 20 (1966): 31–49.

[19] Mudzhar Muhammad Atho, "Fatwas of the Council of Indonesian 'Ulama': A Study of Islamic Legal Thought in Indonesia, 1975–1988," Ph.D. thesis (Los Angeles: University of California, 1990), 6–7.

[20] The IUMS was established in July 2004 in Dublin by a group of scholars under the leadership of Shaykh al-Qaradawi. In October 2010 its headquarters was moved to Doha, and two additional branches were established in Egypt and Tunisia. The structure and composition of the IUMS has been transformed since its creation. Today it is considered the largest-ever Islamic religious body, with around 60,000 members, representing thousands of religious councils and organizations from all over the Arab and Islamic worlds: Sunnis, Shi'ites, Sufis, Ibadis. More on IUMS membership is found at its website: www.iumsonline.net/ar/default.asp?MenuID=3.

[21] More on the emergence of the collective practice of *ifta'* in Masud et al. (eds.), *Islamic Legal Interpretation*, 8–15, 26–32; Jakob Skovgaard-Petersen, *Defining Islam for the Egyptian State: Muftis and Fatwas of the Dar al-Ifta'* (Leiden: E. J. Brill, 1997), 284–286.

asked what to do when approaching a certain problem not treated by the Qur'an or in Hadith tradition. The Prophet instructed 'Ali to consult scholars and other believers familiar with the problem in question and not to make any decisions on his own. Al-Qaradawi also produced several examples of consultations by Abu Bakr (d. 634) and 'Umar Ibn al-Khattab (d. 644), the first two caliphs. Both often summoned scholars to consult with them, to make informed, collective decisions on legal and other religious problems. In any event, al-Qaradawi stresses that collective *ifta'* today should be conducted by an international Islamic scientific council of 'ulama' (*majma' 'ilmi Islami*). Such a council would be an autonomous body, independent of any governmental or political pressure. Most importantly, the decisions made by this council should be accepted as 'binding consensus' (*ijma'*), obligating all Muslims the world over.[22] In the same vein, 'Ali al-Salus, a Shari'a professor at Qatar University, argues that in contemporary global societies individual *ifta'* no longer makes sense; while a mufti is entitled to give his opinion, only a collective body of scholars may issue fatwas on important matters.[23]

Thus, the creation of the unofficial Islamic *ifta'* agencies in Israel seems to be inspired by and in line with this trend of the collective *ifta'* practice. Here, we discuss these agencies, their ideologies, the legal methodologies, and the means by which they interpret Islam for the Muslim minority in Israel.

1   The Islamic Council for Issuing Fatwas, Bayt al-Maqdis (ICIF)

The ICIF was established in 2002 by the NIM in Israel, in an attempt to institutionalize *ifta'*, which had been practiced unofficially since 1996 through the NIM's newspaper *Sawt al-Ḥaqq wa'l Ḥurriyya* (the Voice of Truth and Freedom) as published responses to public queries.[24] For its founders, the creation of the ICIF was inevitable "due to the large number of urgent issues and developments in [Islamic] jurisprudence and to resolve repeated conflicts in jurisprudential views and reduce the level of chaos in some cases."[25] According to the ICIF, the Muslim minority in Israel used to get such answers via satellite broadcasts and correspondence received from regional and international Islamic jurists. However, those jurists were often unfamiliar with the particular realities of the

---

[22] Yusuf al-Qaradawi, *al-Ijtihad al-mu'asir bayna al-indibat wa'l-infirat* (Beirut: al-Maktab al-Islami, 1998), 103–105 [Arabic].

[23] Skovgaard-Petersen, *Defining Islam for the Egyptian State*, 284–285.

[24] www.fatawah.com/Content-96.   [25] Ibid.

Muslim minority in Israel; as such, sometimes their answers were inadequate to meet the actual needs of the Israeli Muslim community.[26]

The ICIF was expected to address the challenges of modernity in various spheres of life that the Muslim minority in Israel faced on a daily basis, as may be seen in its goals and objectives:

1. To answer questions posed by the public, while taking into consideration the realities of the Muslim minority in Israel.
2. To make Islamic law more easily accessible and intelligible to the public (in a realistic and practical way).
3. To handle innovations and developments in daily life that challenge the Muslim minority in Israel through communication with specialized regional and international Islamic bodies.
4. To address recent religious controversies, known as 'fatwa chaos' (fawda al-fatwa).
5. To establish a unified methodology for dealing with religious issues related to the Muslim minority in Israel.
6. To bring different points of view closer together, based on the Qur'an, the Sunna, and the well-known (Sunni) legal schools (madhhabs).
7. To unify Muslim scholars in regard to general public issues of concern to the Muslim community (umma).[27]

Most importantly, the ICIF strives to be the leading religious authority for Muslims in Israel. This was made clear in its 'Vision' statement, in which the founders clearly declared their strategy for the establishment of such an authority. This was to be achieved mainly by "the expansion of the influence of the ICIF over all segments of society and schools-of-thought within the Muslim minority in Israel, thus referring to it as 'the supreme religious authority'."[28] To this end, the ICIF adopted a strategy manifested in "the establishment of mini-committees in community centers all over the country subordinate to the ICIF; and finally to get the membership chair of the Islamic International Fiqh Council."[29]

Indeed, the ICIF was targeting a wide audience from the various strata of the Muslim minority in Israel. Queries might be submitted either in person, by telephone, or in writing, as well as via the ICIF website.[30] For this purpose, weekly schedules are posted with the names of muftis and their contact information, and each list includes a female religious

---

[26] Ibid.; see also Iyad Zahalka, "The development of local Islamic jurisprudence in Israel," *Bayan* 1 (June 2014): 4–8, at 6; Iyad Zahalka, *al-Murshid fi al-qada al-shar'i* (Tel Aviv: Israel Bar Publishing House, 2008) [Arabic].
[27] www.fatawah.com/Content-96.   [28] Ibid.   [29] Ibid.
[30] See for example Abou El Fadl, *Speaking in God's Name*, 173.

counselor to answer women's queries.[31] The answers are posted directly
to the inquirer and also published, in most cases, in the weekly newspaper *Sawt al-Haqq wa'l-Hurriyya*, under the section entitled "Is'alu ahl
al-dhikr" (Ask the [religious] sages); in the monthly magazine *Ishraqa*,
under the section "Fatawa wa-ishraqa," and finally on the ICIF website
and Facebook pages.[32] Thus far, these fatwas have been compiled and
published in two volumes (in 2005 and 2012) under the title *Fatawa al-
Majlis al-Islami li'l-Ifta*[33] which include more than 11,000 fatwas related
to various spheres of life.[34] Other publications have been dedicated to
various local and general Islamic issues, including *Fatawa maqdisiyya*, on
issues related to the al-Aqsa Mosque (2013) and *Mukhtarat fiqhiyya fi
al-hajj wa'l-'umra*, selected *fiqh* issues on pilgrimage (2013). Even more
recently, 2015 saw two important new publications: *Fatawa al-mar'a al-
muslima*, a collection of fatwas for Muslim women, and *Fatawa hira'
hawla ahkam al-Qur'an al-karim wa-adabihi*, comprising fatwas on the
Qur'an and its ethics. In addition, the ICIF holds conferences to discuss Islamic issues, mainly in the socio-cultural and religious spheres.
For example, one such conference, held on November 11, 2013 in Kafr
Kanna, was entitled "A Conference Regarding Islamic Legal Opinions
Related to Worship in the Winter Season."[35]

Methodologically speaking, the ICIF does not seem to confine itself
to a specific Sunni tradition when applying the Islamic principle of preponderance (*tarjih*) as a determining criterion: "When issuing written
and oral fatwas, the ICIF relies on the four schools of thought (*madhhab*s) and departs from their teachings only in cases of private or public
necessity."[36] That is to say, the ICIF supports inter-*madhhab* interpretation and rejects the notion of fidelity to a specific *madhhab*, arguing

---

[31] See www.pls48.net/?mod=articles&ID=1148929#.Vb8GcF1WGJA; also www.fatawah.com/QuestionAdd.aspx

[32] www.fatawah.com/Content-961, www.facebook.com/fatawah.

[33] The latest multivolume edition was published in 2012. See al-Majlis al-Islami li'l-Ifta',
Fatawa al-Majlis al-Islami li'l-Ifta' (Umm al-Fahm: Mu'assasat al-Risala li'l Nashr wa'l
I'lam, 2012) [Arabic]. The online Fatwa Bank is at www.fatawah.com/Fatawah/0/0
.aspx.

[34] See ICIF's Q/A page at www.fatawah.com/Questions/0/0.aspx; Zahalka, "The development of local Islamic jurisprudence in Israel," 6.

[35] www.fatawah.net/Articles/21.aspx.

[36] al-Majlis al-Islami li'l-Ifta', *Fatawa al-mar'a al-muslima* (Umm al-Fahm: Mu'assasat al-
Risala li'l-Nashr wa'l-I'lam, 2015), 6 [Arabic]; see also www.fatawah.com/Content-96.
On *tarjih* see Hallaq, *Authority, Continuity, and Change*, 127, 130–131; Muhammad Abu
Zahra, *'Usul al-fiqh* (Cairo: Dar al-Fikr al-'Arabi, 1957), 350–365 [Arabic]; Bernard
Weiss, "Interpretation in Islamic law: the theory of *ijtihad*," *American Journal of Com-
parative Law* 26 (1978): 199–212; Bernard Weiss, *The Search for God's Law: Islamic
Jurisprudence in the Writings of Sayf al-Din al-Amidi* (Salt Lake City: University of Utah
Press, 1992).

that there is no reason for a Muslim to be constrained by a particular set of determinations. According to the ICIF, a creative interpreter is not bound by the specific opinion of his *madhhab* if he discovers the validity of an opinion found in another *madhhab*. With respect to a specific legal matter, it is not appropriate to prefer one's *madhhab* over another if the other's position is more just. An interpreter should always strive to attain justice for its own sake. Therefore, the seeker of justice, though he identifies himself with a particular legal school, should not abide by it when the truth lies elsewhere.[37]

When a new issue is raised, for which there are no precedents in the four schools, the ICIF prepares and/or utilizes relevant new Islamic research studies. The ICIF also quotes existing decisions "by one of the Islamic international councils, primarily by the Fiqh Council of the Organization of the Islamic Conference [i.e. the International Islamic Fiqh Academy in Jeddah]," and elicits decisions from other fatwa councils in the Muslim world such as the Egyptian Agency for Issuing Fatwas (Dar al-Ifta' al-Masriyya); the Palestinian Council of 'Ulama' in the Diaspora (Hay'at 'Ulama' Filistin fi'l Kharij); and the Permanent Committee for Scientific Research and Legal Opinions (al-Lajna al-Da'ima li'l-Buhuth al-'Ilmiyya wa'l Ifta').[38]

Note that ICIF's fatwas often begin with a statement explaining the reason for issuing the fatwa, and then proceed to name the inquirer and to state the query, followed by the argument, which varies in depth and length according to the case, and, finally, the opinion is given. In general, the argument starts with the Qur'anic precedents followed by relevant Hadiths and quotations from Islamic legal texts. Sometimes, fatwas presented at the meetings are issued without their arguments. Each fatwa is assigned a serial number and is signed by the ICIF, though many are not dated.[39] By not confining itself to a particular *madhhab*, the ICIF strives to utilize the rich Islamic legal tradition in the broadest sense, thus accommodating the legal system to the challenges of modern life.

Indeed, the ICIF's inter-*madhhab* trend is evident in frequent references to the four *madhhab*s in its fatwas. Nevertheless, the ICIF acknowledges the occasional discrepancies between the *madhhab*s and determines that *wasatiyya* ('moderation' or 'the median path') is the right path to be followed when approaching tradition:[40]

[37] al-Majlis al-Islami li'l-Ifta', *Fatawa al-mar'a al-muslima*, 6.
[38] See www.dar-alifta.org/default.aspx?LangID&Home=1&LangID=2;. http://palscholars.com/ar/texts.php?type=3; www.alifta.net/default.aspx.
[39] www.fatawah.com/Content-96.
[40] This Arabic term, *wasatiyya*, which literally means 'centrist; middle; moderate path', is derived from the Qur'an, Sura II, *al-Baqara*, 143: "And thus We have made you a

ICIF found the *wasati* methodology (*manhajiyyat al-wasatiyya*), while shunning extremism, fanaticism and intolerance, when issuing fatwas, and considers reality, local circumstances and customs while applying the four centuries-old, prestigious schools-of-thought (*madhhab*s) in favor of the Muslim Nation.[41]

Though the ICIF chose *wasatiyya* as its methodological path, it seems to have also adopted a conservative attitude, as indicated in its fatwas on various spheres of life, for instance regarding the ban on music. For example, in response to the query: "What is the Islamic rule about music?" the ICIF answered as follows:

The use of or listening to musical instruments, such as the oud, violin and other stringed instruments, or the clarinet, flute and other wind instruments, is forbidden (*haram*). This is the view the majority of scholars, such as Ibn al-Qayyim, al-Suyuti, al-Turtushi and others belonging to various *madhhab*s: Shafiʿi, Maliki and Hanbali. It is also the view of a number of contemporary scholars among them: Dr. Omar Suleiman al-Ashqar, Muhammad Hamid, and Abdul Aziz Bin Baz, the Standing Committee for Scientific Research and Issuing Fatwas in Saudi Arabia and others.[42]

Note that the positions of Muslim scholars toward music may be divided into two major groups. The dominant group follows the view that most music is permissible in principle, as long as the contents and performance accommodate Islamic legal and ethical norms. These jurists perceive singing as melodious words and music as 'noise' that is not wrong in and of itself. Problems only arise if the contents of a song are improper

community of moderation (*wasat*)," and suggests a lenient approach to the integration of almost all the Muslim schools of thought. Note that despite the widespread use of the term *wasatiyya* in modern Islamic theological discourse, there is still no precise and comprehensive definition of this term. Thus, one finds various descriptions of the term, such as 'middle path' or 'moderate way'. Ongoing attempts to define *wasatiyya* have been made by Muslim scholars over the last few years. More on the *wasatiyya* trend in contemporary Arab and Muslim thought in Michaelle Browers, *Political Ideology in the Arab World: Accommodation and Transformation* (Cambridge: Cambridge University Press, 2009); Sagi Polka, "The centrist stream in Egypt and its role in the public discourse surrounding the shaping of the country's cultural identity," *Middle Eastern Studies* 39 (2003): 39–64.

41 al-Majlis al-Islami liʾl-Ifta', *Fatawa al-marʾa al-muslima*, 6.

42 www.fatawah.com/Fatawah/290.aspx?word. In Saudi Arabia, the Standing Committee for Scientific Research and Issuing Fatwas is responsible for conducting research and administering private *ifta'*. More in Muhammad al-Atawneh, *Wahhabi Islam Facing the Challenges of Modernity: Dar al-Ifta in Modern Saudi Arabia* (Leiden: E. J. Brill, 2010), 17–34; Ahmad al-Dawish, *Fatawa al-lajna al daʾima liʾl-buhuth al-ʿilmiyya waʾl-ifta' waʾl-daʿwa waʾl-irshad*, 23 vols. (Riyadh: Maktabat al-ʿIbikan, 2000) [Arabic]; Safwat al-Shawadifi, *Fatawa hayʾat kibar al-ʿulamaʾ biʾl-mamlaka al-ʿarabiyya al-saʿudiyya* (Cairo: Maktabat al-Sunna, 1991) [Arabic].

or if the activities associated with the music are inappropriate, such as mixed dancing or inebriation.[43]

The second group of scholars, best represented by the Wahhabis, outlaws most entertainment involving music. For the Wahhabis almost all types of music are forbidden, since they provide an arena for temptation, seduction, and other immoral practices. This prohibition includes attending parties and musical events and the airing of instrumental music and singing, even in the official Saudi media.[44] In this case, the ICIF has adopted the conservative attitude, while ignoring the dominant one permitting music.

The ICIF's conservative approach is also manifested in fatwas related to women and gender. For example, sexual relations between a man and a woman who have signed a marriage contract (are officially engaged), but are not yet living together as husband and wife, are forbidden. This restriction is contrary to the outlook of more than one *madhhab* authorizing marital intercourse once the marriage contract has been validated, considering the couple as husband and wife in every way.[45]

Another example is that the ICIF forbids Muslim women to completely undress before other women, although most Islamic schools of thought only restrict 'nakedness' from the navel to the knee.[46] The ICIF acknowledges the aforementioned, but states: "this rule is embodied in the authentic traditions, but is not applicable in our time."[47]

In yet another case, the ICIF states that intermarriage between a Muslim man and a Christian or Jewish woman is to be avoided, due to the inherent damage this causes. A relevant fatwa explains why such interfaith marriages should be avoided and provides instruction on how to select an appropriate partner. Again, this attitude is contrary to the religio-legal attitudes found in many other *madhhab*s that permit marriages between Muslims and non-Muslims, particularly the 'People of the Book' (*ahl al-kitab*, i.e. Jews and Christians).[48]

In addition, the intermingling of men and women (*ikhtilat*) is forbidden by ICIF.

---

[43] Muhammad al-Atawneh, "Leisure and entertainment (*malahi*) in contemporary Islamic legal thought: music and the audio-visual media," *Islamic Law and Society* 19 (4) (2012): 397–415.

[44] Ibid.

[45] Majlis al-Islami li'l-Ifta', *Fatawa al-mar'a al-muslima*, 76–79; 'Abd al-Rahman al-Jaziri, *al-Fiqh 'ala al-madhahib al-arba'a* (Beirut: Dar al-Arqam, 1999), IV: 109–124 [Arabic].

[46] Majlis al-Islami li'l-Ifta', *Fatawa al-mar'a al-muslima*, 156. See the relevant fatwa at http://fatwa.islamweb.net/fatwa/index.php?page=showfatwa&Option=FatwaId&Id=115965.

[47] Majlis al-Islami li'l-Ifta', *Fatawa al-mar'a al-muslima*, 156.　[48] Ibid., 190–193.

An ICIF fatwa in this regard reads:

Query:
What is the Islamic rule regarding the intermingling of men and women?

Answer:
In principle, a Muslim must avoid mixing as much as possible, because of the evils and seduction that may result from it... Yet, if intermingling of the two sexes is inevitable, as in schools and colleges in our country [Israel], the following conditions must be maintained:
1. Appearance must be in accordance with the Islamic dress code, avoiding perfume, dyes, and similar forbidden decorations.
2. Lowering the gaze (*ghadd al-basar*) when necessary.
3. Commitment to [Islamic] speech and seating ethics...
4. Never being alone with a non-relative (*khalwa*).
5. Women require the husband's permission and single women [that] of the guardian.

We emphasize the need for separate education in schools, colleges, and other institutions, especially those subject to the control of the Islamic Movement... As long as such separation has not been enforced, special seating arrangements must be made, such that the male students sit in front and the female students sit behind them. Separation must be maintained when entering or exiting the classes, as well as elsewhere in these colleges and schools.[49]

For the ICIF, *ikhtilat* is the major cause of both temptation and seduction (*fitna*), exacerbated when a woman remains alone with a non-*mahram* man, a situation known in Islamic traditions as *khalwa*. According to Islamic law, legal *khalwa* (*khalwa shar'iyya* or *sahiha*) is allowed for couples following their marriage contract (*'aqd nikah*) and between unmarriageable kin, such as fathers, grandfathers, brothers, uncles, etc., and their female relatives. Any other contact between the sexes is illicit *khalwa*. However, there is no consensus amongst modern Muslim jurists on the legal meaning and implications of *khalwa* in the modern context.[50]

Nevertheless, most scholars consider illicit *khalwa* to be the intentional, clandestine meeting between a woman and a non-*mahram* man. For example, a group of muftis (a fatwa team) on the well-known Islamic website Islamweb has defined illicit *khalwa* as follows: " when a non-*mahram* man sits in private with a woman where they are not visible to the public... However, talking to or meeting with one or more women in public should not be considered as illicit *khalwa*."[51] In the same vein, Shaykh al-Qaradawi asserts that nothing is wrong with men and women

---

[49] Ibid., 145–146 [Arabic].
[50] See al-Jaziri, *al-Fiqh 'ala al-madhahib al-arba'a*, IV: 109–120.
[51] www.islamweb.net/ver2/Fatwa/ShowFatwa.php?lang=A&Option=FatwaId&Id=14566.

meeting in public places, as long as they behave in accordance with the relevant Islamic ethics and norms. According to him, contact between men and women is not totally forbidden, and may be commended when their purpose is noble and lawful. For instance, good goals might be: acquiring beneficial knowledge; engaging in charitable projects; performing obligatory *jihad*; or any other good deed that requires the efforts and cooperation of both sexes.[52]

The ICIF has its own, more conservative, definition of *khalwa*, as compared to its aforementioned counterparts: illicit *khalwa* is manifested in almost any contact between a woman and a non-*mahram* man, regardless of whether they are visible to the public or not, based on the Prophetic tradition: "When a man and a woman remain alone in private, the third party is always the Devil."[53]

To conclude, ICIF fatwas reflect a conservative approach, in contrast to its declared methodology of *wasatiyya*. As illustrated above, this is manifested in the adoption of conservative religious attitudes regarding issues such as: intermarriage, *khalwa*, and music, while no attention is paid to the unique circumstances of the Muslim minority in Israel.

2   *Ifta' Center (CIS) at the al-Qasemi College*

The Center for Islamic Studies, Manuscripts, and Issuing Religious Opinions (CIS) was founded in 2005 by the Khalawati Sufi order in Israel (Tariqat al-Qasimi al-Khalwatiyya al-Jami'a) in Baqa al-Gharbiyya. The history of the Khalawati Sufi order in Israel goes back to the late Ottoman period. It was founded by the al-Qawasmeh family from Hebron and is still managed by descendants of this family.[54] In 1989 the order established a college of Shari'a and Islamic studies bearing the family name, al-Qasemi College, which was certified by the Council for Higher Education in Israel in 1993. Today it has more than

---

[52] www.islamonline.net/servlet/Satellite?pagename=IslamOnline-Arabic-Ask_Scholar/FatwaA/FatwaA&cid=1122528600856 [Arabic].

[53] Muhammad b. 'Issa al-Tirmidhi, *Sunan al-Tirmidhi* (Cairo: Matba'at Mustafa al-Babi al-Halabi, 1975–1978), II: 462 [Arabic].

[54] See 'Abd al-Rahman Zu'bi, "The Khalawati Sufi Order in Palestine and Israel," MA thesis (Haifa: Haifa University, 2003), 31–54 [Hebrew]. More on Sufi orders in modern times in Martin van Bruinessen and Julia Day Howell (eds.), *Sufism and the "Modern" in Islam* (London: I. B. Tauris, 2007); Catharina Raudvere and Leif Stenberg (eds.), *Sufism Today: Heritage and Tradition in the Global Community* (London: I. B. Tauris, 2009); Ron Geaves, Markus Dressler, and Gritt Kinkhammer (eds.), *Sufis in Western Society: Global Networking and Locality* (London: Routledge, 2009); Frederick de Jong, "The Sufi orders in nineteenth and twentieth century Palestine," *Studia Islamica* 58 (1983): 148–180; Itzchak Weismann, "Sufi brotherhoods in Syria and Israel: a contemporary overview," *History of Religions* 43 (2004): 303–318.

3,000 students and a faculty of 150, composed of both Arab and Jewish Israeli lecturers. Students are awarded degrees in seven fields: Islamic studies, Arabic language and literature, English language and literature, mathematics and computers, early childhood education, special education, and the sciences.[55]

In fact, the CIS was originally established, and still functions, as an integral part of al-Qasemi College's Department of Islamic Studies.[56] Among its major goals and objectives, as presented in its website, are the following:

1. Spreading Islamic teachings and thoughts.
2. Taking part in investigating important modern-day issues.
3. Issuing collective fatwas to accommodate and resolve problems that Muslims, both local and international, are facing.
4. Producing Islamic research and studies that address emerging issues.
5. Showing the tolerant nature of Islam as a middle path, neither extremist nor intolerant.
6. Introducing Islamic civilization and its contribution to humanity.
7. Urging researchers to approach modern-day issues in various spheres of life: educational, social, economic, medical, etc., and to clarify Islamic attitudes toward them.
8. Fostering the relationship between the CIS and other local and international fatwa agencies.
9. Developing and enriching the CIS's library with studies and various other publications.
10. Occasionally publishing selected fatwas.[57]

According to the CIS chairman, Shaykh Khaled Mahmud, the center aims to serve the Muslim community in Israel by responding to their practical, real-life queries. He claims that thousands of fatwas have been issued following requests received from Muslims across Israel, although most of these fatwas are undocumented, having been given orally. The CIS issues fatwas in an attempt to accommodate Islamic law to the local reality of the Muslim minority in twenty-first-century Israel in a way that preserves the delicate balance between the divergent groups within the community itself.[58]

To this end, the CIS presents itself not only as an *ifta'* center, but as an Islamic research center that also promotes academic studies on religious issues that take into consideration the modernization process

---

[55] www.qsm.ac.il/pr/.   [56] Interview with Khaled Mahmud, August 5, 2015.
[57] http://fatawa.qsm.ac.il/m-04.htm.
[58] Interview with Khaled Mahmud, August 5, 2015.

undergone by the Muslim minority, especially in Israel. Shaykh Mahmud stated:

The age in which we live now is an era of scientific and technical challenges. No nation can compete in this area if it does not employ all its scientific and intellectual energies to build a healthy society and to achieve the intended development.[59]

Accordingly, the CIS also publishes various religious studies dealing with problems encountered in modern society and issues periodic bulletins, such as *Majallat Dirasat Islamiyya* (Magazine of Islamic Studies). In addition, the CIS gives public lectures, conducts seminars and conferences, and utilizes modern media and communications in order to reach a wide audience.[60]

As for the legal methodology adopted by the CIS, it seems to resemble that of the ICIF: it does not confine itself to a certain Sunni school of thought, and applies 'preponderance' (*tarjih*) as a determining criterion. The following are its sources and methods, as presented in the CIS website:

1. Adoption of Sunni legal theory and different methods of argumentation (*turuq al-istidlal*) from various *madhhab*s, especially that of determining the preponderance of opinions (*tarjih*).
2. The sources for issuing fatwas must be those agreed upon by the major Sunni schools of thought.
3. Other controversial sources of legislation (often termed *masdar tashri'i tab'i* [ancillary legislative sources] based on Islamic legal principles) may be: analogy (*qiyas*); seeking good will or striving for betterment for all (*istihsan*); public interest (*al-maslaha al-'amma*); and local custom (*'urf*) – all of which consider real-life situations in line with the spirit of Islam and public welfare.
4. Reliance on reliable Islamic juridical sources.
5. Strong adherence to the fundamental Islamic legal principle that 'the prevention of damage is preferable to the promotion of benefit' (*dar' al-mafasid yataqaddam 'ala jalb al-masalih*), while publishing fatwas that simultaneously accommodate both the current reality of Muslims (in Israel) and the spirit of Islam, by means of a correct interpretation of the intentions of the Shari'a (*maqasid al-Shari'a*).[61]

---

[59] Ibid. [60] http://fatawa.qsm.ac.il/m-07.htm; see also http://alqasimy.com/afta.php.
[61] http://fatawa.qsm.ac.il/m-05.htm. More on these principles in Abu Ishaq al-Shatibi, *al-Muwafaqat fi usul al-ahkam* (Cairo: Maktabat Muhammad 'Ali Sbih, 1969), III: 257, IV: 196, 198 [Arabic].

Clearly, the CIS intends to function as a religious authority able to accommodate the Shari'a to suit the reality of the Muslim minority in Israel, as indicated by the adoption of the flexible methodology cited in item 5 above, and to serve as a body to which Muslims in Israel can turn with their religious queries.

However, the Sufi nature of the CIS suggests another methodology for attaining authority, resembling Friedman's aforementioned notion of "being an authority."[62] That is, the Sufi authority structure of *shaykh–murid* (master–disciple) is manifested by the full submission of the latter to the will of the former as total obedience to all the master's orders and advice. In traditional Sufi teachings, disciples must abandon themselves to the shaykh and his followers "like a dead body to its washer."[63] Shaykh Mahmud described the centrality of dialogue and constant recourse to the Sufi shaykh in these words:

Beneficence and Sufism are in fact synonymous and one can never truly grasp them unless in the company of divine and perfect masters. The master who calls for the truth is the one who propagates in the path of Allah insightfully. He is also the one who calls on Muslims to go in line with the teachings of Prophet Muhammad ... Al-Suhrawardi legitimized the master status based on the saying of Prophet Muhammad: "Among His servants, Allah loves most those who endeavor to make Allah love his servants and make Allah's servants love Allah, and walk on land giving advice to people."[64]

That is, the absolute loyalty of the followers to their charismatic spiritual leader provides the mainstay of this interrelationship, embodied by Sufi 'etiquette' (*adab*). The early followers of the Prophet (the Companions) serve as role models for the Sufi masters:

The rule of the [Sufi] master is to invite people unto God on behalf of the prophets and to purify their souls of their arrogance, in order, as said by the late Shaykh 'Abd al-'Aziz al-Dabbagh, to be able to bear the secret of knowledge. The Shaykhs are the soldiers of Allah, who guide the disciples and those who seek knowledge and renew the activity of faith in their age and rekindle the light of the message of Prophet Muhammad after the passage of time and the successive centuries. This is what Prophet Muhammad meant by "the scholars inherit the prophets." If the Shaykh's job is so important, it is a must that we treat him most politely, if we intend to arrive at the highest level of spiritual perfection. The Companions reached the highest levels for being in the company

---

[62] See note 1 above.
[63] Hans Harder, *Sufism and Saint Veneration in Contemporary Bangladesh: The Maijbhan-daris of Chittagong* (London: Routledge, 2011), 88–95.
[64] Khalid Mahmud, "The ethical behavior of the Sufi disciple with his sheikh in the Khal-wati order," *In the Footsteps of Sufism History: Trends and Praxis: The First International Conference at al-Qasemi College* (Baqa al-Gharbiyya: al-Qasemi College, 2001), 23–24.

of Prophet Muhammad and for being well-behaved and most respectful of him.[65]

Islamic Sufism is a science which abides by the basic sources of Islam. Sufism is all about etiquette, and each state and station has its own special etiquette. Those who abide by the etiquettes of the times may arrive at the status of the Sufi 'knower of God'. However, one who loses these etiquettes becomes distant from that status, rejected, mistakenly thinking that he/she is close and accepted. It has been said: "The one who is shackled by genealogy is freed by etiquette." Some Sufis said: "One who has no etiquette, can never walk the path and will never arrive at the desired destination."[66]

Etiquette with the master involves total obedience and submission to his commands and prohibitions, venerating and respecting him, and never objecting to his spiritual training. The disciples should respect him as an assiduous person who is most qualified to guide. They should initiate service to him, seek his counsel, as much as possible, tolerate his educational positions and transfer none of the Shaykh's sayings, except for those which ordinary people's minds can bear and comprehend.[67]

Indeed, the local community of the CIS mainly consists of those belonging to the Khalawati Sufi order. To be Khalawati means to belong to one of three circles. The first of these is a restricted, elitist circle of students, forming the core of the order. The second, larger, circle consists of followers seeking proximity to the discourse and the blessing rituals in the public sphere, without being required to change their personal lifestyles. Their affiliation is partial and uneven, but they may experience the full scope and significance of Khalawati Sufism when the Shaykh Guide is present. The third circle is harder to define. It may be described as being composed of believers who are able to see the spiritual Shaykh Guide without taking an active part.

To conclude, the fatwas issued by the CIS seem to take much softer positions than those of the ICIF. For example, there is a fatwa concerning the taking of a bank mortgage for the construction of a family home. According to Shaykh Mahmud, Muslims in Israel are entitled to obtain a mortgage, as long as the Islamic principles of 'public interest', 'preventing evil', and 'necessity overcoming a prohibition' (*al-darurat tubih al-mahzurat*) are applied.[68] He claims that the housing situation for Muslims in Israel is very bad. There is little land allocated by the state for residential construction and housing for young Muslim families. There

---

[65] Ibid., 24.   [66] Ibid.   [67] Ibid.
[68] Interview with Khaled Mahmud, August 5, 2015.

is also an insufficient supply of apartments for rent. Muslim society cannot tolerate such crowded living conditions in the long run. Thus, the issue of building a family home has become a 'necessity' without which Muslims find it very difficult to start their families. The shaykh further explains that this ruling is unique to Israeli Muslims, due to the specific, local circumstances.[69]

3   Ad Hoc Committees for Ifta': the Southern Movement (SIM)

In contrast to the institutionalization process that the ICIF and the CIS underwent, the practice of *ifta'* by the SIM has never been formalized, and is still done by ad hoc committees. The head of the SIM, Shaykh Hamad Abu Da'abis, says that this reality stems from certain financial and logistical considerations; however, he stresses that the creation of a southern *ifta'* center is only a matter of time.[70] According to him, there were some previous attempts to do so by establishing the al-Hiwar College in Tira (2001) and the Council of Fatwa and Islamic Studies in Kafr Qasim; however, they no longer exist. In the meantime, the SIM tried to reach decisions on religious issues by convening ad hoc committees on demand.[71] Fatwas may also be given individually and sporadically to those who apply to scholarly religious members of the SIM, such as the *imam*s of mosques, as long as the respondent has sufficiently studied the issue in question.[72]

Moreover, the religious authority of the SIM may even be derived from foreign scholars and religious institutions across the Islamic world. SIM leaders may rely on various agencies and authorities, including the grand mufti of the Palestinian Authority, whose fatwas may be relevant to the Muslim minority in Israel.[73] In principle, the SIM is also not committed to one particular school of thought. Like the ICIF and the CIS, the SIM recognizes all four Sunni *madhhab*s, adopting moderate attitudes from them that may serve the current reality faced by the Muslim community in Israel.

One of the most prominent examples of SIM ad hoc *ifta'* was a fatwa regarding participation in Knesset elections. This particular fatwa was an updated version of a preliminary ruling handed down by leaders of the SIM during the 1996 elections. Shaykh 'Abd Allah Nimr Darwish, a former SIM head, made clear references to developments in Israel and the region with regard to the Muslim minority in Israel. This revised fatwa was signed by the Committee of Fatwa and Islamic Studies (now

---

[69] Ibid.   [70] Interview with Hammad Abu Da'abis, July 29, 15.
[71] Ibid.   [72] Ibid.   [73] Ibid.

defunct), which authorized the participation in the Israeli elections to the Knesset. That committee, aware of the Islamic debate on the issue, argued that, after reviewing the positions of religious scholars for and against participation in the elections, had reached the conclusion that there is no contradiction between participation in political life and the call to Islam. Even if political participation involves some 'harm', it is minimal and does not violate the other principles of Islam; the minor damage would be dwarfed by the benefits derived from active participation. In such cases, the lesser of the two evils is to be chosen. Participation in Israeli elections, as dictated by reality, is not a concession made to 'oppressors', whereas refraining from active participation might leave the Muslim community solely in the hands of 'oppressors'. Indeed, the SIM chose the first option, recognizing that such participation is both essential and permissible, thanks to the flexibility in Islam.[74]

In actual fact, this fatwa is an important manifesto, presenting the SIM's pragmatic approach. Following this fatwa, the indigenous Muslim minority in Israel managed to assert their presence in their homeland, while ignoring the existence of a legitimate Israeli establishment (and avoiding the conflicting state symbols and its definition as a Jewish/democratic state). This fatwa also states that the reference to the issue of elections in the IM is based on two components. The first relates to political action, which is part of a wide range of activities with one primary goal – to preach Islam for the betterment of individuals and society and to maintain their identity and land. Therefore, there is no conflict between legislative work and the community action of the SIM. Moreover, the SIM believes that their incorporation yielded positive results and achieves long-term goals: to serve the Muslim community in Israel; to promote the welfare of individuals and of Muslim society; to protect the Temple Mount mosques; and to amass assets.

The second component is based on the Islamic principle of public interest (*maslaha 'amma*). Thus, participation in the elections is a tool, a means to combat racism and oppressive policies enacted by the Israeli government. Active political participation may pave the way to solving the difficulties of the Muslim public in Israel, whereas leaving the parliamentary domain could result in a significant void that might be filled by non-Islamic parties. Moreover, the aforementioned fatwa emphasizes that avoiding political action might be wrongly interpreted by the Muslim public, who might think that Islamists are only concerned

---

[74] Iyad Zahalka, "The development of Islamic law in Israel," in Meir Hatina and Muhammad al-Atawneh (eds.), *Muslims in the Jewish State* (Tel Aviv: Hakibbutz Hameuchad, forthcoming) [Hebrew].

with Muslim society – prepared to be involved only in matters of religion and responsible solely for the maintenance of proper Islamic practice.

To date, there seems to be no single locus of Islamic religious authority in Israel, while multiple groups are claiming to speak on Islam's behalf simultaneously. This is manifested in the religio-political fragmentation amid the Muslim community in Israel, each group seeking to create its own religious authority: the ICIF of the NIM; the CIS of the al-Qasemi (Khalawati) Sufi order and, finally, the ad hoc SIM *ifta'* committees.

A quick survey of the work and methodologies of these various religious agencies indicates some similarities, as well as discrepancies, when approaching the realities of the Muslim minority in Israel. While the al-Qasemi Sufi order and the SIM demonstrate a pragmatic approach in their attempts to accommodate the Israeli socio-cultural and political arenas, the NIM takes a much harder line, seen not only in its national political participation, but also in regard to the socio-cultural and theological issues addressed in its fatwas.[75] Thus far, none of these three *ifta'* agencies in Israel has yet been able to apply *fiqh al-aqalliyyat* in Israel, continuing to rely heavily on foreign Islamic and Arab religious authorities. Israeli Muslims tend to maintain strong ties with the regional socio-cultural and religious space and with their peers in the Muslim Arab world, as do the work and methods adopted by Israeli *ifta'* institutions. Moreover, the public's search for and reliance on religious authorities and sources for rulings on mundane problems in daily life regularly solicit religio-legal opinions from the international Muslim community, rendering Western *fiqh al-aqalliyyat* irrelevant to the Israeli case.

The next chapter proceeds with this discussion from yet another angle – the public point of view regarding these religious agencies and their authority.

---

[75] See Elie Rekhess, "Fundamentalist Islam among Israeli Arabs," in Kitty Cohen (ed.), *Perspectives in Israeli Pluralism* (New York: Israeli Colloquium, 1991), 34–44.

3   Islam and the Public
Affiliation, Religiosity, and Observance

This chapter discusses Islam in Israel from yet another angle – from the public's perspective. It focuses on attitudes expressed by Muslims in Israel regarding their religious affiliation, religiosity, and observance. It studies the extent to which they are guided by Islamic laws and norms in their daily life and behavior (observance) or question them by submitting special legal appeals to the Islamic authorities for consideration and seeking new rulings (query submission). Emphasis is placed on the symbiotic connection between religiosity and personal religious observance, and how the former affects the latter. How does Islam affect the normative behavior of Muslims in Israel? To what extent has Islam shaped the socio-cultural and political identities of the Muslim minority in Israel? In order to ascertain these attitudes, not merely from the literature, but in the field, the authors of this book surveyed the various sectors of the Muslim public. To this end, people were asked to respond about various matters: religious affiliations, religiosity, and the degree of their personal observance.

Note the critical distinction between 'formal' Islam and 'public' Islam. Following the microsociological approach taken by Clifford Geertz, the discussion in the present chapter deals with individuals' empirical realities as lived.[1] By means of the survey questions presented below we were able to gain insights into personal religious preferences and identities, not resulting exclusively from collective factors, such as tribal lineage, clan, etc.

Affiliation with Islamic Schools of Legal and Theological Thought (*Madhhab*s)

One of the major aims of this book is to explore the nature of Islam in Israel. To this end, the following presents the significant findings on the public's affiliations with different Islamic schools of thought, legal and/or theological. Given the diversity that exists in the Muslim world,

---

[1] Geertz, *Islam Observed*.

Table 3.1 *Legal* madhhab *affiliation (%)*

Legal *madhhab* affiliation	
	Percentage
Hanafi	14.0
Maliki	1.8
Shafi'i	51.5
Hanbali	11.8
Other doctrines	4.6
Unaffiliated	15.6
Total	99.4

this discussion maps the religious affiliations of the Muslim minority in Israel within both the Israeli and the greater Muslim contexts.

It is no surprise that the majority of the Muslim public, 51.5 percent, declared its affiliation to the Sunni Shafi'i legal *madhhab*, while 14.0 percent are Hanafis, 11.8 percent are Hanbalis, 1.8 percent are Malikis and 15.6 percent are unaffiliated (see Table 3.1). Note that, historically, the Shafi'i *madhhab* has dominated countries such as Israel, Syria, and Jordan.[2]

Affiliation to a legal *madhhab* was examined in relation to different factors, including residential region, educational level, and socio-economic status. No correlation was found between *madhhab* and gender ($\chi^2(5) = 3.29$), such that the gender of the respondents was not related to their attitudes regarding the *madhhab*. It was also found that the age of the participants ($\chi^2(20) = 11.84$) and their marital status ($\chi^2(20) = 11.12$) were not correlated to their conceptions of juridical doctrine. However, the residential regions were found to affect the participants' ideas of the *madhhab*; for instance, a high percentage of those residing in the Galilee are affiliated with the Hanafi *madhhab* ($\chi^2(15) = 69.18$; $p < 0.001$ and rc = .23; $p < 0.001$), as shown in Table 3.2.

As for the dominant religion in the participants' various residential communities, living in predominantly Muslim, Christian, or Druze neighborhoods was found to affect legal *madhhab* affiliation ($\chi^2(15) = 70.42$; $p < 0.001$ and rc = 0.22; $p < 0.001$), as shown in Table 3.3.

In addition, no correlation was found between educational level and legal *madhhab* affiliation, meaning that education, too, does not affect affiliation to a certain *madhhab* ($\chi^2(25) = 25.05$). The economic status of the participants also showed no significant influence on the affiliation to a certain legal *madhhab* ($\chi^2(30) = 30.60$). Table 3.4

---

[2] More on the *madhhab* geography in Wael Hallaq, *Shari'a: Theory, Practice, Transformation* (Cambridge: Cambridge University Press, 2009).

Table 3.2 *Cross-tabulation: legal* madhhab *affiliation (%) and residential region*

		Legal *madhhab* affiliation					
		Hanafi	Maliki	Shafi'i	Hanbali	Other	Unaffiliated
Residential region	Galilee	12.9	2.7	46.0	13.7	6.1	18.6
	Triangle	18.6	0.0	59.3	12.4	2.7	7.1
	Negev	0.0	0.0	100.0	0.0	0.0	0.0
	Mixed cities	20.0	2.5	32.5	12.5	0.0	32.5

Table 3.3 *Cross-tabulation: legal* madhhab *affiliation (%) and residential community*

Residential community	Legal *madhhab* affiliation					
	Hanafi	Maliki	Shafi'i	Hanbali	Other	Unaffiliated
All Muslim	14.1	2.4	57.2	11.8	2.7	11.8
Mostly Muslim	16.7	0.6	48.1	8.3	4.5	21.8
Mostly Christian	16.7	0.0	50.0	0.0	0.0	33.3
Mostly Druze	0.0	0.0	16.0	36.0	28.0	20.0

Table 3.4 *Cross-tabulation: legal* madhhab *affiliation (%) and average monthly income*

		Legal *madhhab* affiliation					
		Hanafi	Maliki	Shafi'i	Hanbali	Other	Unaffiliated
The **average** net **monthly** **income** of an Arab family in Israel is 7,300 NIS. Compare this to your family's income.	Much higher	9.1	3.0	45.5	3.0	6.1	33.3
	A little higher	10.1	5.1	53.5	11.1	5.1	15.2
	The same	21.2	.7	43.2	10.3	6.2	18.5
	A little less	8.6	1.4	61.2	15.8	2.2	10.8
	Much less	17.6	0.0	51.4	13.5	5.4	12.2

Table 3.5 *Theological* madhhab *affiliation (%)*

Theological *madhhab* affiliation	
	Percentage
Ash'ari	2.6
Maturidi	0.6
Ahl al-Hadith	46.7
Other	17.0
Unaffiliated	29.9
Total	96.8

presents the participants' responses in light of their average monthly incomes. This table indicates that there are indeed differences between the choices of legal *madhhab* by the average monthly incomes. At all the income levels, the dominant choice of legal *madhhab* is Shafi'i, while the second place choice, even of those with the high incomes, was "unaffiliated." However, among those with average monthly incomes, there was a significant percentage (21.2 percent (of those affiliated with the Hanafi *madhhab*.

However, in the case of the theological *madhhab*s, one observes a different picture: 29.9 percent of the participants were unaffiliated (could not pick a specific theological *madhhab*), while 46.7 percent stated that they were 'orthodox' Muslims (i.e. belonging to Ahl al-Hadith); see Table 3.5.

The affiliation to a theological *madhhab* was examined vis-à-vis the same variables mentioned above: residential region, educational level, and economic status, in addition to marital status and age. No correlations were found between gender ($\chi^2(4) - 1.58$); age ($\chi^2(16) - 21.86$); or marital status and the theological affiliation ($\chi^2(16) = 10.11$) of the participants. However, a correlation was found between the theological affiliation and the degree of religiosity ($\chi^2(20) = 50.95$; p < 0.001 and rc = 0.16; p < 0.001), as may be seen in Table 3.6.

In terms of geographic distribution, the findings indicate that the residential regions are correlated with the participants' theological *madhhab* affiliations, with a Cramer's V of medium strength ($\chi^2(12) = 73.20$; p < 0.001 and rc = 0.23; p < 0.001), as indicated in Table 3.7.

Clearly, residents of the Galilee identify with 'orthodox' Islam (55.7 percent) more than the residents of other regions, such as the Triangle (30.6 percent). However, the residential communities (majority Muslim, Christian, or Druze) showed no correlations with the theological *madhhab*s ($\chi^2(12) = 16.62$).

Table 3.6 *Cross-tabulation: theological* madhhab *(%) and religiosity*

Theological *madhhab*	Very religious	Religious	Sort of religious	Somewhat non-religious	Not religious	Not religious at all
Ash'ari	23.1	30.8	46.2	.0	.0	.0
Maturidi	.0	.0	.0	100.0	.0	.0
Ahl al-Hadith	5.7	33.5	45.2	11.7	3.9	.0
Other	7.3	31.7	30.5	17.1	11.0	2.4
Unaffiliated	10.3	20.5	43.8	12.3	7.5	5.5

Their educational levels (advanced degrees, high-school diploma, or uneducated) do not seem to affect the participants' attitudes toward certain theological *madhhab*s ($\chi^2(20) = 21.58$). Furthermore, their economic status ($\chi^2(24) = 22.84$) and religiosity ($\chi^2(25) = 32.26$) are correlated with their attitudes toward them. In particular, the average monthly salaries of the respondents were found to be correlated with their theological *madhhab* affiliation ($\chi^2(16) = 28.80$; $p < 0.05$ and rc = 0.12; $p < 0.05$). Table 3.8 presents a cross-tabulation in which affiliation with each theological *madhhab* varies with the average monthly salary.

In the same vein, the participants were asked about their adherence to other Islamic ideological groups that currently dominate the Islamic discourse: Salafis, Salafi Jihadists, 'moderates' (*wasati*, following the 'median path') and, finally, 'liberals'.[3] Of all the participants, 55.9 percent declared themselves moderates; 13.6 percent said they are liberals; 5.0 percent are Salafis; and 0.8 claimed to be Salafi Jihadists (see Table 3.9).

Again, some of the above variables, such as residential region, gender, age, and marital status were considered in the analysis. It is evident that no correlations were found between the participants' gender ($\chi^2(5) = 9.48$); age ($\chi^2(20) = 9.83$); or marital status ($\chi^2(20) = 8.76$) and their responses regarding their Islamic ideological affiliation. However, the residential region (Galilee, Negev, Triangle, and mixed cities) was found to affect the participants' responses regarding Islamic ideological affiliation ($\chi^2(15) = 35.62$; $p < 0.01$ and rc = 0.16; $p < 0.01$). Table 3.10 presents a cross-tabulation of the geographical regions versus ideological affiliations, showing the different responses according to the participants'

---

[3] On liberal Islam see Charles Kurzman (ed.), *Liberal Islam: A Sourcebook* (New York: Oxford University Press, 1998); Leonard Binder, *Islamic Liberalism: A Critique of Development Knowledge* (Chicago: University of Chicago Press, 1988).

Table 3.7 *Cross-tabulation: theological* madhhab *(%) and residential region*

		Residential region			
		Galilee	Triangle	Negev	Mixed cities
Theological *madhhab*	Ash'ari	58.3	16.7	0.0	25.0
	Maturidi	100.0	0.0	0.0	0.0
	Ahl-al Hadith	55.7	30.6	8.7	5.0
	Other	53.4	9.6	30.1	6.8
	Unaffiliated	63.8	23.2	0.0	13.0

Table 3.8 *Cross-tabulation: theological* madhhab *(%) and economic status*

		Average of net monthly income of an Arab family in Israel is 7,300 NIS. Compare this to your family's income.				
		Much higher	A little higher	The same	A little less	Much less
Theological *madhhab*	Ash'ari	8.3	25.0	58.3	8.3	0.0
	Maturidi	0.0	33.3	0.0	0.0	66.7
	Ahl al-Hadith	3.5	19.9	26.8	34.6	15.2
	Other	7.1	17.9	29.8	28.6	16.7
	Unaffiliated	10.8	22.3	31.1	22.3	13.5

Table 3.9 *Adherence to Islamic ideological groups (%)*

To which of the current Islamic ideological groups do you adhere?	
	Percent
Salafis	5.0
Salafi Jihadists	0.8
Moderates	55.9
Liberals	13.6
Other	11.2
Unaffiliated	8.8
Total	95.4

Table 3.10 *Cross-tabulation: Islamic ideology (%) and residential region*

		Residential region			
		Galilee	Triangle	Negev	Mixed cities
To which of the current	Salafis	62.5	25.0	4.2	8.3
Islamic ideological	Salafi	50.0	25.0	.0	25.0
groups do you adhere?	Jihadists				
	Moderates	51.0	31.2	12.2	5.7
	Liberals	70.3	9.4	3.1	17.2
	Other	68.1	21.3	4.3	6.4
	Unaffiliated	62.2	13.5	10.8	13.5

residential regions. Notice how adherence to Salafism varies significantly across the regions: Triangle (25 percent), Galilee (62.5 percent), and Negev (4.2 percent).

Note the correlation between Islamic ideology and religiosity ($\chi^2(25) = 93.63$; $p < 0.001$ and rc = 0.2; $p < 0.001$). In this regard, Salafis and Salafi Jihadists consider themselves to be the most religious, as indicated in Table 3.11.

In fact, the Islamic ideological groups chosen by the participants show no correlations with their residential communities ($\chi^2(15) = 17.92$); educational levels $\chi^2(25) = 27.42$); and types of (un)employment ($\chi^2(30) = 35.26$), or with their average monthly salaries ($\chi^2(20) = 26.35$).

Religiosity and Observance of Islamic Norms

The above discussion reflects the significant process of 'Islamic awakening' (aroused religiosity) occurring over the past few decades in Israel,

Table 3.11 *Cross-tabulation: Islamic ideology (%) and religiosity*

Islamic ideological group	Very religious	Religious	Sort of religious	Somewhat non-religious	Not religious	Not religious at all
Salafis	20.8	37.5	33.3	8.3	0.0	0.0
Salafi Jihadists	50.0	25.0	25.0	0.0	0.0	0.0
Moderates	7.3	32.8	45.3	12.0	2.6	0.0
Liberals	1.5	13.2	55.9	13.2	11.8	4.4
Other	5.6	25.9	27.8	20.4	16.7	3.7
Unaffiliated	16.7	28.6	21.4	11.9	9.5	11.9

Table 3.12 *Participants' responses (%) Muslims in Israel preserving important Islamic values*

Muslims in Israel have very important values and must preserve them	
	Percentage
I strongly agree	35.9
I agree	29.3
I agree to a certain extent	20.2
I disagree to a certain extent	6.8
I disagree	5.2
I strongly disagree	2.2
Total	99.6

raising more questions regarding Islamic identity in Israel and the extent to which the Muslim minority there seeks to uphold and preserve Islamic values and norms. The participants in this survey were also asked about their level of support for the various Islamic groups and movements. This is especially important in light of the global events of the Arab Spring, which quickly turned into an 'Islamic Spring', when taken over by various Islamic movements. Notably, during the research period for this book, bloody events began in several Arab countries: Egypt, Syria, Libya, and other Arab states.

This being the case, the respondents were also asked to what extent they agree/disagree with the following statement: "Muslims in Israel have very important values and must preserve them." These responses were ranked on a scale of 1–6. The results were as follows: almost half (49.5 percent) agreed that Muslims have important values that they must preserve and (35.9 percent) agreed to a large extent with this statement. A small percentage (7.4 percent) disagreed, as indicated in Table 3.12.

The effects of various demographic variables were examined vis-à-vis the above statement. On one hand, gender was found to be unrelated to the participants' positions regarding the preservation of Islamic values ($\chi^2(5) = 5.33$); age, on the other hand, did show a Spearman correlation with their positions (rs = 0.14; p < 0.01). Marital status was unrelated to the participants' responses to the above statement ($\chi^2 (20) = 14.66$), although the geographic distribution showed a moderate Cramer's V correlation in this case ($\chi^2 (15) = 46.87$; p < 0.001 and rc = 0.19; p < 0.001). Table 3.13 illustrates the fact that participant responses vary by geographical region.

Another factor, that of the participants' residential community, also showed a moderate Cramer's V correlation with their responses to the

Table 3.13 *Cross-tabulation: residential region (%) and preservation of Islamic values in Israel*

		Residential region			
		Galilee	Triangle	Negev	Mixed cities
Muslims in Israel have	I strongly agree	41.4	34.6	13.0	11.1
very important values	I agree	60.9	20.3	13.0	5.8
and must preserve	I agree to a certain extent	71.3	16.0	2.1	10.6
them	I disagree somewhat	58.6	34.5	0.0	6.9
	I disagree	84.0	12.0	0.0	4.0
	I strongly disagree	70.0	20.0	0.0	10.0

preservation of Islamic values (χ^2 (15) = 73.93; p < 0.001 and rc = 0.23; p < 0.001), as shown in Table 3.14.

However, the educational level showed a negative correlation with the participants' responses to the above statement (rs = −0.14; p < 0.01); in other words, the more educated Muslims tended to disagree more with the statement "The Muslims in Israel have very important values and must preserve them," presenting a more critical attitude toward the preservation of Islamic values. Moreover, the bloody events of the Arab Spring seem to bolster negative attitudes toward political Islam and to support change, rather than preservation.

The responses to another survey item (Q: 1): "I try to observe the Islamic religious laws on a daily basis" also support this negative trend – the educational level showed a negative correlation with personal Shari'a practice in the participants' responses. The response patterns to these two statements demonstrate both the critical approach taken by educated

Table 3.14 *Cross-tabulation: residential community (%) and preservation of Islamic values in Israel*

		Residential community			
		All Muslim	Mostly Muslim	Mostly Christian	Mostly Druze
Muslims in Israel have	I strongly agree	69.4	29.5	0.6	0.6
very important values	I agree	72.5	19.7	2.1	5.6
and must preserve	I agree to a certain extent	45.5	49.5	1.0	4.0
them	I disagree somewhat	44.1	38.2	2.9	14.7
	I disagree	42.3	30.8	0.0	26.9
	I strongly disagree	36.4	63.6	0.0	0.0

Table 3.15 *Factor loading of the results for four survey items (N = 500)*

	Factor 1	Factor 2
I have mastered the Islamic religious laws	**0.882**	0.09
I side with the Sunnites in the conflict against the Shiites	**0.881**	0.103
I am satisfied with the Muslims' condition in the world	0.098	**0.893**
I am satisfied with the Muslims' condition in Israel	0.104	**0.892**

Muslims in Israel and their tendency to support change, rather than the preservation of values and conservative behavior.

In addition, the socio-economic variables correlated with the position regarding the preservation of Islamic values indicate very little impact on the participants' attitudes. Both employment (χ^2 (20) = 14.66) and average salary (χ^2 (20) = 26.63) were not correlated. Apparently, these attitudes stem from a collective religious identity bolstered during the course of the 'Islamic awakening'. Note that the aforementioned outcomes confirm some relevant findings and conclusions reached by the sociologist Sammy Smooha.[4]

In addition, the participants were also asked to respond to four more items regarding their familiarity with Islamic religious laws and their (dis)satisfaction with the situation of Muslims in Israel and abroad. In order to examine the validity of these survey items (Q: 7–10), an exploratory factor analysis (EFA) was conducted using principal components extraction with varimax rotation. The respondents' knowledge of religious law was measured using four items, rated on a 6-point Likert-type scale, ranging from 1 (strongly agree) to 6 (strongly disagree). Table 3.15 describes the results of this factor analysis.

The factor analysis of these four items yielded two subscales· the first subscale (two items, Q: 6–7 – familiarity) presents the extent to which the participants are familiar with Islamic religious law and its observance. The Cronbach alpha (i.e. an estimate of the internal consistency reliability) is 0.72. The second subscale (two items, Q: 8–9 = [dis]satisfaction) presents their (dis)satisfaction with the situation of Muslims in Israel and abroad. Here, the Cronbach alpha is 0.76. An examination of the Pearson correlations between these two factors showed a significant correlation between them: (rp = 0.22; p < 0.001).

The effects of these two variables on both subscales were examined by means of a T-test for two independent samples and a one-way ANOVA. As for the first 'familiarity' subscale, the T-test found a gender difference

---

[4] See Sammy Smooha, *Still Playing by the Rules: Index of Arab–Jewish Relations in Israel, 2012: Findings and Conclusions* (Haifa: University of Haifa/Israel Democracy Institute, 2013).

$(t(483.67) = 2.105; p < 0.05;$ Mean for women $= 2.69$ and Mean for men $= 2.92$). However, no gender difference was found for the second '(dis)satisfaction' subscale $(t(485) = 1.05;$ Mean for women $= 3.85$ and Mean for men $= 3.97$).

Moreover, the participants' responses regarding the extent of their familiarity with Islamic religious law was found to differ between age groups $(F(4) = 3.30; p < 0.05)$. A post-hoc test showed that the mean differences in this scale derive mainly from the difference between the forty to forty-nine age group (Mean $= 2.65$) and the above sixty age group (Mean $= 3.26$). However, no differences were found between age groups regarding the (dis)satisfaction of the participants $(F(4) = 1.02)$. On both scales, marital status did not affect the participants' familiarity $(F(4) = 1.48)$ or (dis)satisfaction $(F(4) = 1.47)$.

As for geographic distribution, differences were found only on the familiarity scale $(F(3) = 15.27; p < 0.001)$. These variables were examined using a post-hoc analysis (Tukey test) and found to be derived mainly from regional differences between the Galilee (Mean $= 3.04$) and the Negev (Mean $= 1.87$); between the Galilee and the mixed cities (Mean $= 2.47$); and between the Galilee and the Triangle (Mean $= 2.61$). Note that significant differences exist between these regional averages.

Also notice that the nature of each residential community (Muslim or Druze majorities, or completely Muslim) does significantly affect the participants' familiarity with Islamic religious law $(F(3) = 6.94; p < 0.001)$. The post-hoc analysis shows that most of these differences are either between Muslim-majority communities (Mean $= 2.89$) and Druze-majority communities (Mean $= 3.78$); or between completely Muslim (Mean $= 2.69$) and Druze-majority communities. Christian-majority communities were negligible in this respect. The average differences between completely Muslim and completely Druze residential communities are significant.

On the (dis)satisfaction scale, no differences were found by residential region $(F(3) = .26)$; however, differences were found according to the residential community $(F(3) = 2.79; p < 0.001)$. A post-hoc analysis showed that significant differences in (dis)satisfaction are primarily found between the completely Muslim communities (Mean $= 4.03$) and those with a Muslim majority (Mean $= 3.69$).

As for the educational level, it was found to affect the (dis)satisfaction scale $(F(5) = 2.41; p < 0.05)$. The one-way ANOVA F-test performed yielded significant results. A post-hoc test showed that the most significant difference in (dis)satisfaction was between the uneducated participants (Mean $= 3.2$) and those with a Master's degree (Mean $= 4.57$).

Table 3.16 *Participants' responses (%) regarding support for IM ideology*

	I strongly agree	I agree	I agree to a certain extent	I disagree to a certain extent	I disagree	I strongly disagree
I support the ideological discourse of the IM	9.8	20.8	35.7	18.2	9.0	6.0
I support the ideological discourse of the NIM	9.2	18.0	31.5	17.4	13.4	8.4
I support the ideological discourse of the SIM	8.8	15.4	30.9	20.0	12.4	10.0

The (un)employment factor did not affect the satisfaction levels when correlated with the situation of Muslims either in Israel or abroad (F(6) = 0.91; p = n.s.), but the average monthly salary level did have an impact. A one-way ANOVA F-test was significant (F(4) = 3.31; p < 0.05). A post-hoc test showed that a significant difference on the (dis)satisfaction scale was found when comparing those with a below-average monthly income (Mean = 3.61) and those with a much lower than average income (Mean = 4.12). Nonetheless, the educational levels of the participants (F(5) = 0.46), their average monthly salaries (F(4) = 1.13; p = n.s.), or (un)employment did not affect their degree of familiarity with Islamic religious law and observance (F(6) = 0.33).

Finally, the extent to which participants support the ideology of the IM was addressed by means of the following three items on the questionnaire (Q: 13) "I support the ideological discourse of the IM"; (Q: 14) "I support the ideological discourse of the NIM"; and (Q: 15) "I support the ideological discourse of the SIM." The Cronbach alpha was measured and found to be 0.81. The Spearman correlations between the items on this scale are significantly high, above 0.5 (see Table 3.16).

No correlation was found either between age (rs = 0.04; p = n.s.) or educational level (rs = 0.04) and the 'IM ideology' scale. However, a significant negative correlation was found between the average monthly salary and support of IM ideology (rs = −0.11; p < 0.05), such that higher average salaries correlate with less support of the IM ideology. Moreover, men and women differed on this factor (men averaged M = 3.36, while women averaged M = 3.15; t(482.74) = 1.92; p = 0.05). However, support of IM ideology did not differ when correlated with (un)employment (F(6) = 1.26).

The nature of the residential community had a negligible effect when correlated with Islamic ideology (F(3) = .69), although support for certain Islamic ideologies did vary in accordance with the residential region

Table 3.17 *Participants' responses (%) regarding reliance on Islamic religious institutions in Israel*

	I strongly agree	I agree	I agree to a certain extent	I disagree to a certain extent	I disagree	I strongly disagree
I rely on the official Islamic institutions in Israel, e.g. the Shariʿa Courts	8.4	28.7	34.1	12.8	11.2	4.4
I rely on the Islamic institutions of the IM	15.4	26.9	32.9	12.4	8.6	3.6

($F(3) = 3.49$; $p < 0.05$). The significant differences were between the Triangle (Mean $= 3.42$) and the Negev (Mean $= 2.71$); and between the Negev and the mixed cities (Mean $= 3.41$). In both cases, the post-hoc tests showed that the differences between the above averages are significant. Lastly, marital status did not affect adherence to an Islamic ideology ($F(4) = 1.8$).

Islamic Religious Authority and Public Submission of Legal Queries

A major issue regarding Islamic religious authority in Israel is to whom the Muslim minority may turn when in need of Shariʿa rulings concerning daily practice and contemporary issues; which Muslim sources, Islamic legal experts, and religious bodies are accessible and deemed to be reliable. To study this phenomenon, the participants in this study were specifically asked to respond to the following statements: (Q: 11) "I rely on the official Islamic institutions established by the State of Israel (such as the Shariʿa courts)"; and (Q: 12) "I rely on the Islamic institutions established by the IM."[5] The extent of the reliance of the participants on these religious institutions was measured using five items, ranked on a six-point Likert-type scale, ranging from 1 (strongly disagree) to 6 (strongly agree). The first scale (Q: 11–12) indicates the extent to which the participants rely on the Islamic religious institutions in Israel. The Cronbach alpha was measured and found to be 76.

---

[5] On the work of the Shariʿa courts in modern times, see Ahmad ʿAli Dawud, *al-Qararat al-istiʾnafiyya fi ʾal ahwal al-shakhsiyya* (Amman: Maktabat Dar al-Thaqafa liʾl Nashr waʾl Tawziʿ, 1999) [Arabic].

Table 3.18 *Participants' responses (%) regarding
personal religious observance*

Personal religious observance	
	Percentage
To a very high degree	14.0
To a high degree	39.5
To a certain degree	30.5
Not to a certain degree	5.0
To a small degree	5.2
Non-observant or secular	4.4
Total	98.6

This 'reliance' scale was examined in relation to various demographic variables. A Spearman test found the level of education to be unrelated to this scale ($rs = 0.04$). A significant negative Spearman correlation was found between this reliance on Islamic institutions and the average monthly income of the participants ($rs = -0.12$; $p < 0.01$), such that those earning a larger average monthly income rely less on Islamic institutions in Israel. As for the participants' gender, men and women differed regarding their levels of reliance; the average level for men was (Mean = 3.05) and for women (Mean = 2.79). A T-test on two independent samples showed a difference between men and women ($t(484) = 2.44$; $p < 0.05$).

In addition, a one-way ANOVA did not find differences in participants' responses to the 'reliance' scale with regard to their marital status ($F(4) = 0.74$). However, the residential region was found to affect the participants' reliance on Islamic institutions in Israel ($F(3) = 3.46$; $p < 0.05$). A post-hoc analysis showed that this significant average difference resulted mainly from the difference between residence in the Galilee (Mean = 3.01) and in the Negev (Mean = 2.43).

There is a positive correlation between the extent to which respondents rely on Islamic institutions in Israel and their degree of personal observance ($rs = 0.29$; $p < 0.01$), such that greater reliance correlated with higher levels of observance. However, the nature of their residential communities did not affect the extent of their reliance ($F(3) = 1.66$). The (un)employment factor showed no correlation whatsoever with the 'reliance' scale ($F(6) = 0.55$).

As for the 'observance' scale, the primary findings indicate that 84 percent of the participants claim to behave in accordance with Islamic religious laws on a daily basis. Table 3.18 shows that only 4.4 percent do not observe Islamic religious laws and norms.

Table 3.19 *Cross-tabulation: age (%) and degree of observance*

		Age				
		18–29	30–39	40–49	50–59	60+
Degree of	To a very high degree	16.7	25.8	27.3	22.7	7.6
observance	To a high degree	24.9	23.8	27.5	13.0	10.9
	To a certain degree	41.2	22.3	18.2	14.2	4.1
	Not to a certain degree	21.7	30.4	30.4	13.0	4.3
	To a small degree	29.2	25.0	20.8	16.7	8.3
	Non-observant or secular	42.9	14.3	4.8	33.3	4.8

The degree of personal observance was correlated with additional demographic variables in order to examine their influence. The following are the factor-by-factor results. To learn the effect of gender on observance, a chi-square test was conducted, which showed no correlation ($\chi^2(5) = 10.37$) between the participants' gender and their commitment to Islamic religious laws as a normative basis for personal behavior.

During the examination of the effect of age on the degree of observance, a negative Spearman correlation was found (rs $= -0.14$; p < 0.01), meaning that older Muslims are less committed to Islamic religious law as a normative basis for their behavior than young Muslims, who are more committed. Table 3.19 presents a cross-tabulation with the age factor and the responses regarding personal observance. It was found that among young adults (aged between eighteen and twenty-nine), 88.2 percent observe Islamic religious law to a very high, a high, and a certain degree. In comparison, among older Muslims (aged between fifty and fifty-nine), only 49.9 percent responded that they observe Islamic law to a very high, a high, and a certain degree.

In order to explain these findings, it is necessary to take into account the fact that the Islamic revival amid the Muslim minority in Israel is relatively young. The adult generation had experienced the initial modernization processes, which distanced them from religion. Meanwhile, their children, the second generation, experienced a more advanced modernization process, which partially spurred the religious revival of the Muslim minority in Israel.[6] Similar phenomena have been experienced by other Muslim minorities in Europe.[7] Studies on the Turkish Muslim

---

[6] Nohad ʿAli, "The Islamic Movement in Israel between religion, nationality and modernity," in Y. Yonah and Y. Goodman (eds.), *Maelstrom of Identities: A Critical Look at Religion and Secularity in Israel* (Jerusalem: Van Leer Institute, 2004), 132–164 [Hebrew].

[7] See Andrew March, "Liberal citizenship and the search for an overlapping consensus: the case of Muslim minorities," *Philosophy and Public Affairs* 34 (4) (2006): 373–421; Muhammad Masud, "Islamic law and Muslim minorities," *ISIM Newsletter* 11 (2002).

Table 3.20 *Cross-tabulation: residential region (%) and degree of observance*

		Residential region			
		Galilee	Triangle	Negev	Mixed cities
Degree of	To a very high degree	60.3	20.6	7.4	11.8
observance	To a high degree	43.5	37.5	16.3	2.7
	To a certain degree	66.9	17.3	2.9	12.9
	Not to a certain degree	70.8	8.3	8.3	12.5
	To a small degree	55.0	20.0	0.0	25.0
	Non-observant or secular	89.5	0.0	0.0	10.5

minority in Germany found a strong correlation between age and obser-vance; the intermediate generation took religion into account to a greater extent than their parents did.

To correlate the effect of marital status on observance, a chi-square test showed that there are indeed no differences between the partici-pants in this regard ($\chi^2(20) = 28.84$). The fact that a participant is sin-gle, married, divorced, or widowed does not affect the degree of obser-vance. However, the residential region was found to affect the partici-pants' commitment to Islamic religious law ($\chi^2(15) = 73.23$; p < 0.001 and rc = 0.23; p < 0.001). Table 3.20 presents a cross-tabulation of the residential region and the responses to this item, showing that residents of the Galilee are more observant than residents of other areas.

Contrary to the Triangle and the Negev, the Galilee has a mixed popu-lation of Muslims, Christians, and Druze, although the Muslims consti-tute the majority. A mixed residential area tends to cause a certain Mus-lim solidarity surrounding a core of Islam, while in mixed cities with Jewish or Christian majorities, the Muslim residents show less solidar-ity In addition, the nature of a participant's residential community (e.g. Muslim or Christian majority) significantly affects the degree of obser-vance ($\chi^2(15) = 30.01$; p < 0.01 and rc = 0.16; p < 0.01). Table 3.21 presents a cross-tabulation of the participants' responses regarding their degree of personal observance and residential communities. If a neigh-borhood is predominantly Muslim, then more people are found to be observant.

These results strengthen the previous findings regarding majority–minority relations within and between communities in Israel. Where the Muslims predominate, they coalesce to a greater extent around their reli-gious values, which they make their primary behavioral reference point. Note that Islam has a crucial effect on Arab culture in Israel and in general. The dominance of religion has blurred the lines between the

Table 3.21 *Cross-tabulation: residential community (%) and degree of observance*

| | | Residential community | | | |
		All Muslim	Mostly Muslim	Mostly Christian	Mostly Druze
Degree of observance	To a very high degree	65.7	32.8	0.0	1.5
	To a high degree	68.9	29.5	0.5	1.0
	To a certain degree	54.8	36.3	2.1	6.8
	Not to a certain degree	52.0	32.0	4.0	12.0
	To a small degree	50.0	26.9	3.8	19.2
	Non-observant or secular	59.1	27.3	0.0	13.6

cultural and the social. However, an examination of the effect of the level of education on the degree to which the respondents are committed to Islamic religious law as a normative basis for behavior shows a significant negative Spearman correlation ($rs = -0.14$; $p < 0.01$), meaning that highly educated Muslims are less committed to Islam. For example, Table 3.22 shows that Muslims with Master's degrees are less observant than those with only a high-school education. This finding suggests that the negative correlation between the educational level and the attitude toward Islam is a significant socio-cultural indicator.

Regarding the (un)employment factor, a Spearman test found no correlation ($\chi^2(30) = 29.86$) between (un)employment and the degree of observance as normative behavior. Finally, a significant negative

Table 3.22 *Cross-tabulation: educational level (%) and degree of observance*

| | | Educational level | | | | | |
		No formal education	Elementary education	Secondary education	BA/ B.Sc.	MA/ M.Sc.	Ph.D.
Degree of observance	To a very high degree	1.4	24.3	47.1	21.4	2.9	2.9
	To a high degree	5.1	14.9	52.8	21.0	5.1	1.0
	To a certain degree	2.7	13.0	55.5	23.3	4.1	1.4
	Not to a certain degree	0.0	12.5	70.8	12.5	4.2	0.0
	To a small degree	0.0	15.4	42.3	42.3	0.0	0.0
	Non-observant or secular	0.0	9.1	68.2	13.6	9.1	0.0

Table 3.23 *Participants' responses (%) regarding the preferred extent of Islamic religious observance in Israel*

Preference for Islamic religious observance in Israel	
	Percentage
To a very great extent	20.4
To a great extent	34.1
To a certain extent	29.5
Not to a certain extent	6.2
To a small extent	3.2
Indifferent	4.0
Total	97.4

correlation was found between the average monthly income and the degree of observance (rs = -0.12; p < 0.01), such that participants with an income over the 7,300 NIS average were significantly less committed to daily observance.

In addition, 84 percent of the respondents would like to see Muslims in Israel observing Islamic practice; of them, 20.4 percent agree to a great extent and only 4 percent are indifferent to this, as indicated in Table 3.23.

The preference for Islamic observance in Israel was also studied in relation to certain demographic variables, as was done in the previous instances. A chi-square test showed that there is no correlation between gender and the preference for observance ($\chi^2(5) = 3.3$). At first sight this seems to be a problematic finding, since the attitude of Muslim women to Islamic law (which discriminates against women) should be different from that of men. However, in the reality of Muslim life, it turns out that Islamic culture grants more rights to women than are afforded to them by the patriarchal, less egalitarian Arab society in general. One example of this is the matter of the right of women to inherit from their parents. While Islam grants women a third part of the parental inheritance, Arab culture deprives women of this right, transferring it to male blood relatives.

In the present survey, the age factor was found not to affect the preference for general Islamic observance (rs = 0.02), although, as stated above, age did negatively impact on the preference for observance in others. In a chi-square test performed, marital status showed no correlation with the extent of preference for observance in Israel ($\chi^2(20) = 18.69$). Nevertheless, the residential region, as in other cases above, was found to

Table 3.24 *Cross-tabulation: residential region (%) and preference for observance*

		Residential region			
		Galilee	Triangle	Negev	Mixed cities
Preference for	To a very great extent	45.7	23.4	23.4	7.4
observance	to a great extent	48.8	39.5	7.4	4.3
	To a certain extent	66.4	18.2	4.4	10.9
	Not to a certain extent	92.6	0.0	3.7	3.7
	To a small extent	71.4	0.0	0.0	28.6
	Indifferent	80.0	0.0	0.0	20.0

affect the preference for Islamic observance ($\chi^2(15) = 87.25$; $p < 0.001$ and rc $= 0.26$; $p < 0.001$). A moderate Cramer's V relationship was also found. Table 3.24 presents a cross-tabulation of the residential regions and the responses to this item (Q: 2), indicating that Galilee residents prefer Muslims in Israel to act in accordance with Islamic law more than do the residents of other areas.

As with the previous item, here too it is important to note that in the Galilee, which has a very heterogeneous population, with Christians, Druze and Muslims living side by side, Muslims tend to be defensive and coalesce around their religious norms. Also, the residential communities in which people live affect the extent to which the respondents prefer Islamic observance in Israel ($\chi^2(15) = 55.50$; $p < 0.001$ and rc $= 0.2$; $p < 0.001$). As such, Muslims residing in Muslim-majority neighborhoods prefer a greater extent of Islamic observance than do Muslim-minority residents.

Table 3.25 *Cross-tabulation: residential community (%) and preference for observance*

		Residential community			
		All Muslim	Mostly Muslim	Mostly Christian	Mostly Druze
Preference for	To a very large extent	76.2	22.8	1.0	0.0
observance	To a large extent	67.1	30.5	0.6	1.8
	To a certain extent	49.3	42.3	2.1	6.3
	Not to a certain extent	58.6	24.1	0.0	17.2
	To a small extent	43.8	31.3	0.0	25.0
	Indifferent	55.0	25.0	5.0	15.0

As for the level of education, it was found to be uncorrelated with the preference for Islamic observance, showing no difference between Muslims with advanced degrees and those with high-school diplomas (rs = −.003). Unlike the previous item, where education impacted attitudes, here its effect was neutralized. It seems evident that both more- and less-educated Muslims are aware that Islamic law is generally inapplicable in their status as a minority in Israel. Additionally, no correlation was found between (un)employment and the preference for general observance ($\chi^2(30) = 34.84$; p = n.s.). And finally, the average monthly salary was also examined in regard to the preference for observance by others, and a negative Spearman correlation was found) rs = −0.15; p < 0.01). This means that the participants with higher than average salaries (higher than 7,300 NIS) are less concerned with Muslims in Israel observing Islam than are those with lower monthly salaries.

In conclusion, during the past four decades Islam has become an important factor in the political and socio-cultural identity of the Arab minority in Israel; thus, Islamic values often serve as behavioral standards. This is manifested in the evolving number of Muslims in Israel who now define their identity, first and foremost, in relation to their religious affiliation, but also in the high degree of personal religious observance, and the greater reliance on Islamic religious institutions. Note that the highly observant group considers its affiliation with Islam to be a proud achievement, and thus it is only natural that they tend to promote the implementation of Shari'a law. Moreover, the latest research findings suggest that there is a growing number of Muslims in Israel who want other Muslims to better observe the tenets of the Shari'a.

However, these findings show that the Muslim community in Israel differs not only by virtue of geography, but also along religious and socio-cultural lines. The significant factors identified were personal observance and the degree of ethno-religious homogeneity in both the residential community and the residential region. This means that when Muslims live in mixed ethno-religious neighborhoods or in heterogeneous geographic regions, they tend to become more religious and more observant. For example, the Muslim Galilee residents live in mixed communities (among Muslims, Druze, and Christians), while most of the Negev and Triangle Muslims live in more homogeneous communities. As such, it is not surprising that we found distinctions in religious perception between these regions, as in regard to Salafism, the preservation of Islamic values and norms, and support for women wearing Islamic religious attire.

4 Muslim Identity and Islamic Practice in Israel

The previous chapter was aimed at deepening our understanding of public affiliation, religiosity, and observance in the Muslim minority in Israel. Clearly, this minority is now part of the global and regional 'Islamic awakening', as expressed by responses regarding various aspects of daily life. This chapter continues the discussion on Islam and the public from yet another angle: the evolving religious identity among Muslims in Israel, as reflected in further data culled from the research survey.[1] Emphasis is placed on personal Islamic daily life practices, such as dress code, marital preference, and other personal data, considering two distinct clusters of demographic variables: (a) geographic and religious factors (e.g. residential region, residential community, religious affiliations, and degree of religiosity); and (b) social and personal factors (such as age, gender, level of education, marital status, (un)employment, average monthly salary, and degree of personal religious observance).

The respondents' knowledge of Islamic identity was measured by means of ten items, rated on a Likert-type frequency scale, ranging from 1 (strongly agree) to 6 (strongly disagree). An exploratory factor analysis was conducted to examine the validity of the questions, with varimax rotation (Q: 39–48). Table 4.1 presents the results of this factor analysis.

This factor analysis yielded four subscales. The first subscale (three items) focuses on the participants' positions regarding intra-religious marriage among Muslims; its Cronbach alpha is 0.84. The second subscale (three items) represents daily observance in the personal sphere; here, the Cronbach alpha is 0.81. The third subscale (two items) asks about Islamic preaching in Israel and 'Pakistani attire' for men; in this case, the reliability of these items by Cronbach alpha is 0.65. Specifically, the item mentioning 'Pakistani attire' for men (though technically belonging to subscale 4) was included in the factor loading for subscale 3, due to the apparent bias caused by that term. And lastly, the

---

[1] On the politics of minority group identity, see Charles Taylor, *Multiculturalism and the Politics of Recognition* (Princeton: Princeton University Press, 1992).

Table 4.1 *Factor loading of the results for ten survey items (N = 500)*

	Factor 1	Factor 2	Factor 3	Factor 4
I support Muslim men only marrying Muslim women	**0.832**	0.055	0.109	0.052
I support Muslims marrying according to traditional Islamic rituals	**0.792**	0.200	0.056	0.189
I support Muslim women only marrying Muslim men	**0.887**	0.071	0.032	0.194
I personally support the daily practice of Islamic Shari'a laws	0.471	**0.629**	0.291	0.146
When choosing my life partner, do I stipulate that he/she must be observant?	0.131	**0.858**	0.218	0.056
When choosing my friends, do I stipulate that they must be observant?	0.022	**0.862**	0.214	0.147
I support Islamic preaching in Israel	0.282	0.338	**0.749**	0.015
I support men wearing Islamic religious attire ('Pakistani attire')	−0.070	0.233	**0.830**	0.215
I believe that Islamic religious attire mainly expresses Islamic identity	0.165	0.098	0.059	**0.930**
I support women wearing Islamic religious attire	0.355	0.212	0.417	**0.641**

fourth subscale (two items) stresses positions on visual identity, as manifested by Islamic attire (symbolic clothing); here, the Cronbach alpha is 0.714.

An examination of the Spearman correlations between the factors on intra-religious marriage and those on observance in the personal sphere shows a significant correlation between them (rs = 0.37; p < 0.01), and also between an observant personal sphere and religiosity (ro = 0.54; p < 0.01). In addition, the factors related to Islamic preaching and 'Pakistani attire' for men (subscale 3) were also found to be related to religiosity (rs = 0.53; p < 0.01). Finally, Islamic attire, in Israel in general, is correlated with religiosity (rs = 0.42; p < 0.01). A majority of the participants seemed to agree that identity and observance are directly correlated – namely, the more observant they are, the more they identify themselves as a part of the Muslim community. Table 4.2 presents the Pearson's correlations between the four subscales.

All Pearson's correlations above 0.25 are considered to be significant, meaning that all four subscales studied here provided significant results; as such, the participants' positions regarding intra-religious marriage, the observant personal sphere, Islamic preaching, and 'Pakistani attire' are all correlated with their degree of religiosity.

Table 4.2 *Correlations between the four subscales*

	Subscale1	Subscale2	Subscale3
Subscale 1			
Subscale 2	0.373**		
Subscale 3	0.256**	0.6**	
Subscale 4	0.45**	0.42**	0.44**

P < 0.01

The first subscale (Muslim intra-religious marriage; Q: 39–41) was examined in relation to demographic variables. A Spearman test found that age (rs = 0.002) and average income (rs = −0.01) are unrelated to this parameter. A significant negative Spearman correlation was found between intra-religious marriage and the participants' level of education (rs = −0.125; p < 0.01), such that the more educated participants show less support for intra-religious marriage. Many studies, as well as modernization theory, cite a negative correlation between the level of education and conservativeness and insularity, i.e. the higher the education, the lower the degree of conservativeness.[2] Moreover, a T-test done with two independent samples showed no difference between men and women (t(482) = 1.75) in this regard. Also, a one-way ANOVA found no difference in attitudes toward intra-religious marriage due to the respondents' personal marital statuses (F(4) = 1.84).

However, the residential region[3] (F(3) = 3.11; p < 0.05) and the residential community (F(3) = 3.12; p < 0.05) did affect the participants' positions on intra-religious marriage. A post-hoc analysis showed that this difference derived mainly from the significant differences between majority-Muslim communities (Mean = 2.39) and majority-Druze communities (Mean = 3.08); and between completely Muslim communities (Mean = 2.36) and majority-Druze ones. In this case, the residential region is a function of the predominance of Muslims in the residential

---

[2] See, for example, Moshe Semyonov, Noah Lewin-Epstein, and Iris Braham, "Changing labour force participation and occupational status: Arab women in the Israeli labour force," *Work, Employment and Society* 13 (1) (1999): 117–131; Majid al-Haj, "Higher education among the Arabs in Israel: formal policy between empowerment and control," *Journal of Higher Education Policy* 16 (2003): 351–368; Hunaida Ganem, Nohad 'Ali, and Ghadah Abu Jabir-Najm, *Attitudes towards the Status and Rights of Palestinian Women in Israel* (Nazareth: Women Against Violence, 2005); Lila Abu-Lughod, "Orientalism and Middle East feminist studies," *Feminist Studies* 27 (1) (2001): 101–113.

[3] Despite the result of the F-test being significant, the post-hoc analysis showed no significant differences between the averages of the two groups.

communities and their hegemony within the region – influencing the extent to which resident Muslims feel secure or threatened by mixed marriages. Notably, the rate of mixed marriages between Muslims and Druze is negligible, since exogamy is entirely forbidden for all adherents of the Druze religion.

The second subscale (observant personal sphere; Q: 43–45) was also analyzed in relation to various demographic variables. A Spearman correlation found that age (rs = −0.042) is unrelated. A significant positive Spearman correlation was found between observant personal sphere and the level of education (rs = 0.11; p < 0.05); participants with more education show more support for personal Islamic practice in their daily lives and want their life partners and friends to be religious as well. However, a significant negative Spearman correlation was found between observant personal sphere and average monthly income (rs = −0.12; p < 0.01), indicating that participants with higher average monthly incomes base their daily lives less on traditional Shari'a law and practice. A T-test done with two independent samples showed no difference between men and women for this parameter (t(481) = −0.669; Mean (women) = 3.24; Mean (men) = 3.17).

Nonetheless, the nature of the residential community (F(3) = 5.43; p < 0.01) was found to affect the participants' positions regarding subscale 2 (observant personal sphere). A post-hoc analysis showed that this significant difference is derived mainly from the differences between majority-Muslim communities (Mean = 3.17) and majority-Druze communities (M = 4.07); and between completely Muslim communities (M = 3.11) and majority-Druze ones. In addition, a significant one-way ANOVA F-test was performed. Differences in the participants' responses were found with regard to their marital status (F(4) = 3.02; p < 0.05) and residential region (F(3) = 7.42; p < 0.01). A post-hoc analysis showed that this significant difference is mostly derived from the regional differences between the Galilee (Mean = 3.26) and the Negev (Mean = 2.74); the Triangle (Mean = 2.91) and the Galilee; the Triangle and the mixed cities (Mean = 3.50); and between the Negev and the mixed cities.

The third subscale, which includes both Islamic preaching and 'Pakistani attire' for men (Q: 46–47), was also studied in relation to the same demographic variables. A Spearman test found that age (rs = 0.004) and average monthly income (rs = −0.067) are unrelated to this parameter. A significant positive Spearman correlation was found between Islamic preaching and the level of education of the participants (rs = 0.1; p < 0.05); in other words, respondents with more education give more support to Islamic preaching in Israel and approve more of 'Pakistani attire' for men than do the less-educated Muslims. Educated Muslims exhibit a level of openness toward the preachers' right to preach and men's right to dress as they wish. In the authors' opinions, this response was given more in support of common civil rights than in regard to the contents of the preaching itself or valuing a certain dress code. A T-test done for two independent samples showed no difference in opinion between men and women about Islamic preaching (t(481) = 0.249; Mean (women) = 3.5; Mean (men) = 3.53.

The religious majority in the residential community, however, (F(3) = 3.68; p < 0.05) was found to affect the participants' positions on subscale 3 (Islamic preaching and 'Pakistani attire'). A post-hoc analysis showed that this significant difference is mainly derived from the differences between majority-Muslim communities (Mean = 3.27) and majority-Druze communities (Mean = 4.04); and between completely Muslim communities (Mean = 3.6) and majority-Muslim ones. Here too, the degree of homogeneity and the minority–majority ratio affects the attitudes of the Muslim minority in Israel. Additionally, a one-way ANOVA also found differences in the responses correlating Islamic preaching with the respondents' marital status (F(4) = 4.68; p < 0.01) and with their residential regions (F(3) = 2.64; p < 0.05). Another post-hoc analysis showed that this significant difference stems primarily from the difference between the Triangle (Mean = 3.73) and the Negev (Mean = 3).

The fourth subscale focuses on elements of overt, visual identity (Q: 48–49), and was also analyzed in relation to the same demographic variables. A Spearman correlation found that age (rs = 0.05) and level of education (rs = 0.000) are unrelated to Islamic attire. However, a significant negative Spearman correlation was found between support of Islamic attire and the average monthly income of the participants (rs = −0.13; p < 0.01), such that respondents with higher average monthly incomes tend to offer less support for dressing in Islamic attire (an overt expression of Islamic identity). A T-test done for two independent samples showed no gender difference (t(481) = 0.92; Mean (women) = 2.83; Mean (men) = 2.95); moreover, a one-way ANOVA did not find any differences in the responses to this subscale with regard to marital status (F(4) = 1.29), nor with residential community (F(3) = 1.88). However, residential region was found to affect the attitudes toward Islamic attire and visual identity (F(3) = 3.6; p < 0.05). In this case, a post-hoc analysis showed that this significant difference is mostly derived from the differences between the Triangle (Mean = 3.03) and the Negev (Mean = 2.25); and between the Galilee (M = 2.91) and the Negev. As mentioned in earlier chapters, the Triangle and Negev are much more

Table 4.3 *Gender separation (%) at public events*

I support the separation of men and women at public events	
	Percentage
I strongly agree	22.2
I agree	16.8
I agree to a certain degree	19.8
I disagree to a certain degree	17.4
I disagree	13.0
I strongly disagree	9.2
Total	98.4

homogeneously Muslim, as opposed to the Galilee, which is mixed with Christians and Druze.

Moving on to matters of Islamic practice that were among the survey items, there is the issue regarding the separation of men and women in the public sphere (Q: 42 and 50). 58.8 percent of the survey participants reported that they support the separation of men and women at public events. Table 4.3 shows that 39.6 percent of the respondents do not support gender separation at public venues. Apparently, the religious revival occurring among the Muslims in Israel and the growing strength of the IM, along with ready access to the Israeli cultural media, have begun to affect the attitudes of Israeli Muslims. Many have begun to acquire Islamic religious and cultural values that were not customary in Israel between the inception of the state and the 1990s. For example, it is currently possible to attend weddings with separate halls for men and women (as exist in Jewish Ultra-Orthodox weddings). In IM educational institutions in Israel, classroom gender separation is commonplace.[4]

Like all the previous survey items, gender separation was examined in relation to the usual demographic variables. A chi-square test produced insignificant correlations with the participants' own gender ($\chi^2(5) = 2.57$), level of education ($rs = 0.04$) or type of (un)employment ($\chi^2(30) = 25.30$). A significant negative Spearman correlation was found between average monthly income and the degree of support for public gender separation ($rs = -0.11$; $p < 0.05$), meaning that those with higher average incomes offered less support for public gender separation.

[4] Nohad 'Ali, "Islamic Movement and the challenge of minority status: the independent community as a case study," in Hatina and al-Atawneh (eds.), *Muslims in the Jewish State.*

Table 4.4 *Cross-tabulation: gender separation at public events (%) and marital status*

		Marital status			
		Single	Married	Divorced/ Separated	Widowed
I support gender separation at public events	I strongly agree	17.3	76.4	5.5	0.9
	I agree	15.0	83.8	1.3	0.0
	I agree to a certain extent	17.3	74.5	4.1	4.1
	I disagree to a certain extent	29.1	66.3	1.2	2.3
	I disagree	24.6	73.8	0.0	1.5
	I strongly disagree	40.0	55.6	2.2	2.2

Also, a significant negative correlation exists between age and agreement with this statement, such that older people showed less support for gender separation (rs = −0.09; p < 0.05). Numerous studies indicate that most of those supporting the Islamic religious revival are young Muslims. Nonetheless, the marital status of the respondents is significantly correlated to support for gender separation at public events (χ^2 (20) = 32.86; p < 0.05; and rc = 0.13; p < 0.05). As may be seen in Table 4.4, a highly significant percentage of those supporting gender separation at public events are married.

The residential region was also found to be correlated with participant support of gender separation (χ^2 (15) = 35.13; p < 0.01; and rc = 0.16; p < 0.01), such that a high percentage of those who agreed or agreed to a large extent were from the Galilee. As previously mentioned, the Galilee is a mixed residential region, where this trend has only recently begun, but continues to grow. In the Triangle and in the Negev, this phenomenon has existed for the past two decades and is highly prevalent (see Table 4.5).

The type of residential community was also found to be significantly correlated with support for gender separation by means of a chi-square test (χ^2 (15) = 26.53; p < 0.05; and rc = .14; p < 0.05), as may be seen in Table 4.6.

In general, a correlation was found between gender separation at public events and religiosity (rs = 0.43; p < 0.01); the more the participants supported public gender separation, the more religious they were found to be.

Regarding the survey item (Q: 50) dealing with gender separation in the Arab school system in Israel, 44 percent of the participants reported

Table 4.5 *Cross-tabulation: gender separation at public events (%) and residential region*

		Residential region			
		Galilee	Triangle	Negev	Mixed cities
I support gender separation at public events	I strongly agree	38.1	36.2	13.3	12.4
	I agree	68.0	24.0	4.0	4.0
	I agree to a certain extent	62.0	22.8	5.4	9.8
	I disagree to a certain extent	65.4	23.5	6.2	4.9
	I disagree	54.4	22.8	14.0	8.8
	I strongly disagree	63.6	9.1	13.6	13.6

that they support this; however, 54.6 percent do not. Although most Israeli Muslims still oppose gender separation in educational institutions, there is a growing trend for support. In a study conducted in 2005,[5] only one-third of the Muslim minority supported gender separation in Arab education; notably, this issue is neither in the hands of the students nor of their parents, but under the authority of the Israeli Ministry of Education and Culture.

A significant negative Spearman correlation was found between the respondents' level of education and the extent of their support of gender separation in the Arab school system (rs = 0.133; p < 0.01), meaning that those with higher education showed less support for gender-separated classrooms. Another significant negative correlation was found between age and support for gender separation in the schools, such that older Muslims expressed less support for classroom separation (rs = −144; p < 0.01). Average income (rs = −0.086) and the respondents' gender ($\chi^2(5)$ = 4.85) were both unrelated to gender-separated education.

By means of a chi-square test, it was found that marital status is significantly correlated to support for gender-separated education (χ^2 (20) = 38.59; p < 0.01; and rc = 0.14; p < 0.01), as it was for gender separation at events. The cross-tabulation in Table 4.8 shows that a significant percentage of those supporting gender separation in the classrooms are married.

The residential region was also found to be correlated with support for gender-segregated education (χ^2 (15) = 35.11; p < 0.01; and

[5] Ganem, 'Ali, and Abu Jabir-Najm, *Attitudes towards the Status and Rights*.

Table 4.6 *Cross-tabulation: gender separation at public events (%) and residential community*

		Residential community			
		All Muslim	Mostly Muslim	Mostly Christian	Mostly Druze
I support gender separation at public events	I strongly agree	68.2	29.9	0.9	0.9
	I agree	59.0	36.1	0.0	4.8
	I agree to a certain extent	51.1	41.5	1.1	6.4
	I disagree to a certain extent	63.2	31.0	3.4	2.3
	I disagree	65.1	22.2	1.6	11.1
	I strongly disagree	65.2	23.9	0.0	10.9

Table 4.7 *Participants' responses (%) on gender separation in Arab schools in Israel*

I support gender separation in Arab schools	
	Percentage
I strongly agree	11.2
I agree	14.6
I agree to a certain extent	18.2
I disagree to a certain extent	18.4
I disagree	17.6
I strongly disagree	18.6
Total	98.6

Table 4.8 *Cross-tabulation: gender separation in Arab education in Israel (%) and marital status*

		Marital status			
		Single	Married	Divorced/ Separated	Widowed
I support gender separation in the Arab schools in Israel	I strongly agree	12.5	76.8	7.1	1.8
	I agree	14.5	78.3	4.3	2.9
	I agree to a certain extent	19.8	79.1	1.1	0.0
	I disagree to a certain extent	22.5	73.0	2.2	2.2
	I disagree	19.3	77.3	1.1	2.3
	I strongly disagree	39.1	57.6	1.1	2.2

Table 4.9 *Cross-tabulation: gender separation in Arab education (%) and residential region*

| | | Residential region | | | |
		Galilee	Triangle	Negev	Mixed cities
I support gender	I strongly agree	54.7	22.6	9.4	13.2
separation in the	I agree	58.2	32.8	6.0	3.0
Arab schools in	I agree to a certain extent	58.0	38.3	0.0	3.7
Israel	I disagree to a certain extent	56.6	22.9	9.6	10.8
	I disagree	55.8	22.1	14.0	8.1
	I strongly disagree	58.8	12.9	14.1	14.1

rc $= 0.16$; p < 0.01). Note that a high percentage of those in support of this item are from the Galilee.

As above in the case of gender separation at public events, there is also a correlation between support for gender-separated Arab education in Israel and Muslim religiosity (rs $= 0.42$; p < 0.01; see Table 4.9).

Finally, the type of (un)employment (χ^2 (30) $= 28.27$) and the residential community (χ^2 (15) $= 18.85$) were found to be unrelated to support for gender-separated education.

Two other examples of popular Islamic practices in Israel are *'aqiqa* and *halaqat al-dhikr*. The *'aqiqa* ritual is "a birth ritual involving shaving of the child's head, distribution of money to the poor, animal sacrifice and naming of the child. The call to prayer is spoken into the child's right ear and the summons to prayer in the left."[6] *Halaqat al-dhikr* or Islamic devotional and study circles are often practiced in the mosques.[7] The survey participants' Islamic ideologies were found to be correlated with their degree of participation in rituals and practices such as *'aqiqa* (χ^2 (25) $= 44.05$; p < 0.05; and rc $= 0.14$; p < 0.05), as well as in devotional and study circles (χ^2 (25) $= 45.51$; p < 0.01; and rc $= 0.14$; p < 0.01), as seen in Tables 4.10 and 4.11.

During the course of the survey, the respondents were also asked to provide their opinions regarding national and religious identities (Q: 51–54). One such item was: "I believe that Islam is more important than the state of Israel." As is evident from the data in Table 4.12, nearly 70.9 percent agreed that their religion is more important than their state, while 7.2 percent disagreed with this statement. Note that, since the Muslim

---

[6] John L. Esposito (ed.), *The Oxford Dictionary of Islam* (Oxford: Oxford University Press, 2003), 22.

[7] For more see ibid., 67 and 105.

Table 4.10 *Cross-tabulation: participation in* 'aqiqa *(%) and Islamic ideologies*

		Participation in 'aqiqa					
		I strongly agree	I agree	I agree to a certain extent	I disagree to a certain extent	I disagree	I strongly disagree
Islamic	Salafis	28.0	20.0	20.0	12.0	16.0	4.0
ideologies	Salafi Jihadists	0.0	75.0	0.0	25.0	0.0	0.0
	Moderates	16	19.6	23.6	25.8	10.2	4.7
	Liberals	10.4	16.4	20.9	26.9	19.4	6.0
	Others	18.2	20.0	23.6	14.5	18.2	5.5
	Unaffiliated	28.6	9.5	14.3	23.8	4.8	19.0

Arab citizens of Israel belong to three distinct groups, their identities also consist of three main components: a religious identity – 'Muslim'; a national identity – 'Palestinian Arab', and a civilian one – 'Israeli'. Sometimes these identities conflict with each other. In the 1970s–1990s, the nationalistic Palestinian Arab identity was dominant. This trend (putting Islam before Israel) is bolstered and validated by the item regarding personal observance of Islamic practice (Q: 1): "I try to observe Islamic religious laws on a daily basis."

Another correlation was found between personal religiosity and the belief that being a part of 'the community of Islam' is more important than being an Israeli national citizen (rs = 0.46; p < 0.01); in other

Table 4.11 *Cross-tabulation: participation in* halaqat al-dhikr *(%) and Islamic ideologies*

		Participation in *halaqat al-dhikr*					
		I strongly agree	I agree	I agree to a certain extent	I disagree to a certain extent	I disagree	I strongly disagree
Islamic	Salafis	20.0	12.0	16.0	28.0	20.0	4.0
ideologies	Salafi Jihadists	25.0	0.0	25.0	25.0	25.0	0.0
	Moderates	8.0	12.7	25.5	28.0	15.3	10.5
	Liberals	1.5	9.0	17.9	29.9	19.4	22.4
	Others	9.1	18.2	20.0	12.7	20.0	20.0
	Unaffiliated	14.3	19.0	14.3	11.9	9.5	31.0

Table 4.12 *Participants' responses (%) regarding national and religious identity*

I believe that Islam is more important than the state of Israel	
	Percentage
I strongly agree	22.0
I agree	22.4
I agree to a certain extent	26.5
I disagree to a certain extent	16.8
I disagree	7.2
I strongly disagree	3.4
Total	98.4

words, the more religious the respondent, the more he/she values Islam above the state of Israel. When correlating the importance of Islam with the other demographic variables, the Spearman tests showed correlations with the level of education (rs = 0.049), age (rs = 0.006), and average monthly income (rs = −0.05). However, the results of a chi-square test showed that the participants' genders were significantly correlated with their positions on the importance of Islam (χ^2 (5) = 15.03; p < 0.05; and rc = 0.18; p < 0.01), as shown in Table 4.13.

The participants' types of (un)employment were also correlated with their positions on the importance of Islam (χ^2 (30) = 47.61; p < 0.05; and rc = 0.14; p < 0.05), as may be seen in Table 4.14.

Although the residential community had no effect on the importance of Islam (χ^2 (15) = 20.54), the residential region was found to be correlated (χ^2 (15) = 39.92; p < 0.001; and rc = 0.17; p < 0.001), as shown in Table 4.15.

Table 4.13 *Cross-tabulation: gender (%) and the importance of Islam*

		Gender	
		Male	Female
I believe that	I strongly agree	59.0	41.0
Islam is more	I agree	44.0	56.0
important than	I agree to a certain extent	44.7	55.3
the state of Israel	I disgree to a certain extent	56.6	43.4
	I disagree	57.1	42.9
	I strongly disagree	82.4	17.6

Table 4.14 *Cross-tabulation: Type of (un)employment (%) and the importance of Islam*

		Employee or clerk	Self-employed	Unemployed, seeking a job	Unemployed, not seeking a job	Retired	College student	Housewife
I believe that Islam is more important than the state of Israel	I strongly agree	50.0	14.5	9.1	3.6	2.7	7.3	12.7
	I agree	44.0	12.8	11.0	8.3	5.5	6.4	11.9
	I agree to a certain extent	39.7	11.5	18.3	5.3	3.1	2.3	19.8
	I disagree to a certain extent	50.6	8.4	18.1	7.2	1.2	3.6	10.8
	I disagree	50.0	19.4	2.8	0.0	13.9	2.8	11.1
	I strongly disagree	64.7	0.0	17.6	0.0	5.9	11.8	0.0

Table 4.15 *Cross-tabulation: residential region (%) and the importance of Islam*

| | | Residential region | | | |
		Galilee	Triangle	Negev	Mixed cities
I believe that Islam is more important than the state of Israel	I strongly agree	49.0	21.6	16.7	12.7
	I agree	47.6	30.1	15.5	6.8
	I agree to a certain extent	61.8	30.1	2.4	5.7
	I disagree to a certain extent	69.3	21.3	1.3	8.0
	I disagree	68.6	14.3	8.6	8.6
	I strongly disagree	60.0	13.3	6.7	20.0

Lastly, marital status showed no correlation with the perceived importance of Islam (χ^2 (20) = 29.31).

The second survey item in this cluster (Q: 52) also referred to religious identity relative to civilian identity: "I believe that being Muslim is more important than being Israeli." Note that Israeli civilian identity is the weakest of the three aforementioned identities.[8] The participants' responses are detailed in Table 4.16. In response, 82 percent of the participants agreed that their Muslim religious identity is more important to them than their Israeli citizenship. It seems that Israeli identity is marginal among most Israeli Muslims, due to the marginalization of the Muslim minority in the 'Jewish State'.[9]

In this case as well, a Spearman correlation was found between religiosity and the primacy of the Islamic identity (rs = 0.36; p < 0.01); obviously, those who believe that their religious identity is more important also consider themselves to be more religious. The demographic variables found to be unrelated to the primacy of the Islamic identity are the level of education (rs = −0.07); average monthly income (rs = −0.05); gender (χ^2 (5) = 6.22); marital status (χ^2 (20) = 17.50); and age (rs = 0.085). Nonetheless, the type of (un)employment was correlated (χ^2 (30) = 47.75; p < 0.05; and rc = 0.14; p < 0.05), as shown in Table 4.17.

---

[8] See Sammy Smooha, "Are the Palestinian Arabs in Israel radicalizing?" *Bitterlemons-International* 24 (2) (2004); Smooha, *Still Playing by the Rules*; Nohad 'Ali, "The notion of 'el-mogtama' el-aisami' of the Islamic Movement," in Elie Reckess (ed.), *The Arab Minority in Israel and the 17th Knesset Elections* (Tel Aviv: Moshe Dayan Center for Middle East and Africa Studies, 2007), 100–111 [Hebrew]; 'Ali, "Political Islam."

[9] Smooha, "Are the Palestinian Arabs in Israel radicalizing?"

Table 4.16 *Participants' responses (%)*
regarding the primacy of Islamic identity

I believe that being Muslim is more important than being
Israeli

	Percentage
I strongly agree	29.7
I agree	27.5
I agree to a certain extent	24.8
I disagree to a certain extent	11.6
I disagree	2.8
I strongly disagree	1.4
Total	97.8

Both residential community (χ^2 (15) = 35.18; p < 0.01; and rc = 0.16; p < 0.01; see Table 4.18) and residential region (χ^2 (15) = 40.23; p < 0.001; and rc = 0.17; p < 0.001; see Table 4.19) correlate with positions regarding the primacy of Islamic identity.

As for the survey question (Q: 53): "Which of the following identities do you prefer?" – over half of the respondents (57.5 percent) said that it is most important for them to be 'Muslim', while only 17 percent said that it is important for them to be 'Israeli' and another 23.4 percent stated that it is important for them to be 'Palestinian'. Thus, it appears that religious identity is more important than the others (civil or national, respectively). These findings reflect the identity changes that the IM (NIM and SIM) has managed to bring about in the Muslim minority in Israel.[10]

A correlation was found between the religiosity of each respondent and his/her identity preference (χ^2 (10) = 75.07; p < 0.001; and rc = 0.28; p < 0.001), as shown in Table 4.20.

Regarding identity preference, a chi-square test indicated that both gender (χ^2 (2) = 0.44) and marital status (χ^2 (8) = 12.11) are unrelated. However, age (χ^2 (8) = 23.81; p < 0.01; and rc = 0.16; p < 0.01);

---

[10] See Nohad 'Ali, "Changes in the identity and attitudes of the supporters and opponents of the Islamic Movement in Israel," in Rassem Khamaissa (ed.), *Arab Society in Israel: Population, Society, Economy* III (Jerusalem: Van Leer Jerusalem Institute, 2009), 304–324 [Hebrew]; 'Ali, "Islamic Movement and the challenge of minority status"; Smooha, *Still Playing by the Rules*; Elie Rekhess, "Islamization of Arab identity: the Islamic Movement, 1972–1996," in Rekhess and Rudnitzky (eds.), *Muslim Minorities*, 63–74; Nimrod Luz, "The Islamic Movement and the seduction of sanctified landscapes: using sacred sites to conduct the struggle of land," in Rekhess and Rudnitzky (eds.), *Muslim Minorities*, 75–84.

Table 4.17 *Cross-tabulation: type of (un)employment (%) and the primacy of Islamic identity*

		Type of (un)employment					
		Employee or clerk	Self-employed	Unemployed, seeking a job	Unemployed, not seeking a job	Retired	College student	Housewife
I believe that being Muslim is more important than being Israeli	I strongly agree	51.4	9.5	14.2	3.4	3.4	6.1	12.2
	I agree	40.6	16.5	12.8	9.8	3.0	5.3	12.0
	I agree to a certain extent	43.1	14.6	13.0	4.1	3.3	4.9	17.1
	I disgree to a certain extent	53.4	3.4	17.2	5.2	5.2	3.4	12.1
	I disagree	42.9	0.0	7.1	0.0	28.6	0.0	21.4
	I strongly disagree	71.4	14.3	0.0	0.0	0.0	0.0	14.3

Table 4.18 *Cross-tabulation: residential community (%) and the primacy of Islamic identity*

| | | Residential community | | | |
		All Muslim	Mostly Muslim	Mostly Christian	Mostly Druze
I believe that being	I strongly agree	69.0	28.9	0.7	1.4
Muslim is more	I agree	65.9	29.6	1.5	3.0
important than	I agree to a certain extent	56.2	36.4	0.8	6.6
being Israeli	I disgree to a certain extent	46.6	34.5	3.4	15.5
	I disagree	71.4	14.3	0.0	14.3
	I strongly disagree	28.6	71.4	0.0	0.0

residential region (χ^2 (6) = 22.86; p < 0.01; and rc = 0.16; p < 0.01); and residential community (χ^2 (6) = 32.93; p < 0.001; and rc = 0.19; p < 0.001) are each correlated with the identity preferences of the participants, as shown in Tables 4.21–4.23.

The level of education (χ^2 (10) = 15.98) and type of (un)employment (χ^2 (12) = 16.18) were unrelated to the participants' identity preferences. However, the average monthly income was found to be correlated with identity preference (χ^2 (8) = 19.88; p < 0.05; and rc = 0.14; p < 0.05). The cross-tabulation in Table 4.24 shows that participants with below-average incomes valued their Israeli identity; those with an average monthly income gave primacy to their Muslim identity.

In response to the question (Q: 54): "How do you identify yourself, when asked to choose one of the following possibilities?" some

Table 4.19 *Cross-tabulation: residential region (%) and the primacy of Islamic identity*

| | | Residential region | | | |
		Galilee	Triangle	Negev	Mixed cities
I believe that being	I strongly agree	47.8	25.7	12.5	14.0
Muslim is more	I agree	50.0	29.2	13.8	6.9
important than	I agree to a certain extent	61.5	28.2	5.1	5.1
being Israeli	I disgree to a certain extent	81.6	10.2	0.0	8.2
	I disagree	84.6	15.4	0.0	0.0
	I strongly disagree	83.3	0.0	0.0	16.7

Table 4.20 *Cross-tabulation: religiosity (%) and identity preference*

	Being an Israeli citizen	Being a Muslim	Being a Palestinian
Very religious	10.3	76.9	12.8
Religious	11.3	76.1	12.7
Somewhat religious	17.0	58.5	24.5
Somewhat non-religious	27.0	39.7	33.3
Non-religious	37.9	13.8	48.3
Not religious at all	27.3	0.0	72.7

36.5 percent of the respondents defined themselves as 'Palestinian Arabs living in Israel'. In Smooha's studies (2013; 2015), the percentage of those identifying themselves in this way was only 31–33 percent. Note, however, that Smooha's studies included Arab Christians and Arab Druze, who patently do not define themselves as 'Palestinian'.

Again, a correlation was found between religiosity and identity preference ($\chi^2(20) = 38.32$; $p < 0.01$ and $rc = 0.14$; $p < 0.01$), as shown in Table 4.26.

This survey item was also examined in relation to the studied demographic variables. A chi-square test showed a correlation between the

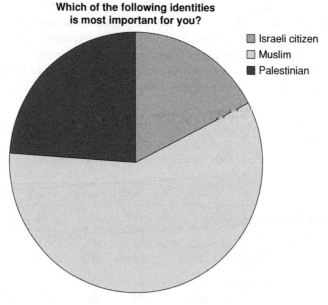

Figure 4.1 Identities

Table 4.21 *Cross-tabulation: age (%) and identity preference*

		Age				
		18–29	30–39	40–49	50–59	60+
Which identity do you prefer?	Being an Israeli citizen	15.9	23.2	26.8	25.6	8.5
	Being a Muslim	28.1	26.6	23.7	13.7	7.9
	Being a Palestinian Arab	43.8	17.9	19.6	13.4	5.4

Table 4.22 *Cross-tabulation: residential region (%) and identity preference*

		Residential region			
		Galilee	Triangle	Negev	Mixed cities
Which identity do you prefer?	Being an Israeli citizen	59.7	32.5	2.6	5.2
	Being a Muslim	51.7	26.0	13.2	9.1
	Being a Palestinian Arab	69.7	16.5	3.7	10.1

Table 4.23 *Cross-tabulation: residential community (%) and identity preference*

		Residential community			
		All Muslim	Mostly Muslim	Mostly Christian	Mostly Druze
Which identity do you prefer?	Being an Israeli citizen	61.9	26.2	0.0	11.9
	Being a Muslim	68.3	27.7	0.7	3.2
	Being a Palestinian Arab	44.8	46.6	3.4	5.2

Table 4.24 *Cross-tabulation: average monthly income (%) and identity preference*

		Average income				
		Much higher than average	A little higher than average	Average	Slightly below average	Much below average
Which identity do you prefer?	Being an Israeli citizen	4.8	20.2	27.4	44.0	3.6
	Being a Muslim	6.0	20.1	31.3	25.0	17.6
	Being a Palestinian Arab	9.4	19.7	29.1	25.6	16.2

Table 4.25 *Participants' responses (%)*
regarding identity preference

How do you identify yourself, when asked to choose one of the following possibilities?	
	Percentage
Arab	14.8
Israeli Arab	15.8
Palestinian Arab	19.6
Palestinian in Israel	10.6
Palestinian Arab in Israel	36.5
Total	97.3

ages of the participants and their identity preferences (χ^2 (16) $= 26.81$; $p < 0.05$; and rc $= 0.12$; $p < 0.05$; see Table 4.27), indicating that those in the age groups between eighteen and twenty-nine and between forty and forty-nine tend to identify themselves as 'Arab' (similar percentages). The highest percentage of those who identify themselves as 'Israeli Arab' are in the age group between thirty and thirty-nine, and the highest percentage of those who identify themselves as 'Palestinian Arab' are between the ages of eighteen and twenty-nine.

With regard to the identity preference in this survey, it was found that marital status (χ^2 (16) $= 25.44$) and gender (χ^2 (4) $= 3.19$) are unrelated, but residential region is correlated (χ^2 (12) $= 51.60$; $p < 0.001$; and rc $= 0.2$; $p < 0.001$). Table 4.28 shows that those who define themselves as 'Arab', 'Israeli Arab', and 'Palestinian Arab' are mostly from the Galilee.

Residential community was also found to be correlated with the participants' identity preference (χ^2 (12); 20.72; $p = 0.05$; and rc $= 0.12$; $p = 0.05$). Table 4.29 presents data showing that those who identify themselves as 'Arab' live in mostly or completely Muslim communities;

Table 4.26 *Cross-tabulation: religiosity (%) and identity preference*

	Arab	Israeli Arab	Palestinian Arab	Palestinian in Israel	Palestinian Arab in Israel
Very religious	20.5	5.1	41.0	5.1	28.2
Religious	20.7	11.4	17.9	7.9	42.1
Somewhat religious	13.9	16.3	18.8	13.4	37.6
Somewhat non-religious	8.1	27.4	16.1	9.7	38.7
Not religious	10.3	27.6	20.7	17.2	24.1
Not religious at all	0.0	27.3	18.2	9.1	45.5

Table 4.27 *Cross-tabulation: age (%) and identity preference*

		Age				
		18–29	30–39	40–49	50–59	60+
How do you	Arab	26.5	25.0	26.5	10.3	11.8
identify yourself,	Israeli Arab	19.7	35.5	25.0	15.8	3.9
when asked to	Palestinian Arab	28.9	23.7	22.7	18.6	6.2
choose one of the	Palestinian in Israel	32.7	7.7	21.2	23.1	15.4
following	Palestinian Arab in	33.7	23.0	23.6	14.0	5.6
possibilities?	Israel					

while a high percentage of those who identify themselves as 'Israeli Arab' are from completely Muslim communities.

The level of education was also found to correlate with identity preference (χ^2 (20) = 32.14; p < 0.05; and rc = 0.13; p < 0.05). Table 4.30 presents data indicating that those who completed a high-school education tend to identify themselves either as 'Arabs' or as 'Palestinian Arabs'.

While the type of (un)employment was found to be unrelated (χ^2 (24) = 29.54) to identity preference, the average monthly incomes are correlated (χ^2 (16) = 28.06; p < 0.05; and rc = 0.12; p < 0.05). Table 4.31 shows that a high percentage of those with average monthly incomes identify themselves as 'Arabs'.

Note, for the sake of clarification, that the terms 'Sunni' and 'Shi'ite' had not been significant parts of the Israeli Muslim discourse. These terms only entered this discourse after the Gulf War in the 1990s. In fact, in Mandatory Palestine, and even after the establishment of the

Table 4.28 *Cross-tabulation: residential region (%) and identity preference*

		Residential region			
		Galilee	Triangle	Negev	Mixed cities
How do you	Arab	66.7	11.6	5.8	15.9
identify yourself,	Israeli Arab	72.5	14.5	2.9	10.1
when asked to	Palestinian Arab	58.9	17.8	16.7	6.7
choose one of	Palestinian in Israel	47.1	49.0	3.9	0.0
the following	Palestinian Arab in	49.7	31.4	10.7	8.3
possibilities?	Israel				

Table 4.29 *Cross-tabulation: residential community (%) and identity preference*

| | | Residential community | | | |
		All Muslim	Mostly Muslim	Mostly Christian	Mostly Druze
How do you identify yourself, when asked to choose one of the following possibilities?	Arab	52.1	47.9	0.0	0.0
	Israeli Arab	60.8	29.1	1.3	8.9
	Palestinian Arab	68.4	26.3	2.1	3.2
	Palestinian in Israel	65.4	25.0	0.0	9.6
	Palestinian Arab in Israel	62.5	30.7	1.1	5.7

state of Israel, Israeli Muslims considered themselves to be Sunnis.[11] As for the survey item (Q: 55) questioning the participants' more specific religious identity, 86 percent of the respondents identified themselves as 'Sunni', 2.2 percent as 'Shiite', and 8 percent indicated the option 'Other'. 'Other' is an appropriate response either for those who do not consider themselves as being either Shi'ite or Sunni, for those who simply do not want to affiliate themselves with any specific branch of Islam and prefer to only make a general statement acknowledging that they are Muslims, or for those who reject this categorization entirely, because they only identify themselves as being 'Arab' (perhaps due to certain political positions, such as adherence to communism).

A different interpretation of this data may suggest that this group of respondents (8 percent) is a sort of 'protest group', opposing the division of Muslim identity between 'Sunni' and 'Shi'ite'; as such, they reject the new terminology introduced following the Gulf War and the burgeoning influence of the Islamic Republic of Iran. By no means can they be considered not to know their identity; on the contrary, these Muslims are fully aware of it.

Another possible explanation is that religious people are especially aware of the ramifications of religious connotations and the politics of identity. As such, the definition of a Sunni identity is significant for them in light of the ongoing conflict in the Islamic world between rival groups and, especially, after the Gulf War and the occupation of Iraq by the United States and Western Coalition armies.

---

[11] More on Shi'ite Islam in Israel in Khaled Sindawi, "The Shiite community in Israel: past and present," in Hatina and al-Atawneh (eds.), *Muslims in the Jewish State.*

Table 4.30 *Cross-tabulation: level of education (%) and identity preference*

		Level of education					
		No formal education	Elementary education	Secondary education	BA	MA	Ph.D.
How do you identify yourself, when asked to choose one of the following possibilities?	Arab	5.6	18.1	55.6	18.1	1.4	1.4
	Israeli Arab	3.8	16.5	62.0	13.9	3.8	0.0
	Palestinian Arab	3.1	17.5	49.5	24.7	5.2	0.0
	Palestinian in Israel	7.5	20.8	50.9	18.9	0.0	1.9
	Palestinian Arab in Israel	0.0	10.6	53.1	27.9	6.7	1.7

It was found that the specific religious affiliations of the participants ('Sunni', 'Shi'ite', or 'Other') are unrelated to: age (χ^2 (16) = 10.29); gender (χ^2 (4) = 1.29); level of education (χ^2 (20) = 10.01); marital status (χ^2 (16) = 14.94); type of (un)employment (χ^2 (24) = 11.46); and average monthly income (χ^2 (16) = 23.76). However, residential region is significantly correlated with specific religious affiliation, according to a chi-square test (χ^2 (12) = 34.52; p < 0.01; and rc = 0.16; p < 0.01; see Table 4.32). For instance, a high percentage of the participants from the Galilee identify themselves as 'Sunni'.

Table 4.31 *Cross-tabulation: average monthly income (%) and identity preference*

		Average income				
		Much higher than average	Somewhat higher than average	Average	Somewhat less than average	Much less than average
How do you identify yourself, when asked to choose one of the following possibilities?	Arab	9.5	12.2	37.8	23.0	17.6
	Israeli Arab	3.8	16.7	34.6	37.2	7.7
	Palestinian Arab	7.1	19.4	23.5	31.6	18.4
	Palestinian in Israel	3.8	11.3	35.8	34.0	15.1
	Palestinian Arab in Israel	7.8	28.3	26.7	22.8	14.4

Table 4.32 *Cross-tabulation: residential region (%) and specific religious affiliation*

		Residential region			
		Galilee	Triangle	Negev	Mixed cities
I specifically	Sunni	56.2	26.7	10.3	6.8
consider myself	Shi'ite	60.0	40.0	0.0	0.0
to be...	Other	68.6	2.9	0.0	28.6

Furthermore, with regard to issues of identity, the survey participants were also asked to answer two additional questions emphasizing their minority status, as belonging both to a national and a religious minority (Q: 57–58). They were also queried about their attitudes towards the caliphate (*khilafa*; a form of Islamic government) and whether they support the idea of a caliphate either in the Arab/Islamic world or in the state of Israel (items Q: 59–60).

An exploratory factor analysis was conducted to examine the validity of the items Q: 57–60 (found in Table 4.33). The results of this analysis appear in Table 4.34.

My specific religious affiliation is:

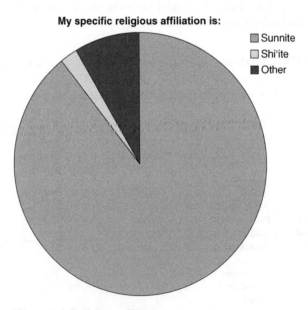

Figure 4.2 Religious affiliations

Table 4.33 *Participant responses (%) regarding the caliphate and minority status*

	I strongly agree	I agree	I agree to a certain extent	I disagree to a certain extent	I disgree	I strongly disagree
I support the idea of a caliphate ruling the Muslims in Israel	**9.6**	17.4	24.2	19.8	13.6	12.6
I support the idea of a caliphate ruling the Arab/Islamic world	**12**	20.2	24.2	21.0	10.6	10.0
I belong to a national minority in Israel	18.4	**42.5**	**22.4**	**10.4**	**3.2**	**1.4**
I belong to a religious minority in Israel	18.4	**39.1**	**24.2**	**10.6**	**4.6**	**1.4**

This factor analysis yielded two subscales. The first subscale (the caliphate; two items) reflects the participants' attitudes towards the caliphate and whether they support the idea of a caliphate ruling in the Arab/Islamic world or in Israel; its Cronbach alpha is 0.71. The second subscale (minority status; also two items) focuses on the respondents' sense of belonging either to a national or a religious minority; its Cronbach alpha is 0.68.

An examination of the Pearson correlations between these two factors (the caliphate and minority status) shows a significant correlation between them ($rp = 0.23$; $p < 0.001$). This means that the

Table 4.34 *Factor loading of the results for the four survey items (N = 500) in Table 4.33*

	Factor 1	Factor 2
I support the idea of a caliphate ruling the Muslims in Israel	**0.901**	−0.101
I support the idea of a caliphate ruling the Arab/Islamic world	**0.887**	0.141
I belong to a national minority in Israel	−0.015	**0.875**
I belong to a religious minority in Israel	0.213	**0.828**

participants' conceptions regarding their minority groups are correlated with their thoughts on the caliphate and the idea of an Islamic caliphate in the Arab/Islamic world or in Israel.

Moreover, a correlation was found between personal religiosity (Q: 56) and the first (caliphate) subscale (rs = 0.16; p < 0.01). The more positive the participants' attitude toward the caliphate, the more religious they claim to be, according to their responses. Finally, a correlation was also found between religiosity (rs = 0.4; p < 0.01) and the second (minority status) subscale.

The effects of the demographic variables on both subscales were further examined by means of a T-test, done for two independent samples, and a one-way ANOVA. An analysis of the data shows that participants': age (F(4) = 2.205); gender (t(480) = 0.368); marital status (F(4) = 2.17); type of (un)employment (F(6) = 1.56); residential community (F(3) = 0.979); residential region (F(3) = 1.39); and level of education (F(5) = 2.01) are all not related to the participants' conceptions of the caliphate (Factor 1). However, another one-way ANOVA test indicated significant differences for average monthly income (F(4) = 3.08; p < 0.05), especially between the groups with a somewhat below-average monthly income (Mean = 3.04) and with an average income (Mean = 3.5); and between those with somewhat below-average monthly incomes and those with somewhat above-average ones (Mean = 3.52).

The second subscale (Factor 2, minority status) was also studied in relation to the usual demographic variables. An analysis of the data shows that the respondents' age (rs = 0.02); gender (t(482) = 0.71; male (Mean = 2.48); female (Mean = 2.41)); marital status (F(4) = 0.65); and average monthly income (rs = 0.02) are all not related to this subscale. Moreover, the level of education was found to be significantly, negatively correlated to minority status (rs = −0.16; p < 0.01), such that higher education is associated with a reduced sense of belonging to both the national and the religious minorities.

A one-way ANOVA (F-test) did, however, indicate significant differences according to residential region (F(3) = 3.55; p < 0.05), and analysis of the post-hoc test showed that these differences mainly result from the significant attitudinal difference found between the Galilee residents (Mean = 2.55) and the Negev residents (Mean = 2.13). Similarly, the residential community was also found to be correlated with minority status (F(3) = 6.80; p < 0.001). Its post-hoc test indicated that these differences are mainly derived from the differences between completely Muslim communities (Mean = 2.31) and majority Druze communities (M = 3.06); and between majority Muslim communities (M = 2.61) and completely Muslim ones.

Table 4.35 *Cross-tabulation: residential region (%) and support for a return to Islamic practice in Israel*

		Residential region			
		Galilee	Triangle	Negev	Mixed cities
I support the	I strongly agree	49.4	27.0	15.7	7.9
return of lapsed	I agree	48.4	24.6	16.7	10.3
Israeli Muslims	I agree to a certain extent	68.1	18.5	3.4	10.1
to their religious	I disagree to a certain	72.7	15.9	2.3	9.1
observance	extent				
	I disagree	67.7	24.3	2.7	5.4
	I strongly disagree	44.4	52.8	0.0	2.8

Moreover, the type of (un)employment is also correlated with Factor 2 (the minority status subscale; (F(6) = 2.04; p = 0.05)). The post-hoc test showed that these differences result mainly from the differences between salaried employees (Mean = 2.3) and those that are unemployed, but looking for work (M = 2.76).

An analysis of the responses to another survey item, dealing with support for the return of lapsed Israeli Muslims to their religious observance (Q: 61), shows that 18.8 percent highly support a return to Islamic practice; 28.1 percent are in support of this; 25.3 percent are somewhat supportive; 10 percent are somewhat unsupportive; 7.8 percent do not support this; and 8 percent are against this. In total, 72.2 percent support the return to Islamic practice for Muslims in Israel. The survey results also show that religiosity is, naturally, correlated with the hope for a return to Islamic practice in Israel (rs = 0.28; p < 0.01).

Again, an analysis of the demographic variables, using a chi-square test, shows that age ($\chi^2(20)$ = 20.54); gender ($\chi^2(5)$ = 1.01); marital status ($\chi^2(20)$ = 19.34); type of (un)employment ($\chi^2(30)$ = 31.63); average monthly income ($\chi^2(20)$ = 17.45); and level of education ($\chi^2(50)$ = 52.47) are all unrelated to the participants' positions on a return to Islamic practice. However, the residential region ($\chi^2(15)$ = 49.86; p < 0.001; and rc = 0.19; p < 0.001) and the residential community ($\chi^2(15)$ = 41.56; p < 0.001; and rc = 0.17; p < 0.001) are significantly correlated with a return to Islamic practice, as shown in Tables 4.35 and 4.36.

In conclusion, the above discussion aimed at exploring the extent to which Islam has shaped the identity and the daily practice of the Muslim minority in Israel.

To this end, a number of survey items were dedicated to assessing the impact of Islam in the state of Israel (Q: 1–10). Then, those items were examined in relation to issues of identity (Q: 39–61). Various types

Table 4.36 *Cross-tabulation: residential community (%) and support for a return to Islamic practice in Israel*

| | | Residential community | | | |
		All Muslim	Mostly Muslim	Mostly Christian	Mostly Druze
I support the return of lapsed Israeli Muslims to their religious observance	I strongly agree	69.6	29.3	1.1	0.0
	I agree	64.7	34.6	0.7	0.0
	I agree to a certain extent	53.7	35	1.6	9.8
	I disagree to a certain extent	42.0	42.0	2.0	14.0
	I disagree	63.2	26.3	0.0	10.5
	I strongly disagree	79.5	15.4	0.0	5.1

of analyses were performed on the survey data: Spearman correlations, Pearson correlations, and chi-square tests (with the strengths of these correlations assessed by means of Cramer's V).

The first data studied were taken from the results of items Q: 39–48, that formed four subscales, dealing with attitudes to intra-religious marriage among Muslims; daily observance in the personal sphere; Islamic preaching in Israel and 'Pakistani attire' for men; and, lastly, Muslim attire (overt visual identity). The tested survey data from the first subscale show that there is a significant Spearman correlation between the extent of the respondents' commitment to Islamic law (Shari'a) as the basis for their normative behavior and their attitudes to intra-religious marriage (Q: 39–41; rs = 0.358; p < 0.01), meaning that the more the respondents are committed to practicing the Shari'a, the more they are of the opinion that Muslims should only marry Muslims in accordance with Islamic rituals.

Another significant positive Spearman correlation was found between the respondents' preference for Islamic observance by Muslims in Israel and their attitudes to intra-religious marriage (Q: 39–41; rs = 0.37; p < 0.01). People who prefer that the Muslims in Israel act according to the Shari'a also agree that Muslims should only marry Muslims and that they should do so in Islamic ceremonies.

As for the correlation between the extent to which each respondent is personally committed to Islamic law as a basis for his/her own normative daily behavior and prefers daily observance by the others in the personal sphere (the second substrate; Q: 42–44), a strong significant Spearman correlation was found (rs = 0.6; p < 0.01). Moreover, the overall preference for Islamic observance by Muslims in Israel was also found to be positively correlated with the desire to see daily observance by significant others in the personal sphere (rs = 0.56; p < 0.01). In other words, the more the respondents are personally committed to the Shari'a, and want the other Muslims in Israel to act accordingly, the more they also desire their close personal friends and immediate family to do so on a daily basis.

Regarding the third subscale (Q: 46–47), dealing with attitudes to Islamic preaching and the dissemination of religious values, this was found to be correlated with the extent to which the respondents reported their commitment to the Shari'a and normative Muslim behavior (rs = 0.37; p < 0.01), and also significantly correlated with the extent to which they would like the other Muslims in Israel to do so as well (rs = 0.33; p < 0.01). This means that the more the participants base their personal behavior on the Shari'a and want other Muslims to do the same, the more they tend to support Islamic preaching and the dissemination of Islamic values, including Muslim men wearing 'Pakistani attire'.

Finally, with regard to the fourth subscale (Q: 48–49), which emphasizes attitudes towards overt, visual identity (e.g. dress codes), the Spearman test showed a significant correlation between this parameter and the extent to which the respondents indicated their personal observance of daily Islamic practice (rs = 0.28; p < 0.01), as well as a significant correlation with the extent of their general preference for Islamic observance by Muslims in Israel (rs = 0.34; p < 0.01). As such, participants committed to the Shari'a for themselves and for all Muslims in Israel want to see Israeli Muslims in religious Islamic attire, overtly associated with a devout Islamic identity.

Clearly, those participants who live by the Shari'a tend to support gender segregation in Arab education (rs = 0.37; p < 0.01) and at public events (rs = 0.42; p < 0.01), as do those who want the other Muslims in Israel to act according to the Shari'a as well: gender segregation in education (rs = 0.28; p < 0.01) and at public events (rs = 0.37; p < 0.01).

5 The Muslim Minority and the Israeli Establishment
Acceptance and/or Alienation

This chapter discusses the relations between the Muslim minority in Israel and the Israeli establishment.[1] The previous chapter on identity indicated the complex and difficult dilemmas experienced by the Muslims in Israel regarding their participation in the modern Israeli public sphere while maintaining their Islamic socio-cultural norms and values. Such dilemmas are common mainly among Muslims living in non-Muslim or Western environments. Some key questions that arise are: How do Muslims relate to the Israeli institutions and authorities? How do Muslims accommodate contradictions between Islamic law, Israeli law and governance, and local customs?

The answers to the above and other related questions were culled from the empirical fieldwork done to assess these issues. In principle, a majority of the respondents support the establishment of Islamic religious, social, cultural, and economic institutions in general, and most of them wish this to be done by the IM; only a small percentage of the respondents feel that this should be done by the Israeli government (Q: 11–12 and 16–19).[2] These findings also indicated a sweeping dissatisfaction with the existing official Islamic institutions, their funding, management, and performance. Nonetheless, most of the respondents are content with the work of the existing IM institutions that they perceive to be more authentic – preferable alternatives to those provided by the state of Israel. Such results foster the notion of forming an 'autonomous [Islamic] society' (*mujtama' 'isami*) in Israel, as promoted by the IM over the last two decades.[3] Yet note that a signficant number of survey participants responded that it does not matter to them who establishes Islamic institutions in Israel, as long as they exist and function.

---

[1] On the official Israeli policy toward Islam in Israel see Rubin-Peled, *Debating Islam in the Jewish State.*

[2] See 'Issam Aburaiya, "Concrete religiosity versus abstract religiosity: the case of the division of the Islamic Movement in Israel," *Megamot* 43 (4) (2005): 682–698 [Hebrew]; and 'Ali, "Religious Fundamentalism."

[3] 'Ali, "The notion of 'el-mogtama' el-aisami'."

Table 5.1 *Preferential support (%) for the establishment of Islamic institutions in Israel*

	I support the establishment of Islamic religious institutions by	I support the establishment of Islamic cultural institutions by	I support the establishment of Islamic social institutions by	I support the establishment of Islamic economic institutions (e.g. banks) by
State of Israel	9.2	11.8	14.6	19.6
Islamic Movement (NIM or SIM)	41.6	38.5	34.7	30.5
Regardless of the founders	38.9	40.3	40.1	35.3
I do not support the establishment of Islamic institutions	10.0	8.2	9.0	13.8

When analyzing the relevant survey items (Q: 16–19), Table 5.1 indicates different levels of support for the establishment of different types of Islamic institutions and a clear preference regarding who should be the founders of those institutions, regardless of the type. Only 9.2 percent feel that the state of Israel should establish the official Islamic religious institutions (Q: 16) and, similarly, only 19.6 percent support its founding of Islamic banks and such (Q: 19). In the same vein, many (41.6 percent) of the respondents prefer that Islamic religious institutions be established in Israel by the IM (NIM or SIM) and, similarly, 30 percent want the IM to found the Islamic financial institutions. The interviewees and survey participants consider these institutions to be much more than merely buildings, and expressed concerns regarding their ethical and educational impacts on the Muslim public. As such, the religious education provided by the IM is much preferred to that given by the state of Israel, although the formal, state-owned and -run institutions are the 'official' ones and are currently run by officially recognized and authorized Israeli Islamic religious scholars.

Other survey items focused on the different impacts of various demographic parameters on the preferential support for the establishment of Islamic religious institutions in Israel (Q: 16) and the analyzed results are as follows. Participants' age (χ^2 (12) = 12.88) and gender (χ^2 (3) = 3.08) did not affect the preferences. However, marital status (single, married, divorced, widowed; see Table 5.2) did affect certain responses to this item (χ^2 (12) = 30.31; p < 0.01 and rc = 0.14; p < 0.01). Significant

Table 5.2 *Cross-tabulation: preferential support (%) for religious institutions and marital status*

		Marital status			
		Single	Married	Divorced/ Separated	Widowed
I support the establishment of Islamic religious institutions by:	State of Israel	21.7	69.6	6.5	0.0
	Islamic Movement (NIM or SIM)	18.2	78.3	2.0	1.5
	Regardless of whom	21.1	73.2	2.6	3.2
	I do not support this	42.9	55.1	2.0	0.0

differences were found, for instance, between single (21.7 percent) and married respondents (69.6 percent) in the degree of their support for the establishment of such Islamic institutions.

The residential region was also correlated (χ^2 (9) = 16.96; p < 0.05 and rc = 0.11; p < 0.05). Table 5.3 presents a cross-tabulation of preferential support and residential region, indicating the different regional preferences. For instance, over half the respondents from the Galilee preferred that the IM establish Islamic religious institutions in Israel, compared to a third of the participants from the Triangle.

However, the residential communities (χ^2(9) = 3.36), levels of education (χ^2 (15) = 21.79), and average monthly incomes of the participants were not related to their choices of who should establish Islamic religious institutions in Israel (χ^2 (12) = 10.41).

Nonetheless, the type of (un)employment did affect the respondents' choices regarding the establishment of religious institutions, as shown in Table 5.4 (χ^2 (18) = 28,68; p = 0.05 and rc – 0,14; p – 0.05).

Table 5.3 *Cross-tabulation: preferential support (%) for religious institutions and residential region*

		Residential region			
		Galilee	Triangle	Negev	Mixed cities
I support the establishment of Islamic religious institutions by:	State of Israel	65.0	25.0	10.0	0.0
	Islamic Movement (NIM or SIM)	54.1	28.9	6.7	10.3
	Regardless of whom	57.1	20.9	13.2	8.8
	I do not support this	66.7	21.4	0.0	11.9

Table 5.4 *Cross-tabulation: preferential support (%) for religious institutions and type of (un)employment*

				Type of (un)employment			
		Employee or clerk	Self-employed	Unemployed, seeking employment	Unemployed, not seeking employment	Retired	College student	Housewife
I support the establishment of Islamic religious institutions by:	State of Israel	37.8	8.9	15.6	4.4	2.2	8.9	22.2
	Islamic Movement (NIM or SIM)	51.0	16.2	9.3	4.9	4.4	3.4	10.8
	Regardless of whom	39.4	10.4	17.1	6.7	4.1	5.2	17.1
	I do not support this	61.2	6.1	12.2	2.0	4.1	8.2	6.1

Table 5.5 *Cross-tabulation: preferential support (%) for cultural institutions and level of education*

		Level of education					
		No formal education	Elementary education	Secondary education	BA	MA	Ph.D.
I support the establishment of Islamic cultural institutions by:	State of Israel	5.1	23.7	54.2	15.3	1.7	0.0
	Islamic Movement (NIM or SIM)	3.7	16.0	45.5	29.4	3.7	1.6
	Regardless of whom	2.0	11.7	65.0	15.2	5.1	1.0
	I do not support this	2.4	17.1	46.3	24.4	7.3	2.4

As for the results regarding preferences for the establishment of Islamic cultural institutions in Israel (Q: 17), by either the Israeli government or the IM – the participants' gender (χ^2 (3) = 2.46); age (χ^2 (12) = 17.46); marital status (χ^2 (12) = 15.96); average monthly income (χ^2 (12) = 14.70); residential region (χ^2 (9) = 13.50), residential community (χ^2 (9) = 11.19); and type of (un)employment – all had no impact on their responses (χ^2 (18) = 21.06).

What did prove somewhat influential was the level of education (χ^2 (15) = 27.60; p < 0.05 and rc = 0.14; p < 0.05) of the participants. A chi-square test showed a weak, but significant, correlation with the establishment of Islamic cultural institutions. Table 5.5 presents a cross-tabulation of the level of education and the responses regarding support for the establishment of Islamic cultural institutions in Israel, showing that they vary with the degree of education of the respondent.

The survey results regarding public support for the establishment of Islamic social institutions (Q: 18) were also analyzed against the same demographic variables as above. It was found that none of the following: gender (χ^2 (3) = 1.11); age (χ^2 (12) = 11.86); marital status (χ^2 (12) = 14.02); average monthly income (χ^2 (12) = 13.93), residential region (χ^2 (9) = 10.66); residential community (χ^2 (9) = 0.80); type of (un)employment (χ^2 (18) = 16.22); and level of education (χ^2(15) = 20.05) affected the responses regarding the establishment of Islamic social institutions. In this case, the findings indicate that this issue supersedes all the demographic variables; there appears to be a consensus, based on a general feeling of dissatisfaction, brought on by beliefs that the Islamic institutions established by the state of Israel are of poor quality and receive insufficient funding. It also seems that the IM knows how

Table 5.6 *Cross-tabulation: preferential support (%) for economic institutions and level of education*

		Level of education					
		No formal education	Elementary education	Secondary education	BA	MA	Ph.D.
I support the establishment of Islamic economic institutions by:	State of Israel	4.1	16.5	62.9	14.4	2.1	0
	Islamic Movement (NIM or SIM)	4.0	17.4	38.9	30.9	6.7	2.0
	Regardless of whom	1.7	14.0	61.6	16.9	4.7	1.2
	I do not support this	2.9	11.8	57.4	25.0	1.5	1.5

to identify this dissatisfaction amid the Muslim minority and so it offers institutional alternatives to remedy this situation, going from the stage of identifying problems to the more proactive stage of providing solutions. The fundamentalist movements in general, and the IM in Israel, seek to fill the vacuum generated by the Israeli establishment.[4]

Another survey item dealt with preferential support of the establishment of Islamic economic institutions (for example, Islamic banks; Q: 19). This, too, was examined in correlation with the same demographic variables as above. Also in this case, a chi-square test showed that participants' gender (χ^2 (3) = 1.72); age (χ^2 (12) = 14.14); marital status (χ^2 (12) = 12.15); residential region (χ^2 (9) = 10.66); residential community (χ^2 (9) = 11.69; p = n.s.); and type of (un)employment (χ^2 (18) = 17.67) did not affect the preferences. One factor that did impact the responses is the level of education (χ^2 (15) = 29.83; p < 0.05; and rc = 0.14; p < 0.05), as shown in Table 5.6.

Average monthly income was also found to be correlated with support for the establishment of Islamic economic institutions. Table 5.7 presents a cross-tabulation of average monthly income with the responses to this item, showing that participants with an above- or a below-average income differ in their responses (χ^2 (12) = 22.35; p < 0.05 and rc = 0.12; p < 0.05).

The attitudes indicated by the survey population sample regarding economic matters are especially important and have two interrelated, but opposing, causes. On the one hand, the state of Israel has made

[4] For more details see 'Ali, *Between 'Ovadia and 'Abdallah.*

Table 5.7 *Cross-tabulation: preferential support (%) for economic institutions and average monthly income*

		Average income				
		Much above average	Slightly above average	Average	Slightly below average	Much below average
I support the establishment of Islamic economic institutions by:	State of Israel	5.1	16.3	32.7	29.6	16.3
	Islamic Movement (NIM or SIM)	10.0	26.0	20.0	30.7	13.3
	Regardless of whom	5.2	15.5	38.5	24.7	16.1
	I do not support this	2.9	25.0	26.5	29.4	16.2

concerted efforts to make the Arab Israeli minority totally dependent on Jewish Israeli mainstream economy.[5] On the other hand, the intention to achieve financial independence for the Muslim minority is a mainstay of many IM projects for the improvement of self-management and autonomy (*al-mujtama' al-'isami*), particularly by means of the establishment of financial institutions, such as Islamic banks. However, thus far, attempts to establish such banks have been thwarted by the state.[6]

With regard to survey items Q: 20–24, dealing with support of active political participation in municipal and/or state government, a confirmatory factor analysis (CFA) was conducted. The results appear in Table 5.8.

The factor analysis of these five items yielded two subscales. The first subscale (three items; Q: 20–22) emphasizes the respondents' support of political participation on both the local and national levels, as expressed by their support for running Muslim candidates and parties in various Israeli elections. The Cronbach alpha for this subscale is 0.77.

The second subscale (two items; Q: 23–24) refers to a preference for living under an Islamic authority (i.e. a Muslim regime). In this case, the Cronbach alpha is 0.8. It was found that the correlation between religiosity and political participation is (rs = 0.14; p < 0.01) and between religiosity and living under Islamic authority is (rs = 0.48; p < 0.01).

---

[5] See Lustick, *Arabs in the Jewish State*; Adriana Kemp, "From politics of location to politics of signification: the construction of political territory in Israel's first years," *Journal of Area Studies* 6 (12) (1998): 74–96; Ramsees Gharrah (ed.), *Arab Society in Israel: Population, Society, Economy* VII (Jerusalem: Van Leer Institute, 2015) [Hebrew]; 'Ali, "The Islamic Movement in Israel between religion, nationality and modernity"; Rubin-Peled, *Debating Islam in the Jewish State.*

[6] 'Ali, "The notion of 'el-mogtama' el-aisami'."

Table 5.8 *Factor loading for items Q: 20–24 (N = 500)*

	Factor 1	Factor 2
I support the idea of Muslim political participation in Knesset elections	**0.930**	−0.03
I support the idea of Muslim political participation in municipal elections	**0.860**	0.11
I support the idea of an Islamic party running for the Israeli Knesset	**0.650**	0.40
I support Islamic political parties that rule in Arab countries	0.106	**0.897**
I prefer to live in a state with an Islamic religious orientation	0.104	**0.899**

The overall correlation between these two subscales is (rp = 0.31; p < 0.001).

The 'Muslim political participation' subscale (subscale 1) was then examined in relation to the usual demographic variables. Spearman tests showed that average monthly income (rs = 0.03); level of education (rs = −0.05); and age (rs = 0.02) are unrelated to the stated positions regarding political participation. Additionally, a T-test for two independent samples showed no difference between men (Mean = 2.69) and women (Mean = 2.63) (t(483) = 0.65;p = n.s.). A one-way ANOVA also showed no differences in participant responses by residential region (F(3) = 0.99); residential community (F(3) = 0.102); marital status (F(4) = 0.84); nor by the type of (un)employment (F(6) = 0.56).

As for the 'living under Islamic authority' subscale (subscale 2), Spearman tests showed that average monthly income (rs = 0.013); level of education (rs = 0.013); and age (rs = −0.05) are not correlated with attitudes to living under an Islamic authority. T-tests were also done for two independent samples and showed no differences between the attitudes of Muslim men and Muslim women (t(483) = −0.25). Again, a one-way ANOVA showed that participants' positions on living under Islamic authority do not vary by residential region (F(3) = 1.14); residential community (F(3) = 1.61); nor by the type of (un)employment (F(6) = 0.217). Marital status, however, was found to affect the participants' positions on this matter (F(4) = 4.47; p < 0.05).

When analyzing the responses to the item (Q: 25) in Table 5.9: "How much do you support/reject the Islamic party regimes existing in some 'Arabic Spring' countries?" the Spearman tests showed no correlations between positions taken on this statement and the level of education (rs = 0.04), nor with the average monthly income (rs = 0.02); however, age was found to be correlated (rs = 0.16; p < 0.01). Also, a chi-square test did not show any differences on this issue by the gender ($\chi^2(5)$ = 4.14) or marital status ($\chi^2(20)$ = 24.34; p = n.s.) of the participants.

Table 5.9 *How much (%) do you support/reject Islamic party regimes?*

	Strongly reject	Reject	Reject to a certain degree	Support to a certain degree	Support	Strongly support
How much do you support/reject Islamic party regimes?	8.4	12.6	22.0	20.4	18.0	17.4

Of the respondents, only 43 percent indicated any degree of rejection of Islamic party regimes (such as exist in some Arab Spring countries).

Nonetheless, participants' positions did vary significantly by residential region ($\chi^2(15) = 32.30$; $p < 0.01$ and $rc = 0.15$; $p < 0.01$), as shown in Table 5.10.

A chi-square test ruled out any correlation between the residential communities and the participants' positions regarding Islamic party regimes ($\chi^2 (15) = 15.12$). Another chi-square test also found no correlation between this issue and the participants' type of (un)employment ($\chi^2 (30) = 16.73$).

Personal observance does not, however, show a significant correlation ($rs = -0.06$) with support for an Islamic regime. However, the extent of commitment to the observance of Shari'a law does correlate with the participants' preferences regarding the establishment of Islamic religious institutions, either by the state of Israel or by the IM ($\chi^2(15) = 76.24$; $p < 0.001$ and $rc = 0.23$; $p < 0.001$). Table 5.11 shows the percentages of participants supporting the establishment of Islamic religious institutions in relation to their degree of personal observance.

Table 5.10 *Cross-tabulation: support/rejection of Islamic party regimes (%) and residential region*

		Residential region			
		Galilee	Triangle	Negev	Mixed cities
I support/reject	Strongly reject	70.3	16.2	10.8	2.7
Islamic party	Reject	61.9	15.9	15.9	6.3
regimes	Reject to a certain degree	60.6	21.2	11.1	7.1
resulting from	Support to a certain degree	61.1	18.9	6.3	13.7
the 'Arab	Support	50.6	31.8	5.9	11.8
Spring'	Strongly support	46.8	41.6	6.5	5.2

Table 5.11 *Cross-tabulation: support for Islamic religious institutions (%) and degree of observance*

| | | I support the establishment of Islamic religious institutions by: | | | |
		State of Israel	Islamic Movement (NIM or SIM)	Regardless of whom	I do not support this
I observe	To a very high degree	10.0	64.3	22.9	2.9
Shari'a	To a high degree	8.7	40.3	44.4	6.6
law	To a certain degree	9.3	43.7	38.4	8.6
	Not to a certain degree	20.0	28.0	40.0	12.0
	To a small degree	3.8	23.1	46.2	26.9
	Non-observant or secular	9.1	13.6	27.3	50.0

The extent to which the respondents are committed to Islamic observance is also correlated with their support for the establishment of Islamic cultural institutions in Israel ($\chi^2(15) = 98.16$; $p < 0.001$ and rc $= 0.26$; $p < 0.001$), such as theaters.[7] Table 5.12 presents the percentages of participants supporting the establishment of Islamic cultural institutions (either by the state of Israel or by the IM).

In addition, the extent to which the respondents are committed to Islamic observance correlates with their support for the establishment of Islamic social institutions, such as sports clubs, in Israel ($\chi^2(15) = 95.21$; $p < 0.001$ and rc $= 0.26$; $p < 0.001$), as shown in Table 5.13.

Moreover, the extent to which the respondents are committed to Islamic observance correlates with their support for the establishment of Islamic economic institutions in Israel, such as Islamic banks ($\chi^2(15) = 54.54$; $p < 0.001$ and rc $= 0.19$; $p < 0.001$). Table 5.14 shows the percentages of the respondents supporting the establishment of Islamic economic institutions (either by the state of Israel or by the IM).

Further analysis of the data was done to determine the extent to which personal religious observance affects the respondents' perceptions of their relationships with the state of Israel. Spearman tests showed a correlation (rs $= 0.1$; $p < 0.05$) between the respondents' degrees of observance and levels of support for political participation (Q: 20–22, Knesset elections and Islamic political parties) and also with living under Islamic authority (Q: 23–24; rs $= 0.4$; $p < 0.01$). This indicates that the more the participants are committed to the Shari'a (i.e. the

---

[7] 'Ali, "Religious Fundamentalism."

Table 5.12 *Cross-tabulation: support for Islamic cultural institutions (%) and degree of observance*

		I support the establishment of Islamic cultural institutions by:			
		State of Israel	Islamic Movement (NIM or SIM)	Regardless of whom	I do not support this
I observe Shari'a law	To a very high degree	11.4	57.1	30.0	1.4
	To a high degree	11.8	37.9	43.1	7.2
	To a certain degree	12.8	40.9	43.0	3.4
	Not to a certain degree	28.0	28.0	36.0	8.0
	To a small degree	3.8	26.9	46.2	23.1
	Non-observant or secular	4.5	4.5	36.4	54.5

Table 5.13 *Cross-tabulation: support for Islamic social institutions (%) and degree of observance*

		I support the establishment of Islamic social institutions by:			
		State of Israel	Islamic Movement (NIM or SIM)	Regardless of whom	I do not support this
I observe Shari'a law	To a very high degree	11.6	63.8	21.7	2.9
	To a high degree	14.9	32.8	44.1	8.2
	To a certain degree	14.7	35.3	43.3	6.7
	Not to a certain degree	40.0	24.0	32.0	4.0
	To a small degree	8.0	12.0	60.0	20.0
	Non-observant or secular	9.1	9.1	31.8	50.0

Table 5.14 *Cross-tabulation: support for Islamic economic institutions (%) and degree of observance*

		I support the establishment of Islamic economic institutions by:			
		State of Israel	Islamic Movement (NIM or SIM)	Regardless of whom	I do not support this
I observe Shari'a law	To a very high degree	10.0	48.6	34.3	7.1
	To a high degree	16.4	33.3	36.4	13.8
	To a certain degree	26.0	29.3	34.7	10.0
	Not to a certain degree	32.0	16.0	32.0	20.0
	To a small degree	23.1	19.2	34.6	23.1
	Non-observant or secular	27.3	0.0	22.7	50.0

Table 5.15 *Cross-tabulation: support for Islamic social institutions (%) and degree of observance*

		I support the establishment of Islamic social institutions by:			
		State of Israel	Islamic Movement (NIM or SIM)	Regardless of whom	I do not support this
Degree of observance	To a very high degree	10.0	51.0	36.0	3.0
	To a high degree	16.1	35.7	39.9	8.3
	To a certain degree	15.1	33.6	45.9	5.5
	Not to a certain degree	36.7	13.3	36.7	13.3
	To a small degree	6.3	18.8	43.8	31.3
	Non-observant or secular	5.0	15.0	25.0	55.0

more observant they are), the more they support Islamic political action within Israel and would prefer living in an Islamic (rather than a Jewish) state. Regarding Q: 25, no correlation was found between the degree of personal observance and the rejection of Islamic party regimes in Arab Spring countries (rs = −0.02).

Similarly, the degrees of personal observance of the survey participants were found to be correlated to their levels of support for the establishment of Islamic social institutions ($\chi^2(15) = 90.95$; $p < 0.001$ and rc = 0.25; $p < 0.001$), as shown in Table 5.15. Clearly, those who choose the Islamic way of life want to strengthen the Muslim community by educating the Muslim public in Shari'a law and values via the establishment of Islamic social institutions, especially those established by the IM.

In fact, it was found that the extent to which the participants want Israeli Muslims to act according to Shari'a law is correlated with their support for the establishment of Islamic religious institutions in Israel ($\chi^2(15) = 99.42$; $p < 0.001$ and rc = 0.26; $p < 0.001$). Table 5.16 presents a high percentage of respondents who support the establishment of Islamic religious institutions by the IM. In general, it appears that the observance of Islamic religious law is a crucial, formative value and that observant Muslims in Israel are quite willing to live in seclusion in order to maintain an Islamic lifestyle.

The extent to which the survey participants preferred that Muslims in Israel behave according to Islamic religious laws (Q: 2) was also found to be correlated with support for the establishment of Islamic cultural institutions in Israel ($\chi^2(15) = 115.49$; $p < 0.001$ and rc = 0.28; $p < 0.001$). Such institutions assist the Muslim minority community in nurturing

Table 5.16 *Cross-tabulation: preferential support for religious institutions (%) and preference for Islamic observance*

		I support the establishment of Islamic religious institutions by:			
		State of Israel	Islamic Movement (NIM or SIM)	Regardless of whom	I do not support this
Preference for observance	To a very high degree	5.9	55.9	35.3	2.9
	To a high degree	11.8	41.4	37.9	8.9
	To a certain degree	6.8	43.8	43.2	6.2
	Not to a certain degree	25.8	22.6	38.7	12.9
	To a small degree	6.3	18.8	37.5	37.5
	Non-observant or secular	5.0	5.0	30.0	60.0

an Islamic lifestyle by fostering Shari'a-based Islamic norms and values. Table 5.17 provides a cross-tabulation of the percentages of participants supporting the establishment of Islamic cultural institutions (either by the state of Israel or by the IM) correlated with their preferences for Islamic observance in Israel.

It was found (see Table 5.18) that half of those not interested in implementing Islamic laws in their personal daily lives nonetheless support the establishment of economic institutions for Muslims in Israel. Not surprisingly, the extent to which the survey participants prefer that Muslims observe Islam in Israel was also found to be correlated with their support for the establishment of Islamic economic institutions (χ^2 (15) = 49.24; $p < 0.001$ and rc = 0.19; $p < 0.001$).

Table 5.17 *Cross-tabulation: preferential support for cultural institutions (%) and preference for Islamic observance*

		I support the establishment of Islamic cultural institutions by:			
		State of Israel	Islamic Movement (NIM or SIM)	Regardless of whom	I do not support this
Preference for observance	To a very high degree	8.8	52.0	37.3	2.0
	To a high degree	15.0	37.7	40.1	7.2
	To a certain degree	10.3	40.7	44.8	4.1
	Not to a certain degree	25.8	19.4	48.4	6.5
	To a small degree	6.3	31.3	25.0	37.5
	Non-observant or secular	0.0	5.0	35.0	60.0

Table 5.18 *Cross-tabulation: preferential support for economic institutions (%) and preference for Islamic observance*

		I support the establishment of Islamic economic institutions by:			
		State of Israel	Islamic Movement (NIM or SIM)	Regardless of whom	I do not support this
Preference for observance	To a very high degree	15.8	39.6	35.6	8.9
	To a high degree	19.0	35.7	31.0	14.3
	To a certain degree	19.2	30.8	39.7	10.3
	Not to a certain degree	38.7	9.7	29.0	22.6
	To a small degree	31.3	18.8	25.0	25.0
	Non-observant or secular	20.0	0.0	30.0	50.0

The analysis of the relevant Spearman test also shows a correlation between the degree of preference for observance and the respondents' support for political participation (Q: 20–22; rs = 0.12; p < 0.001) and also with the willingness to live under an Islamic authority (Q: 23–24; rs = 0.41; p < 0.001). This means that the more the participants want Muslims in Israel to be observant, the more they support local, regional, and national political participation and the establishment of Islamic political parties to stand in various Israeli elections. However, no correlation was found between the preference for observance in Israel and the rejection of Islamic party regimes elsewhere, like those that exist in some Arab Spring countries (Q: 25; rs = −0.07).

In fact, a positive and significant correlation was found between the degree of preference for observance and the sense of alienation felt by some Muslims in Israel (Q: 30–33; rs = 0.35; p < 0.001), meaning that the more the participants want the Muslims in Israel to act according to Shari'a law, the more they may feel alienated from the state of Israel.

Madhhab Affiliation and the Israeli Establishment

No correlation was found between the survey participants' legal *madhhab* affiliation (Q: 3) and support for the establishment of Islamic religious institutions (χ^2 (15) = 18.24). However, legal *madhhab* affiliation was found to be correlated with support for the establishment of Islamic cultural institutions ($\chi^2(15) = 27.07$; p < 0.05 and rc = 0.14; p < 0.05), as observed in Table 5.19.

Table 5.19 *Cross-tabulation: preferential support for the establishment of cultural institutions (%) and legal* madhhab *affiliation*

		I support the establishment of Islamic cultural institutions by:			
		State of Israel	Islamic Movement (NIM or SIM)	Regardless of whom	I do not support this
Legal *madhhab* affiliation	Hanafi	7.6	37.9	43.9	10.6
	Maliki	11.1	44.4	44.4	0.0
	Shafi'i	14.5	34.5	43.5	7.5
	Hanbali	27.6	32.8	32.8	6.9
	Other doctrines	13.0	30.4	56.5	0.0
	Unaffiliated	13.0	39.0	28.6	19.5

In addition, a correlation was found between legal *madhhab* affiliation and the respondents' preferential support for the establishment of Islamic social institutions ($\chi^2(15) = 28.90$; $p < 0.05$ and rc = 0.14; $p < 0.05$). Table 5.20 shows the percentage of participants supporting the establishment of Islamic social institutions according to their legal *madhhab* affiliations.

The survey findings also indicate a correlation between legal *madhhab* affiliation and the respondents' preferential support for the establishment of Islamic economic institutions $\chi^2(15) = 28.14$; $p < 0.05$ and rc = 0.14; $p < 0.05$). Table 5.21 presents the percentage of participants

Table 5.20 *Cross-tabulation: preferential support for the establishment of social institutions (%) and legal* madhhab *affiliation*

		I support the establishment of Islamic social institutions by:			
		State of Israel	Islamic Movement (NIM or SIM)	Regardless of whom	I do not support this
Legal *madhhab* affiliation	Hanafi	7.6	37.9	43.9	10.6
	Maliki	11.1	44.4	44.4	0.0
	Shafi'i	14.5	34.5	43.5	7.5
	Hanbali	27.6	32.8	32.8	6.9
	Other doctrines	13.0	30.4	56.5	0.0
	Unaffiliated	13.0	39.0	28.6	19.5

Table 5.21 *Cross-tabulation: preferential support for the establishment of economic institutions (%) and legal* madhhab *affiliation*

		I support the establishment of Islamic economic institutions by:			
		State of Israel	Islamic Movement (NIM or SIM)	Regardless of whom	I do not support this
Legal *madhhab*	Hanafi	13	24.6	53.6	8.7
affiliation	Maliki	22.2	55.6	22.2	0.0
	Shafi'i	17.2	33.6	35.9	13.3
	Hanbali	29.3	29.3	27.6	13.8
	Other doctrines	21.7	30.4	30.4	17.4
	Unaffiliated	27.3	24.7	26.0	22.1

supporting the establishment of Islamic economic institutions by their legal *madhhab* affiliations.

Lastly, when comparing the respondents' legal *madhhab* affiliations with the extent of their support for political participation by means of a chi-square test, a correlation was found (Q: 20–22; $\chi^2(75) = 118.86$; $p < 0.001$). The strength of this correlation, as measured by Cramer's V, was (rc $= 0.22$; $p < 0.001$), meaning that the respondents' legal *madhhab* affiliations do impact the extent to which they support political participation, such as supporting Muslim candidates for local or regional councils, or for the Knesset, or supporting the establishment of an Islamic party in Israel.

Furthermore, the survey results indicate a relation between the respondents' legal *madhhab* affiliations and their preference for living under an Islamic authority (Q: 23–24; $\chi^2(50) = 88.8$; $p < 0.001$ and rc $= 0.19$; $p < 0.001$). However, no correlation was found between respondents' legal *madhhab* affiliations and the sense of alienation felt by Muslims in Israel (Q: 30–33; $\chi^2(130) = 149.19$). Also, no correlation was found between the respondents' legal *madhhab* affiliations and the extent to which the survey participants reject Islamic party regimes (Q: 25; $\chi^2(25) = 20.44$).

Theological *Madhhab* and the Israeli Establishment

The extent to which the participants are committed to specific theological *madhhab*s was not found to be correlated with support for the establishment of Islamic religious institutions ($\chi^2 (12) = 9.07$).

Table 5.22 *Cross-tabulation: preferential support for the establishment of cultural institutions (%) and theological* madhhab

| | | I support the establishment of Islamic cultural institutions by: | | | |
		State of Israel	Islamic Movement (NIM or SIM)	Regardless of whom	I do not support this
Theological	Ash'ari	16.7	25.0	58.3	0.0
madhhab	Maturidi	66.7	0.0	33.3	0.0
	Ahl al-Hadith	12.6	39.8	42.4	5.2
	Other	11.8	43.5	35.3	9.4
	Unaffiliated	9.6	37.0	39.7	13.7

However, a correlation was found between the theological *madhhab* and support for the establishment of Islamic cultural institutions ($\chi^2(12) = 21.76$; $p < 0.05$ and rc = 0.12; $p < 0.05$), as shown in Table 5.22.

Nonetheless, no correlation was found between the participants' theological *madhhab*s and their support for the establishment of Islamic social institutions ($\chi^2 (12) = 15.25$), nor with their preference for the establishment of Islamic economic institutions ($\chi^2 (12) = 7.86$).

The effects of the respondents' theological *madhhab*s on their positions regarding the Israeli establishment were also examined. A chi-square test yielded insignificant outcomes, ruling out both the possibility of a correlation between respondents' theological *madhhab*s and support for Muslim political participation (Q: 20–22; $\chi^2 (60) = 61.40$) and with the parameter of living under Islamic authority (Q: 23–24; $\chi^2 (40) = 41.66$). In addition, no correlation was found between the respondents' theological *madhhab*s and the rejection of Islamic party regimes (Q: 35; $\chi^2 (20) = 22.99$); nor was a correlation found between theological *madhhab*s and the sense of alienation felt by some Muslims in Israel (Q: 30–33; $\chi^2(100) = 112.07$). Lastly, no correlation was found between theological *madhhab*s and the extent to which participants believe that 'there is a lot to learn from the West and less from Arab countries' (Q: 34; $\chi^2 (20) = 12.39$).

Islamic Ideologies and the Israeli Establishment

Other current Islamic ideologies held by the survey participants were also analyzed versus their preferences for the establishment of Islamic religious institutions ($\chi^2 (15) = 37.50$; $p < 0.01$ and rc = 0.16; $p < 0.01$,

Table 5.23 *Cross-tabulation: current Islamic ideologies (%) and support for the establishment of Islamic religious institutions*

		I support the establishment of Islamic religious institutions by:			
		State of Israel	Islamic Movement (NIM or SIM)	Regardless of whom	I do not support this
Current Islamic ideologies	Salafis	12.0	68.0	16.0	4.0
	Salafi Jihadists	0.0	75.0	25.0	0.0
	Moderates	8.7	43.7	41.2	6.5
	Liberals	7.4	23.5	52.9	16.2
	Other ideologies	12.5	41.1	32.1	14.3
	Unaffiliated	13.6	43.2	22.7	20.5

see Table 5.23); cultural institutions (χ^2 (15) = 38.78; $p < 0.01$ and rc = 0.17; $p < 0.01$, see Table 5.24); and social institutions (χ^2(15) = 41.59; $p < 0.001$ and rc = 0.17; $p < 0.001$, see Table 5.25) – in all three cases, some correlation was found. However, none was found between the current Islamic ideologies to which they adhere and their preferences for the establishment of Islamic economic institutions (χ^2 (15) = 20.21).

Table 5.23 shows the percentages of participants supporting the establishment of Islamic religious institutions by their current Islamic ideologies.

Table 5.24 *Cross-tabulation: current Islamic ideologies (%) and support for the establishment of Islamic cultural institutions*

		I support the establishment of Islamic cultural institutions by:			
		State of Israel	Islamic Movement (NIM or SIM)	Regardless of whom	I do not support this
Current Islamic ideologies	Salafis	16.0	60.0	16.0	8.0
	Salafi Jihadists	0.0	75.0	25.0	0.0
	Moderates	13.8	38.2	43.3	4.7
	Liberals	11.9	20.9	56.7	10.4
	Other ideologies	7.3	47.3	29.1	16.4
	Unaffiliated	7.3	47.3	29.1	16.4

Table 5.25 *Cross-tabulation: current Islamic ideologies (%) and support for the establishment of Islamic social institutions*

| | | I support the establishment of Islamic social institutions by: | | | |
		State of Israel	Islamic Movement (NIM or SIM)	Regardless of whom	I do not support this
Current Islamic ideologies	Salafis	4.0	72.0	16.0	8.0
	Salafi Jihadists	0.0	75.0	25.0	0.0
	Moderates	19.6	33.8	40.0	6.5
	Liberals	13.4	19.4	55.2	11.9
	Other ideologies	10.9	36.4	36.4	16.4
	Unaffiliated	7.0	32.6	44.2	16.3

In addition, a correlation was found between the current Islamic ideologies and the extent to which the survey respondents feel that "there is a lot to learn from the West and less from Arab countries" (Q: 32; χ^2 (25) = 37.55; p = 0.051 and rc = 0.13; p = 0.051, see Table 5.26).

Furthermore, the participants' current Islamic ideologies were examined by means of a chi-square test and a correlation was found with support for Muslim political participation (Q: 20–22; (χ^2 (75) = 114.97; p < 0.01). The strength of this correlation, as measured by Cramer's V, was (rc = 0.22; p < 0.01). Additionally, the analyzed results show

Table 5.26 *Cross-tabulation: current Islamic ideologies (%) and "there is a lot to learn from the West"*

| | | There is a lot to learn from the West | | | | | |
		I strongly agree	I agree	I agree to a certain extent	I disagree to a certain extent	I disagree	I strongly disagree
Current Islamic ideologies	Salafis	0.0	24.0	16.0	16.0	16.0	28.0
	Salafi Jihadists	0.0	25.0	25.0	0.0	25.0	25.0
	Moderates	14.1	19.5	25.3	20.6	12.6	7.9
	Liberals	22.1	32.4	17.6	13.2	7.4	7.4
	Other ideologies	16.4	9.1	21.8	21.8	16.4	14.5
	Unaffiliated	16.3	11.6	25.6	18.6	11.6	16.3

Table 5.27 *Cross-tabulation: current Islamic ideologies (%) and practical conflicts in normative behavior, between local custom and Shari'a law*

		When local custom conflicts with Islamic religious law, I follow:			
		Local custom and tradition	Islamic religious law (Shari'a)	I try to integrate them	I reject both
Current	Salafis	16.0	64.0	20.0	0.0
Islamic	Salafi Jihadists	0.0	75.0	25.0	0.0
ideologies	Moderates	9.1	51.1	38.3	1.5
	Liberals	12.1	27.3	56.1	4.5
	Other ideologies	12.5	33.9	32.1	21.4
	Unaffiliated	7.1	33.3	38.1	21.4

a correlation between the current Islamic ideology and a preference for living under an Islamic regime (Q: 23–24; χ^2 (50) = 100.66; p < 0.001 and rc = 0.21; p < 0.001). Nevertheless, no correlation was found between current Islamic ideology and the sense of alienation felt by some Muslims in Israel (Q: 30–33; χ^2 (135) = 146.73; p = n.s.), nor with the extent to which they reject Islamic party regimes (Q: 25; χ^2 (25) = 37.43; p = n.s.).

Table 5.27 focuses on the clash between local custom and Islamic law (Q: 62) as resolved by supporters of various current Islamic ideologies. A correlation was found between current Islamic ideologies and the participants' preferences in cases of conflict between local customs and Islamic religious laws (χ^2 (15) = 73.42; p < 0.001 and rc = 0.23; p < 0.001). It is possible to see that a large percentage of those identifying themselves as Salafis or Salafi Jihadists (64–75 percent) prefer following the Shari'a laws in such cases of conflict. However, the moderates and liberals show a more flexible approach for coping with such a conflict by seeking a balance between the Shari'a and local custom.

Another correlation was found between current Islamic ideologies and the respondents' preferences in cases of religio-legal conflicts between the laws of the state of Israel and the Shari'a (Q: 63; χ^2 (15) = 63.14; p < 0.001; and rc = 0.21; p < 0.001). However, no correlation was found between support for specific Islamic ideologies and the participants' preferences in cases in which a state-imposed law clearly contradicts obligatory Islamic law (Q: 64; χ^2 (15) = 19.91). Table 5.28 indicates similar tendencies to those above. In cases of conflict between Shari'a law and Israeli state law, 100 percent of the Salafi Jihadists will choose

Table 5.28 *Cross-tabulation: current Islamic ideologies (%) and religio-legal conflicts between Israeli and Islamic law*

| | | When Israeli law conflicts with Islamic religious law, I follow: | | | |
		Israeli law	The Shari'a	I try to integrate them	I reject both
Current	Salafis	4.0	68.0	24.0	4.0
Islamic	Salafi Jihadists	0.0	100.0	0.0	0.0
ideologies	Moderates	12.8	49.1	37.7	0.4
	Liberal	15.2	27.3	54.5	3.0
	Other ideologies	10.9	36.4	36.4	16.4
	Unaffiliated	11.9	38.1	35.7	14.3

to follow the Shari'a, compared with 68 percent of those identifying themselves as Salafis.

Finally, a correlation was found between Islamic ideologies and the ways in which Muslims seek a reliable religious authority in order to obtain specific religio-legal opinions (Q: 65; χ^2 (21) = 61.25; p < 0.001; rc = 0.18; p < 0.001).

Knowledge of Islam and the Israeli Establishment

The extent to which the survey participants are familiar with Islamic religious laws (Q: 7–8) is correlated with their preferential support for the establishment of Islamic institutions: religious (χ^2 (30) = 125.96;

Table 5.29 *Cross-tabulation: current Islamic ideologies (%) and reliable religious authority*

| | | For reliable religious authority, I turn to: | | | | |
		Local Islamic figures	Foreign Islamic figures	Islamic judges or courts	Personal study	Other
Current	Salafis	36.0	8.0	16.0	36.0	4.0
Islamic	Salafi Jihadists	100.0	0.0	0.0	0.0	0.0
ideologies	Moderates	36.5	29.2	12.8	16.8	4.7
	Liberals	19.7	31.8	12.1	33.3	3.0
	Other ideologies	26.8	17.9	12.5	25.0	17.9
	Unaffiliated	35.7	23.8	7.1	9.5	23.8

$p < 0.001$ and $rc = 0.29$; $p < 0.001$); cultural (χ^2 (30) = 116.46; $p <$ 0.001 and $rc = 0.28$; $p < 0.001$); social ($\chi^2(30)$ = 112.31; $p < 0.001$ and $rc = 0.28$; $p < 0.001$); and economic (χ^2 (30) = 62.21; $p < 0.001$ and $rc = 0.21$; $p < 0.001$). Also, the extent to which a respondent is (dis)satisfied with the situation of the Muslims in Israel and abroad (Q: 9–10) was also found to be correlated with his/her preferential support for the establishment of Islamic institutions: religious ($\chi^2(30) = 54.1$; $p <$ 0.01 and $rc = 0.19$; $p < 0.01$); cultural ($\chi^2(30) = 52.59$; $p < 0.01$ and $rc = 0.18$; $p < 0.01$); social ($\chi^2(30) = 51.83$; $p < 0.01$ and $rc = 0.18$; $p <$ 0.01); and economic ($\chi^2(30) = 52.14$; $p < 0.01$ and $rc = 0.18$; $p < 0.01$).

The two subscales regarding Islam in Israel (the first being support for Muslim political participation and the second, living under an Islamic authority; see Table 5.8) were then examined in relation to various other parameters. For example, the survey results showed a Pearson correlation between the extent of personal knowledge of Islam, its laws and strictures (Q: 7–8) and support for Muslim political participation (Q: 20–22; $rp = 0.29$; $p < 0.01$); a preference for living under Islamic authority (Q: 23–24; $rp = 0.43$; $p < 0.01$); and a sense of alienation in Israel (Q: 30–33; $rp = 0.35$; $p < 0.01$). This means that the more familiar the respondents are with the Shari'a (i.e. the more practical knowledge of Islam they have) – the more they support Muslim political participation at all the various levels (local, regional, and national) and the establishment of an Islamic party to run in Israeli state elections; the greater their desire to live in an Islamic state; and the more they feel alienated from the (Jewish) state of Israel and more like foreigners than citizens.

In line with the respondents' perceptions, it is possible to conclude that there is no actual conflict between Islamic law and participation in Israeli politics, and there does seem to be a feeling that their situation can be improved by means of democratic legislation. Despite the perceived 'foreignness', the Muslim minority still seeks active involvement in the Israeli political sphere.

Moreover, the two survey items reflecting the respondents' (dis)satisfaction with the situation of Muslims in Israel and abroad (Q: 9–10) were examined by means of a Pearson correlation test and no correlations were found with support for political participation (Q: 20–22; $rp = -0.01$); living under Islamic authority (Q: 23–24; $rp = 0.08$); or with the sense of alienation (Q: 30–33; $rp = 0.02$).

The extent to which the survey participants were familiar with Islamic religious laws (Shari'a) showed no correlation whatsoever with the extent to which they reject Islamic party regimes ($rs = 0.000$). However, a correlation does exist between their (dis)satisfaction with the situation of

Table 5.30 *Cross-tabulation: preservation of Islamic values (%) and preferential support for the establishment of Islamic religious institutions*

| | | I support the establishment of Islamic religious institutions by: | | | |
		State of Israel	Islamic Movement (NIM or SIM)	Regardless of whom	I do not support this
Muslims in Israel have very important values and must preserve them	I strongly agree	5.6	48.3	37.6	8.4
	I agree	12.4	47.6	33.8	6.2
	I agree to a certain extent	12.9	34.7	44.6	7.9
	I disagree to a certain extent	2.9	26.5	50.0	20.6
	I disagree	3.8	26.9	46.2	23.1
	I strongly disagree	27.3	0.0	27.3	45.5

Muslims in Israel and abroad and their degree of rejection of Islamic party regimes, both in Israel and abroad (Q: 25; rs = 0.12; p < 0.01).

Those supporting the preservation of Islamic values in Israel (Q: 8) were also found to support the establishment of Islamic institutions: religious (χ^2 (15) = 52.23; p < 0.001 and rc = 0.19; p < 0.001, Table 5.30); cultural (χ^2(15) = 64.88; p < 0.001 and rc = 0.21; p < 0.001, Table 5.31); social (χ^2(15) = 56.66; p < 0.001 and rc = 0.2;

Table 5.31 *Cross-tabulation: preservation of Islamic values (%) and preferential support for the establishment of Islamic cultural institutions*

| | | I support the establishment of Islamic cultural institutions by: | | | |
		State of Israel	Islamic Movement (NM or SIM)	Regardless of whom	I do not support this
Muslims in Israel have very important values and must preserve them	I strongly agree	9.0	48.0	39.0	4.0
	I agree	12.6	44.8	37.1	5.6
	I agree to a certain extent	20.0	29.0	44.0	7.0
	I disagree to a certain extent	5.9	26.5	47.1	20.6
	I disagree	7.7	7.7	53.8	30.8
	I strongly disagree	9.1	18.2	36.4	36.4

Table 5.32 *Cross-tabulation: preservation of Islamic values (%) and preferential support for the establishment of Islamic social institutions*

		I support the establishment of Islamic social institutions by:			
		State of Israel	Islamic Movement (NIM or SIM)	Regardless of whom	I do not support this
Muslims in Israel have very important values and must preserve them	I strongly agree	9.1	43.8	40.9	6.3
	I agree	18.1	38.9	37.5	5.6
	I agree to a certain extent	22.2	28.3	42.4	7.1
	I disagree to a certain extent	8.8	17.6	52.9	20.6
	I disagree	15.4	15.4	34.6	34.6
	I strongly disagree	20.0	10.0	40.0	30.0

p < 0.001, Table 5.32); and economic (χ^2 (15) = 39.01; p < 0.001 and rc = 0.16; p < 0.001, Table 5.33).

A Pearson test found correlations between support for the preservation of Islamic values and all the following: support for Muslim political participation (Q: 20–22; rs = 0.3; p < 0.01); a preference for living under Islamic authority (Q: 23–24; rs = 0.27; p < 0.01); and the sense of alienation felt within the Muslim minority in Israel (Q: 30–33; rs = 0.31; p < 0.01). However, the preservation of Islamic values was not significantly

Table 5.33 *Cross-tabulation: preservation of Islamic values (%) and preferential support for the establishment of Islamic economic institutions*

		I support the establishment of Islamic economic institutions by:			
		State of Israel	Islamic Movement (NIM or SIM)	Regardless of whom	I do not support this
Muslims in Israel have very important values and must preserve them	I strongly agree	15.8	36.7	36.2	11.3
	I agree	20.1	29.2	42.4	8.3
	I agree to a certain extent	26.7	28.7	30.7	13.9
	I disagree to a certain extent	20.6	29.4	17.6	32.4
	I disagree	23.1	7.7	38.5	30.8
	I strongly disagree	9.1	27.3	27.3	36.4

correlated with the acceptance/rejection of Islamic party regimes (Q: 25; rs = −0.007).

In conclusion, the relations between the Muslim minority in Israel and the Israeli establishment seem to be impacted by the increasing religiosity and observance amidst the Muslim population. The survey results also indicated a certain degree of ambivalence in the relations between the Muslim minority and the Israeli establishment. This is evidenced by the participants' responses to questions regarding the control of Islamic institutions; Islamic political parties; the preference for living under Islamic authority; and, finally, by the sense of alienation and feeling of dissatisfaction with the situation of Muslims in Israel. For example, though the observant participants prefer living in a state with an Islamic religious orientation, they support the idea of participating in various Israeli elections; they see no conflict between Islamic law and active involvement in the Israeli democratic 'game'.

Also, only a small percentage of respondents support the establishment of religious, social, cultural, economic, and political Islamic institutions by the Israeli government; here, one observes a sweeping dissatisfaction with the existing official Islamic institutions, their funding, management, and performance. For most of the respondents, the existing IM's institutions are more authentic and preferable alternatives to those provided by the Jewish state.

6   Being Muslim in the Israeli
Socio-Cultural Space

Chapter 5 dealt with the relations between the Muslim minority in Israel and the Israeli establishment. This chapter investigates the interactions between Muslims in Israel and their socio-cultural space, within the Jewish Israeli majority environment in which they live.[1] Emphasis is placed on the question: To what extent do religiosity and observance influence relationships between Muslims and other aspects of Israeli society? Given the fact that modern Israeli society is Western oriented,[2] this discussion (based on the survey findings) examines the following topics: the mastery and use of the Hebrew language; interaction with Jewish Israelis; Muslim–Jewish friendships; and socio-cultural role models for success.

Table 6.1 presents the survey participants' responses to nine statements (Q: 26–34) that reveal their sense of alienation as opposed to attitudes on Muslim–Jewish coexistence in the state of Israel.

An exploratory factor analysis was conducted to examine the validity of eight of the above items and the results are presented in Table 6.2.

This factor analysis yielded two subscales. The first subscale (four items, Q: 30–31, 33–34) deals with the sense of alienation felt by Muslims in Israel, who may feel rejected or like foreigners in their homeland. The Cronbach alpha was 0.66 and a correlation was found between religiosity and a sense of alienation (rs = 0.37; p < 0.01).

The second subscale (four items, Q: 26–29) investigates the social relations between Muslims and Jews in Israel – for instance, the extent to which the participants are willing to have Jewish neighbors and/or friends.[3] Here, the Cronbach alpha is 0.64 and a negative correlation was also found between religiosity and social relations (rs = −0.16; p < 0.01).

---

[1] On Jewish–Arab relations in Israel, see Sammy Smooha, *Jews and Arabs in Israel* (Boulder and London: Westview Press, 1992); Arnon Soffer, "Jewish and Islamic fundamentalism in Israel: reasons, processes and results," *Geographia Religionum* 13 (1989): 155–174.
[2] See Sammy Smooha, "Is Israel Western?" in Eliezer Ben-Rafael and Yitzhak Sternberg (eds.), *Comparing Modernities: Pluralism versus Homogeneity: Essays in Homage to Shmuel N. Eisenstadt* (Leiden and Boston: Brill, 2005), 413–442.
[3] See Smooha, *Still Playing by the Rules*.

Table 6.1 *Responses regarding a sense of alienation (%) versus coexistence in Israel*

	I strongly agree	I agree	I agree to a certain extent	I disagree to a certain extent	I disagree	I strongly disagree
The country between the Jordan River and the Mediterranean Ocean is a common homeland for Jews and Arabs	7.8	21.8	30.1	17.6	10.6	10.4
I am willing to have Jewish friends	15.6	33.9	30.3	10.2	6.8	2.6
I am willing to have Jewish neighbors	17.4	27.1	26.3	14.6	7.8	4.0
Muslim Israelis act more like Jewish Israelis than like the Palestinians in the West Bank and Gaza Strip	13.0	24.0	32.5	13.4	9.4	6.2
As a Muslim in Israel, I feel like a rejected stranger, an outsider	8.2	19.0	29.7	20.6	13.2	7.6
I prefer to live in a village or town in which only Muslims reside	13.4	16.4	22.4	20.0	16.2	9.2
There is a lot to learn from the West and very little from Arab/Islamic countries	14.6	19.6	22.8	19.0	12.6	10.4
Palestine is an Islamic *waqf** land	19.2	24.8	26.7	14.6	7.6	5.2
Palestine, between the Jordan River and the Mediterranean Ocean, is only for Muslims and Arabs	16.0	17.4	23.2	21	14.2	6.6

* *waqf* = an inalienable religious endowment in Islamic law.

Table 6.2 *Factor loading of eight items (N = 500)*

	Factor 1	Factor 2
Palestine, between the Jordan River and the Mediterranean Ocean, is only for Muslims and Arabs	**0.714**	−0.218
I prefer to live in a village or town in which only Muslims reside	**0.679**	−0.200
As a Muslim in Israel, I feel like a rejected stranger, an outsider	**0.674**	0.054
Palestine is an Islamic *waqf** land	**0.628**	−0.067
I am willing to have Jewish friends	−0.132	**0.853**
I am willing to have Jewish neighbors	−0.262	**0.793**
Muslim Israelis act more like Jewish Israelis than like the Palestinians in the West Bank and Gaza Strip	0.359	**0.597**
The country between the Jordan River and the Mediterranean Ocean is a common homeland for Jews and Arabs	−0.328	**0.479**

The correlation obtained between these two subscales is ($rp = -0.26$; $p < 0.001$). A Spearman test of the first subscale (sense of alienation) found it to be unrelated to age ($rs = 0.04$); gender ($t(484) = 0$); marital status ($F(4) = 1.80$); type of (un)employment ($F(6) = 0.52$) average monthly income ($rs = -0.06$); level of education ($rs = -0.004$); residential region ($F(3) = 2.57$; $p = 0.05$); nor is it correlated with residential community ($F(3) = 1.63$).

An examination of the second subscale (social relations) found that the only demographic variable affecting the respondents' positions on Muslim–Jewish interaction is the residential region ($F(3) = 3.39$; $p < 0.05$). A post-hoc test showed that these differences are mainly between participants from the mixed cities (Mean = 2.52) and those from the Galilee (M = 3) or from the Triangle (M = 3.02). A Spearman test indicated that the willingness of Muslim Israelis to interact socially with Jewish Israelis is not correlated with age ($rs = 0.02$); gender ($t(484) = -0.05$); marital status ($F(4) = 0.213$); type of (un)employment ($F(6) = 0.94$); average monthly income ($rs = 0.03$); level of education ($rs = -0.05$); or residential community ($F(3) = 0.85$).

In addition, the survey participants were asked to respond to statements about their positions regarding the Hebrew language and interaction with Jews in Israel. The first item analyzed (Q: 35) was: "I have mastered the Hebrew language and can discuss various issues with Jewish Israelis." Table 6.3 presents their responses regarding the mastery of Hebrew. As may be seen, a large percentage (85.1 percent) of the respondents claim to have mastered the Hebrew language and state that they can conduct a conversation with Jewish Israelis on various subjects.

Table 6.3 *Responses regarding mastery of the Hebrew language (%)*

I have mastered the Hebrew language and can discuss various issues with Jewish Israelis	
	Percentage
I strongly agree	29.1
I agree	29.5
I agree to a certain extent	26.5
I disagree to a certain extent	9.8
I disagree	2.2
I strongly disagree	1.8
Total	98.9

Surprisingly, a significant negative Spearman correlation was found between the level of education (rs = −0.24; p < 0.01) and the mastery of Hebrew, meaning that higher education does not necessarily indicate a mastery of Hebrew, or more conversation with Jews.[4] Many educated Muslims return to work in their Arabic-speaking communities, while the less-educated laborers tend to work in Hebrew-speaking environments.

A large majority (85.1 percent) of the interviewees have mastered the Hebrew language and are able (at different levels of proficiency) to converse with Jewish Israelis about various issues. This finding indicates a high degree of exposure to Jewish Israeli society. The respondents acquired their knowledge of the Hebrew language in school, on the streets, and at work. They are not disconnected from mainstream Jewish Israeli society. They read and hear Hebrew and are familiar with Jewish Israeli popular culture.

The age parameter shows no correlation with the mastery of Hebrew (rs − 0.03), although the average monthly income does show a positive correlation (rs = 0.12; p < 0.01). A chi-square test indicates a correlation between the type of (un)employment and a mastery of Hebrew (χ^2 (30) = 60.11; p < 0.01 and rc = 0.16; p < 0.01). Table 6.4 shows that salaried workers (clerks) present a greater mastery of the Hebrew language, enabling them to communicate at work and to talk to Jews about various matters. This table shows that the large percentage of those who can conduct a conversation in Hebrew are the salaried employees who tend to work in Jewish Israeli surroundings.

---

[4] See Claude Klein, *Israel as a Nation-State and the Problem of the Arab Minority: In Search of a Status* (Tel Aviv: International Center for Peace in the Middle East, 1987).

Table 6.4 *Cross-tabulation: type of (un)employment (%) and mastery of Hebrew*

		Type of (un)employment						
		Employee or clerk	Self-employed	Unemployed, seeking a job	Unemployed, not seeking a job	Retired	College student	House-wife
I have mastered the Hebrew language and can discuss various issues with Jewish Israelis	I strongly agree	60.4	10.4	9.7	4.2	4.2	4.9	6.3
	I agree	49.3	15.8	12.3	6.2	1.4	4.8	10.3
	I agree to a certain extent	38.5	10.0	12.3	6.9	6.2	5.4	20.8
	I disagree to a certain extent	25.0	12.5	29.2	2.1	4.2	4.2	22.9
	I disagree	27.3	18.2	9.1	9.1	0.0	9.1	27.3
	I strongly disagree	33.3	11.1	22.2	0.0	22.2	0.0	11.1

Residential community was found to be correlated with a mastery of Hebrew (χ^2 (15) = 40.40; p < 0.001 and rc = 0.17; p < 0.001), as shown in Table 6.5.

Residential region was also found to be correlated with a mastery of Hebrew (χ^2 (15) = 53.93; p < 0.001 and rc = 0.2; p < 0.001), as seen in Table 6.6, which shows that a high percentage of those who are well versed in Hebrew live in the Galilee.

A chi-square test showed that marital status was also significantly correlated with a mastery of Hebrew (χ^2 (20) = 41.79; p < 0.01 and

Table 6.5 *Cross-tabulation: residential community (%) and mastery of Hebrew*

		Residential community			
		All Muslim	Mostly Muslim	Mostly Christian	Mostly Druze
I have mastered the Hebrew language and can discuss various issues with Jewish Israelis	I strongly agree	69.1	30.2	0.0	0.7
	I agree	70.3	22.1	0.7	6.9
	I agree to a certain extent	55.5	35.9	2.3	6.3
	I disagree to a certain extent	40.8	49.0	2.0	8.2
	I disagree	45.5	36.4	9.1	9.1
	I strongly disagree	22.2	66.7	0.0	11.1

Table 6.6 *Cross-tabulation: residential region (%) and mastery of Hebrew*

		Residential region			
		Galilee	Triangle	Negev	Mixed cities
I have mastered the	I strongly agree	45.9	28.6	6.8	18.8
Hebrew language	I agree	55.6	25.9	14.1	4.4
and can discuss	I agree to a certain extent	65.0	26.0	4.1	4.9
various issues	I disagree to a certain extent	71.7	15.2	6.5	6.5
with Jewish	I disagree	50.0	10.0	40.0	0.0
Israelis	I strongly disagree	87.5	0.0	12.5	0.0

rc $= 0.15$; p < 0.01). Table 6.7 shows that a high percentage of those who agreed with this statement are married.

The participants' genders were not found to be related to their mastery of Hebrew (χ^2 (5) $= 6.93$). However, a correlation was found between Muslim–Jewish friendship (including social visits) and a mastery of Hebrew (χ^2 (8) $= 18.17$; p < 0.05 and rc $= 0.14$; p < 0.05).

Regarding the survey question (Q: 36): "How often do you interact with Jewish Israelis?" almost 43.3 percent of the participants replied "daily"; 27.6 percent indicated "frequently"; and only 25.1 percent "seldom" meet Jews. A large majority of Muslim respondents, more than 70 percent, meet frequently and sometimes regularly with Jews, indicating the openness of the Muslim community toward the Jewish community. This finding supports the clear trend previously observed regarding mastery of Hebrew. Note that this survey did not delve into the nature and contents of these interactions and meetings (whether they were commercial, academic, social, medical, etc., or planned, random, public, or

Table 6.7 *Cross-tabulation: marital status (%) and mastery of Hebrew*

		Marital status			
		Single	Married	Divorced/ Separated	Widowed
I have mastered the	I strongly agree	26.1	68.3	4.9	0.7
Hebrew language	I agree	19.9	78.1	1.4	0.7
and can discuss	I agree to a certain extent	17.8	78.3	0.8	3.1
various issues	I disagree to a certain extent	27.1	64.6	4.2	2.1
with Jewish	I disagree	18.2	63.6	0.0	18.2
Israelis	I strongly disagree	22.2	66.7	11.1	0.0

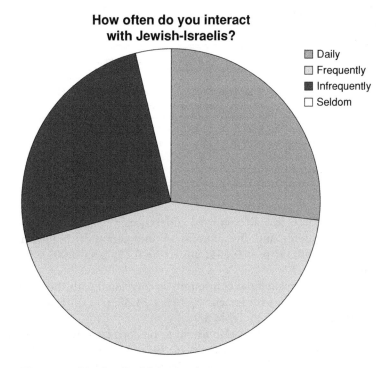

How often do you interact with Jewish-Israelis?

- Daily
- Frequently
- Infrequently
- Seldom

Figure 6.1 Muslim–Jewish interactions

private); the very fact that such interactions and meetings exist reflects openness toward others.[5] Nonetheless, these data indicate that Muslim employees meet the most with Jewish Israelis, suggesting that the nature of these meetings is primarily functional, which also explains why the large majority of those who do meet with Jews are Muslim men, and not Muslim women.

A Spearman test showed that the frequency of interaction with Jewish Israelis was unrelated to age ($rs = 0.01$) and average monthly income ($rs = 0.05$). However, a significant negative Spearman correlation was found with the level of education ($rs = -0.11$; $p < 0.05$), meaning that more highly educated respondents meet Jewish Israelis less often.[6]

---

[5] See Smooha, *Still Playing by the Rules.*
[6] Ilana Kaufman, "Escalation in the demands of the minority: the 'future vision' documents of the Arab Palestinians in Israel," *State and Society* 7 (1) (2010): 11–35 [Hebrew]; Yitzhak Reiter, *National Minority, Regional Majority: Palestinian Arabs Versus Jews in Israel* (Syracuse: Syracuse University Press, 2009); Arik Rudnitzky, *The Arab Minority in Israel and the "Jewish State" Discourse* (Jerusalem: Israel Democracy Institute, 2015) [Hebrew].

Table 6.8 *Cross-tabulation: type of (un)employment (%) and interaction with Jewish Israelis*

		Type of (un)employment					
		Employee or clerk	Self-employed	Unemployed, seeking a job	Unemployed, not seeking a job	Retired	College student
How often do you interact with Jewish Israelis?	Daily	58.6	12.0	7.5	1.5	4.5	7.5
	Frequently	46.5	15.0	15.0	5.6	2.8	5.6
	Infrequently	36.6	8.9	14.6	8.1	5.7	1.6
	Seldom	26.3	5.3	26.3	10.5	5.3	0.0

A chi-square test also showed differences (%) between the type of (un)employment and the amount of interaction with Jewish Israelis (χ^2 (18) = 50.39; p < 0.001; and rc = 0.19; p < 0.001), as seen in Table 6.8.

In addition, residential community is correlated with the frequency of interaction with Jewish Israelis (χ^2 (9) = 24.32; p < 0.01 and rc = 0.13; p < 0.01), as shown in Table 6.9.

Residential region was also found to be correlated with the frequency of interaction with Jewish Israelis (χ^2 (9) = 82.41; p < 0.001 and rc = 0.25; p < 0.001). For instance, a large percentage of those who interact with Jews daily live in the Galilee (41 percent), as illustrated in Table 6.10.

While a chi-square test showed no correlation between marital status and interaction with Jewish Israelis (χ^2 (12) = 18.98), the participants' genders are correlated; Table 6.11 shows that Muslim men have more contact with Jews than Muslim women (χ^2 (3) = 11.10; p < 0.05 and rc = 0.15; p < 0.03), perhaps due to the fact that more Muslim men than women are employed in the Jewish sector.

Table 6.9 *Cross-tabulation: residential community (%) and interaction with Jewish Israelis*

		Residential community			
		All Muslim	Mostly Muslim	Mostly Christian	Mostly Druze
How often do you interact with Jewish Israelis?	Daily	59.7	39.5	0.8	0.0
	Frequently	60.4	32.5	1.4	5.7
	Infrequently	68.9	21.3	1.6	8.2
	Seldom	38.9	44.4	0.0	16.7

Table 6.10 *Cross-tabulation: residential region (%) and interaction with Jewish Israelis*

		Residential region			
		Galilee	Triangle	Negev	Mixed cities
How often do you interact	Daily	41.0	27.4	5.1	26.5
with Jewish Israelis?	Frequently	64.7	25.9	6.5	3.0
	Infrequently	58.3	20.8	18.3	2.5
	Seldom	76.5	23.5	0.0	0.0

Moving on to another survey item (Q: 36), it was found that a large percentage of the participants (63.9 percent) have Jewish friends, whom they have visited within the past two years (23.6 percent). These findings shed light on the social nature of most Muslim–Jewish relations and meetings; almost two-thirds of the Muslim respondents indicated that they have Jewish friends. This significantly reflects actual, personal behavior, rather than merely describing general, theoretical attitudes toward the Jews in Israel. Many interviewees indicated that they have Jewish friends, supporting the openness of the Muslim community toward the Jewish community. This stands in opposition to a common stereotypical perception in Israel regarding Muslim self-segregation and self-imposed social isolation. In fact, one-quarter of the respondents claim that they visit their Jewish friends in their homes, again indicating Muslim–Jewish social interaction.

As for other survey items focusing on social relations with Jewish Israelis, it was found that legal *madhhab* affiliation (Q: 3) is correlated with the frequency of interaction with Jewish Israelis ($\chi^2(15) = 32.05$; $p < 0.01$ and rc = 0.15; $p < 0.01$), as presented in Table 6.12.

Moreover, the participants' current Islamic ideologies were found to be correlated with the frequency of interaction with Jewish Israelis

Table 6.11 *Cross-tabulation: gender (%) and interaction with Jewish Israelis*

		Gender	
		male	female
How often do you interact with Jewish Israelis?	Daily	61.1	38.9
	Frequently	54.0	46.0
	Infrequently	42.1	57.9
	Seldom	36.8	63.2

Table 6.12 *Cross-tabulation: interaction with Jewish Israelis (%) and legal* madhhab *affiliation*

| | | How often do you interact with Jewish Israelis? | | | |
		Daily	Frequently	Infrequently	Seldom
Madhhab affiliation	Hanafi	34.8	43.5	21.7	0.0
	Maliki	44.4	33.3	22.2	0.0
	Shafi'i	20.8	51.0	24.3	3.9
	Hanbali	22.8	35.1	33.3	8.8
	Other doctrines	30.4	21.7	39.1	8.7
	Unaffiliated	40.3	35.1	22.1	2.6

(χ^2 (15) = 30.25; p < 0.05 and rc = 0.15; p < 0.05), as presented in Table 6.13.

A chi-square test showed differences in religiosity when correlated with survey item (Q: 37) on Muslim–Jewish friendship and social visiting (χ^2 (10) = 23.86; p < 0.01 and rc = 0.16; p < 0.01), as presented in Table 6.14.

Also with regard to this item (Q: 37) on the questionnaire, a chi-square test showed that age (χ^2 (8) = 13.65); marital status (χ^2 (8) = 7.72); average monthly income (χ^2 (8) = 10.34); and residential community (χ^2 (6) = 2.08) are all unrelated to Muslim–Jewish friendship and social visiting. However, the participants' gender (χ^2 (2) = 12.91; p < 0.01 and rc = 0.14; p < 0.01) and residential region (χ^2 (6) = 52.75; p < 0.001 and rc = 0.24; p < 0.001) were both found to be correlated. As may be seen in Table 6.16, a high percentage of those residing in the Galilee and in the Triangle responded positively to the statement on Muslim–Jewish friendship and social visiting, compared to the low percentage of respondents residing in the Negev.

Table 6.13 *Cross-tabulation: interaction with Jewish Israelis (%) and Islamic ideologies*

| | | How often do you interact with Jewish Israelis? | | | |
		Daily	Frequently	Infrequently	Seldom
Islamic ideologies	Salafis	32.0	48.0	20.0	0.0
	Salafi Jihadists	50.0	50.0	0.0	0.0
	Moderates	21.0	50.0	25.7	3.3
	Liberals	35.3	42.6	19.1	2.9
	Other	33.9	25.0	33.9	7.1
	Unaffiliated	33.3	23.8	33.3	9.5

Table 6.14 *Cross-tabulation: religiosity (%) and Muslim–Jewish friendship*

	Very religious	Religious	Somewhat religious	Somewhat non-religious	Not religious	Not religious at all
I do not have Jewish friends	56.4	41.8	30.3	27.9	31	18.2
I have Jewish friends, but I have not visited them at home in the last two years	33.3	39.0	45.3	44.3	27.6	36.4
I have Jewish friends and have visited them at home within the last two years	10.3	19.1	24.4	27.9	41.4	45.5

Table 6.15 *Responses regarding Muslim–Jewish friendship (%)*

Do you have Jewish friends and have you visited them at home within the last two years?

	Percentage
I do not have Jewish friends	34.3
I have Jewish friends, but I have not visited them at home in the last two years	40.3
I have Jewish friends and have visited them at home within the last two years	23.6
Total	98.2

Table 6.16 *Cross-tabulation: residential region (%) and Muslim–Jewish friendship*

		Residential region			
		Galilee	Triangle	Negev	Mixed cities
Do you have Jewish friends and have you visited them at home within the last two years?	I do not have Jewish friends	53.8	19.6	21.5	5.1
	I have Jewish friends, but I have not visited them at home in the last two years	60.4	28.3	3.2	8.0
	I have Jewish friends and have visited them at home within the last two years	57.4	26.9	0.9	14.8

Table 6.17 *Cross-tabulation: level of education (%) and Muslim–Jewish friendship*

		Level of education					
		Uneducated	Elementary education	Secondary education	BA	MA	Ph.D.
Do you have Jewish friends and have you visited them at home within the last two years?	I do not have Jewish friends	1.8	19.8	57.5	16.8	4.2	0.0
	I have Jewish friends, but I have not visited them at home in the last two years	4.5	13.6	56.1	21.7	2.5	1.5
	I have Jewish friends and have visited them at home within the last two years	2.5	11.0	47.5	30.5	6.8	1.7

In addition, the level of education was significantly positively correlated with item Q: 37 (χ^2 (10) = 19.60; p < 0.05 and rc = 0.14; p < 0.05), such that the higher the education of the participants, the more friendships and visits were reported.[7] Table 6.17 shows that a high percentage of those who have Jewish friends and visit Jewish homes are those who completed high school or have advanced academic degrees.

Finally, the type of (un)employment was also found to be correlated with Muslim–Jewish friendship and social visiting. Table 6.18 shows the differences for the different types of (un)employment. For instance, a high percentage of the respondents with Jewish friends were salaried employees (χ^2 (12) = 36.96; p < 0.001 and rc = 0.2, p < 0.001).

It is logical that commitment to the Shari'a, personally practicing Islam on a daily basis, will cause less integration, more segregation, and some fear of contact with non-Muslim cultures and societies, particularly with the modern Israeli host society, that of the Jewish majority. There is an obvious tendency for self-protection from the influence of the 'secular' environment, perceived to pose a threat to crucial Islamic values. This may also include a certain fear of the assimilation process, of adopting an Israeli lifestyle, as manifested by knowledge of the Hebrew language and having and visiting Jewish friends in their homes.

[7] Smooha, *Still Playing by the Rules.*

Table 6.18 Cross-tabulation: type of (un)employment (%) and Muslim–Jewish friendship

		Type of (un)employment					
	Employee or clerk	Self-employed	Unemployed, seeking a job	Unemployed, not seeking a job	Retired	College student	Housewife
Do you have Jewish friends and have you visited them at home within the last two years? I do not have Jewish friends	34.1	10.6	17.6	5.9	5.3	4.7	21.8
I have Jewish friends, but I have not visited them at home in the last two years	51.3	10.2	10.7	7.1	3.6	6.1	11.2
I have Jewish friends and have visited them at home within the last two years	55.9	17.8	11.9	1.7	3.4	3.4	5.9

Table 6.19 *Cross-tabulation: Muslim–Jewish friendship (%) and degree of personal observance*

		I do not have Jewish friends	I have Jewish friends, but I have not visited them at home in the last two years	I have Jewish friends and have visited them at home within the last two years
		I have Jewish friends and have visited them at home within the past two years		
Degree of	To a very high degree	56.7	26.9	16.4
personal	To a high degree	36.5	43.7	19.8
observance	To a certain degree	27.9	44.9	27.2
	Not to a certain degree	29.2	54.2	16.7
	To a small degree	23.1	30.8	46.2
	Non-observant or secular	22.7	36.4	40.9

Moreover, a correlation was found between the extent to which participants want other Muslims in Israel to act according to the Shari'a and Muslim–Jewish friendship and social visiting (χ^2 (10) = 34.43; p < 0.001 and rc = 0.1; p < 0.001), as shown in Table 6.20.

However, no correlation was found between Muslim–Jewish friendship and survey item Q: 32 – the extent to which participants believe

Table 6.20 *Cross-tabulation: Muslim–Jewish friendship (%) and preference for Islamic observance*

		I do not have Jewish friends	I have Jewish friends, but I have not visited them at home in the last two years	I have Jewish friends and have visited them at home within the last two years
		Do you have Jewish friends and have you visited them at home in the last two years?		
I would like Muslims	To a very great extent	51.0	31.0	18.0
in Israel to observe	To a great extent	34.9	45.6	19.5
Islamic practice	To a certain extent	24.5	46.9	28.7
(i.e. to act	Not to a certain extent	43.3	36.7	20.0
according to the	To a small extent	31.3	25.0	43.8
Shari'a)	Indifferent	10.0	40.0	50.0

Table 6.21 *Cross-tabulation: Muslim–Jewish friendship (%) and Islamic ideologies*

		Do you have Jewish friends and have you visited them at home in the last two years?		
Islamic ideologies	Salafis	44.0	56.0	0.0
	Salafi Jihadists	33.3	33.3	33.3
	Moderates	36.4	42.5	21.1
	Liberals	17.9	50.7	31.3
	Other	30.4	33.9	35.7
	Unaffiliated	47.6	23.8	28.6

that "There is a lot to learn from the West and less from Arab countries" (χ^2 (20) = 12.39).

The extent to which the survey participants are committed to the Shari'a (Q: 1) was also found to be significantly negatively correlated with the frequency of their interaction with Jewish Israelis (Q: 36; rs = −0.15; p < 0.01), such that highly observant participants generally interact less often with Jewish Israelis. Also, no correlation was found between personal observance and mastery of Hebrew (Q: 35; rs = −0.06; p = n.s). Nonetheless, a correlation was found between the level of commitment to Islamic religious law and Muslim–Jewish friendship (χ^2(10) = 31.68; p < 0.001 and rc = 0.18; p < 0.001). Perhaps those who are highly educated, have mastered Shari'a law, and are themselves observant feel more secure in their faith and are less fearful of assimilation and, thus, more comfortable with their select Jewish friends.

Furthermore, no correlation was found between current Islamic ideologies (such as Salafi, Salafi Jihadist, etc.; Q: 5) and mastery of the Hebrew language, for the purpose of speaking with Jewish Israelis (χ^2 (25) = 34.69). However, a correlation was found between Islamic ideologies and Muslim–Jewish friendship (χ^2 (10) = 27.53; p < 0.01 and rc = 0.17; p < 0.01), as may be seen in Table 6.21.

When asked about their role models (Q: 38) – who best exemplify economic and social success – 31.5 percent of the respondents indicated that they compared themselves with Jews, while only 4 percent referred to Christians within the Arab sector. Table 6.22 presents these responses, comparing personal achievements with those of other ethno-religious groups within Israeli society and with other Muslims elsewhere in the world.

When comparing their personal achievements with the success of others, no correlations were found with age (χ^2(20) = 29.32); gender (χ^2(5) = 3.26); or marital status (χ^2(20) = 29.30).

Table 6.22 *Responses regarding personal achievements (%)*

When you evaluate your own social and economic achievements, with whom do you compare yourself?	Percentage
With the Christians in Israel	4.0
With the Jews in Israel	31.5
With the Druze in Israel	1.0
With Muslims in Arab countries	25.3
With Muslim minorities in the West	12.2
Other	23.6
Total	97.6

These results reflect how the Muslim community perceives itself, and indicate which groups serve as role models. The data suggest that the main reference group is, indeed, the Jewish majority group (31.5 percent), followed by Muslims in the Arab/Muslim world (25.3 percent); 57 percent of the Muslims surveyed in Israel compare their achievements to those of majority groups, rather than other minority groups. In other words, the Muslim minority in Israel has a 'majority' orientation.

What was found to be correlated with personal achievements was residential region ($\chi^2(15) = 80.18$; $p < 0.001$ and rc = 0.244; $p < 0.001$). As may be seen in Table 6.23, most of the Muslims residing in the Galilee and the Triangle attribute their economic and social success to Jewish role models.

Table 6.23 *Cross-tabulation: residential region (%) and personal achievements*

		Residential region			
		Galilee	Triangle	Negev	Mixed cities
When you evaluate your own social and economic achievements, with whom do you compare yourself?	With the Christians in Israel	100.0	0.0		
	With the Jews in Israel	62.6	17.0	11.6	8.8
	With the Druze in Israel	100.0			
	With Muslims in Arab countries	42.7	42.7	12.8	1.7
	With Muslim minorities in the West	74.1	8.6	12.1	5.2
	Other	50.0	29.2	1.9	18.9

Table 6.24 *Cross-tabulation: residential community (%) and personal achievements*

		Residential community			
		All Muslim	Mostly Muslim	Mostly Christian	Mostly Druze
When you evaluate your own social and economic achievements, with whom do you compare yourself?	With the Christians in Israel	57.9	31.6	0.0	10.5
	With the Jews in Israel	66.0	23.7	1.3	9.0
	With the Druze in Israel	40.0	60.0	0.0	0.0
	With Muslims in Arab countries	71.7	25.8	0.0	2.5
	With the Muslim minorities in the West	41.7	56.7	1.7	0.0
	Other	56.9	35.3	2.6	5.2

The residential community is also correlated with personal achievements, as presented in Table 6.24. Note that survey respondents from completely Muslim communities attribute their success to Jewish role models, while participants from majority Druze communities attribute their success to Christian exemplars ($\chi^2(15) = 38.80$; $p < 0.01$ and rc = 0.17; $p < 0.01$).

Both level of education ($\chi^2(25) = 32.26$) and type of (un)employment ($\chi^2(30) = 41.51$) were not correlated with the success of others. However, the average monthly income of the participants was correlated with the success of others ($\chi^2(20) = 37.15$; $p < 0.05$ and rc = 0.14; $p < 0.05$). As may be observed in Table 6.25, 50 percent of the respondents who attribute their success to the Christians are in the average income range (7300 NIS) and about 31 percent of those who attribute their success to Jewish role models are also in the average range. Also note that only a very small percentage of the participants attributed their success to the Druze, but that those who did so have incomes that are slightly above average. The high percentage of those who attribute their success to Muslim role models in Arab countries are those who have below-average incomes.

Another correlation was found between the degree of personal observance and emulation of the success of others (Q: 38; $\chi^2(25) = 92.28$; $p < 0.001$ and rc = .2; $p < 0.001$), as presented in Table 6.26.

In other words, the Muslim majority in Arab countries is the preferred reference group of the Muslim minority in Israel, rather than other

Table 6.25 *Cross-tabulation: average monthly income (%) and personal achievements*

		Average income				
		Much higher	A little higher	Average	A little less	Much less
When you evaluate your own social and economic achievements, with whom do you compare yourself?	With the Christians in Israel	20.0	10.0	50.0	15.0	5.0
	With the Jews in Israel	7.1	25.0	30.8	23.1	14.1
	With the Druze in Israel	0.0	20.0	80.0	0.0	0.0
	With Muslims in Arab countries	4.8	22.6	20.2	32.3	20.2
	With Muslim minorities in the West	1.6	14.8	32.8	36.1	14.8
	Other	8.5	15.4	33.3	29.9	12.8

minority groups in Israel, and Muslim Israelis prefer to compare their achievements to those of the Jewish Israeli majority and not to those of other Arab minorities within Israel. The Islamic minority in Europe was the third-place choice. It seems that Muslims in Israel know very little about this minority, as indicated by their inconsistent answers.

Table 6.26 *Cross-tabulation: personal achievements (%) and degree of personal observance*

		When you evaluate your own social and economic achievements, with whom do you compare yourself?					
		With the Christians in Israel	With the Jews in Israel	With the Druze in Israel	With Muslims in Arab countries	With Muslim minorities in the West	Others
Personal observance	To a very high degree	4.4	20.6	0.0	44.1	17.6	13.2
	To a high degree	0.5	31.1	0.5	34.7	14.3	18.9
	To a certain degree	5.5	33.8	1.4	17.2	11.7	30.3
	Not to a certain degree	21.7	30.4	4.3	8.7	4.3	30.4
	To a small degree	0.0	53.8	0.0	0.0	3.8	42.3
	Non-observant or secular	9.1	45.5	4.5	4.5	4.5	31.8

Table 6.27 *Cross-tabulation: personal achievements (%) and preference for Islamic observance*

		When you evaluate your own social and economic achievements, with whom do you compare yourself?					
		With the Christians in Israel	With the Jews in Israel	With the Druze in Israel	With Muslims in Arab countries	With Muslim minorities in the West	Others
Preference for Islamic observance: I would like Muslims in Israel to appeal to the Islamic religious laws in their behaviors	To a very high degree	3.0	23.8	0.0	40.6	16.8	15.8
	To a high degree	0.0	29.8	0.6	31.0	13.7	25.0
	To a certain degree	6.4	35.7	1.4	20.7	10.7	25.0
	Not to a certain degree	23.3	36.7	3.3	6.7	6.7	23.3
	To a small degree	0.0	68.8	0.0	0.0	0.0	31.3
	Non-observant or secular	5.0	45.0	5.0	5.0	5.0	35.0

No correlation was found between the extent to which the survey participants prefer that other Muslims in Israel observe Islam (act according to the Shariʿa; Q: 46) and the frequency with which they themselves interact with Jewish Israelis (rs = −0.08), nor was there any correlation between a preference for Islamic observance and a mastery of Hebrew (rs = 0.02). However, a correlation was found between a preference for Islamic observance by other Muslim Israelis and the attribution of their personal achievements to the success of others (χ^2 (25) = 85.93; p < 0.001 and rc = 0.19; p < 0.001), as presented in Table 6.27.

In addition, no correlation was found between legal *madhhab* affiliation (Q: 3) and the mastery of Hebrew (χ^2 (25) = 29; p = n.s.), nor with Muslim–Jewish friendship (χ^2 (10) = 15.64). However, a correlation was found between the participants' *madhhab* affiliations and their attributions of personal achievements to the success of others (χ^2(25) = 67.49; p < 0.001 and rc = 0.17; p < 0.001), as appears in Table 6.28.

Moreover, a correlation was found between participants' Islamic ideologies (Q: 4) and their attributions of personal achievements to the success of others (χ^2 (25) = 53.47; p < 0.01 and rc = 0.15; p < 0.01), as seen in Table 6.29.

Nonetheless, there is a correlation between the extent to which the respondents believe that the Muslims in Israel have values worth

Table 6.28 *Cross-tabulation: personal achievements (%) and legal* madhhab *affiliation*

		When you evaluate your own social and economic achievements, with whom do you compare yourself?					
		With the Christians in Israel	With the Jews in Israel	With the Druze in Israel	With the Muslims in Arab countries	With Muslim minorities in the West	Others
Legal	Hanafi	7.2	15.9	0.0	21.7	14.5	40.6
madhhab	Maliki	11.1	22.2	0.0	44.4	0	22.2
affiliation	Shafi'i	2.8	36.1	0.4	27.0	14.7	19.0
	Hanbali	0.0	38.2	0.0	30.9	5.5	25.5
	Other doctrines	21.7	34.8	0.0	13.0	4.3	26.1
	Unaffiliated	2.6	29.9	5.2	23.4	13.0	26.0

preserving (Q: 8) and their attributions of personal achievements to the success of others (χ^2 (25) = 44.71; p < 0.01 and rc = 0.14; p < 0.01), as seen in Table 6.30.

Additionally, those who practice Islam in accordance with the Shari'a (Q: 6–7) do not believe there is much to learn from the West (Q: 32; rs = −0.11; p < 0.05) and tend to reject Western culture and norms

Table 6.29 *Cross-tabulation: personal achievements (%) and Islamic ideologies*

		When you evaluate your own social and economic achievements, with whom do you compare yourself?					
		With the Christians in Israel	With the Jews in Israel	With the Druze in Israel	With the Muslims in Arab countries	With Muslim minorities in the West	Others
Islamic	Salafis	4.0	4.0	0.0	40.0	28.0	24.0
ideologies	Salafi Jihadists	0.0	25.0	0.0	50.0	25.0	0.0
	Moderates	3.3	34.1	0.4	28.9	13.6	19.8
	Liberals	7.6	45.5	1.5	10.6	7.6	27.3
	Other	3.6	26.8	5.4	21.4	14.3	28.6
	Unaffiliated	7.1	21.4	0.0	28.6	4.8	38.1

Table 6.30 *Cross-tabulation: personal achievements (%) and the preservation of Islamic values*

		When you evaluate your own social and economic achievements, with whom do you compare yourself?					
		With the Christians in Israel	With the Jews in Israel	With the Druze in Israel	With the Muslims in Arab countries	With Muslim minorities in the West	Others
Preservation of Islamic values	I strongly agree	2.3	25.4	0.0	32.4	12.7	27.2
	I agree	6.3	40.8	0.7	21.8	6.3	23.9
	I agree to a certain degree	5.0	30.7	1.0	25.7	15.8	21.8
	I disagree to a certain degree	0.0	33.3	6.1	21.2	15.2	24.2
	I disagree	3.8	46.2	3.8	11.5	15.4	19.2
	I strongly disagree	9.1	9.1	0.0	27.3	36.4	18.2

as role models.[8] The extent to which the survey participants expressed (dis)satisfaction with the situation of Muslims in Israel and the world (Q: 9–10) is also unrelated to their beliefs regarding the gleaning of wisdom from the West, rather than from Arab countries (rs = 0.01).

Furthermore, the extent of the respondents' familiarity with Islamic religious law (Q: 6–7) was not found to be correlated with their frequency of interaction with Jewish Israelis (rs = −0.06); nor with their mastery of Hebrew (rs = 0.08); nor with their attributions of personal achievements to the success of others (χ^2 (50) = 66.17). However, a correlation is indicated between familiarity with Islamic religious law and Muslim–Jewish friendship and home visiting (χ^2 (20) = 40.06; p < 0.01 and rc = 0.2; p < 0.01). In general, it seems that those who are highly educated and personally observant, and who feel secure in their own beliefs, are able to enjoy personal friendships with Jewish Israelis.

And finally, the extent to which the participants expressed (dis)satisfaction with the situation of Muslims in Israel and abroad

[8] See Olivier Roy, "EuroIslam: the *jihad* within," *The National Interest* 71 (2003): 63–73; Tariq Ramadan, *Western Muslims and the Future of Islam* (Oxford: Oxford University Press, 2004).

(Q: 9–10) was not found to be correlated with the frequency of interaction with Jewish Israelis (rs = −0.05); nor with their mastery of Hebrew (rs = −0.07; p = n.s.); nor with their attributions of personal achievements to the success of others (χ^2 (50) = 62.98); nor even with Muslim–Jewish friendship (χ^2 (20) = 28.06).

To summarize, the above discussion indicates that the Muslim minority is generally open to the Jewish majority. This is manifested by various research variables, such as a mastery of Hebrew, frequent interaction and friendly visiting, the choice of role models, etc. A majority (>70 percent) of the respondents claim that they either frequently or regularly meet with Jewish Israelis, and a vast majority (~85 percent) have mastered Hebrew and are able to converse. The survey results also show that Muslim employees have functional interactions with Jewish Israelis in the workplace.

It was found that approximately two-thirds of the participants have Jewish friends with whom they interact and about a quarter of them have visited these Jewish friends within the past two years. This is a significant reflection of actual, personal behavior, rather than a mere general description of theoretical attitudes toward the Jews in Israel. Many interviewees blatantly support the openness of the Muslim community toward the Jewish community; this stands opposed to a common, stereotypical perception in Israel regarding Muslim self-segregation and self-imposed social isolation.

However, the Muslim minority does seem to be aware of a certain amount of assimilation with the Israeli Jewish majority. Correlations were found between the extent to which the participants agreed that Muslims in Israel have values worth preserving and their attitudes towards political participation; living under an Islamic regime; and their sense of alienation. Such tendencies are most obvious among observant Muslims, as indicated by their more limited interaction with Jews. Clearly, a personal commitment to daily Islamic observance may lead to a greater degree of segregation, stemming from a fear of contact with non-Muslim influences (cultures and societies), especially that of the Jewish Israeli majority; this is a natural form of self-protection from the seemingly threatening impact of Israeli secular culture.

Conclusions

The present study explores a largely neglected aspect of Muslim life in Israel – that of the Muslim community's attitudes toward and connections with Islam. To this end, the study was undertaken from two major perspectives: (1) Islam as an evolving religious identity among Muslims in Israel; and (2) the extent to which Islam affects the socio-cultural and political conduct of the Muslim minority in Israel. The present discussion covered significant issues regarding Muslim daily life, attitudes, beliefs, levels of (dis)satisfaction, and positions regarding the Israeli establishment and Israeli society. These issues were examined in relation to two distinct clusters of demographic variables: (a) personal and social factors (such as age, gender, level of education, marital status, (un)employment, average monthly salary, and degree of personal religious observance); and (b) geographic and religious factors (such as residential community, residential region, religious affiliations, and degree of religiosity).

Clearly, over the past four decades Islam has become an important factor in the political and socio-cultural identity of the Arab minority in Israel. Moreover, the number of Muslims in Israel who now define their identity first and foremost in relation to their religious affiliation has steadily grown. Among other things, this is manifested by a sharp increase in the number of Islamic associations, mosques, cultural centers, schools, and academic religious institutions in Israel, such as al-Qasemi College in Baqa al-Gharbiyya and the Da'wa College for Islamic Studies in Umm al-Fahm. Some students may even travel abroad to study Islam, mainly to the West Bank, Egypt, Jordan, Malaysia, and Turkey.

Moreover, substantial findings show that, despite the changes and developments in the Muslim community in Israel, due to modernization, Islam is still a very important factor in the formulation of its ethical and social norms. That is, Islam is affecting the behavior of the Muslim minority in Israel, with Islamic values often serving as behavioral standards. This is evidenced by the degree to which the participants are

149

personally committed to the Shari'a as a basis for their normative behavior (observant practice) and in light of the extent of their reliance on the religious institutions established by the IM and the state of Israel. The above analysis showed that, the higher the degree of personal observance, the greater the reliance on these Islamic religious institutions, whether they fall under the auspices of the IM or of the state of Israel. Doubtless, the phenomenon of the global and Israeli 'Islamic awakening' has increased the public's need for a variety of religious services.

The above findings also indicated that the effects of the personal and social demographic variables were relatively smaller than those of the geographic and religious variables. The degree of religiosity was one of the main factors that most affected the other parameters. Other significant factors identified were personal observance and the degree of ethno-religious homogeneity in both residential community and residential region. This means that when Muslims live in mixed ethno-religious neighborhoods or in heterogeneous geographic regions, they tend to become more religious and more observant.

Moreover, the latest research findings suggest that there is a growing number of Muslims in Israel who want other Muslims to better observe the tenets of the Shari'a. Note that the highly observant group considers its affiliation with Islam to be a proud achievement, not merely a parental inheritance. As such, it is only natural that they tend to promote the implementation of Shari'a law. Moreover, the extent to which the participants in this study prefer that Muslims in Israel practice Islam by acting according to the Shari'a is correlated with the extent of their reliance on the IM and the official religious institutions, such as the Shari'a courts.

With regard to the nature of Islam in Israel, this study hypothesized that devout Muslims in non-Muslim countries would seek new religio-legal/theological interpretations, ones that would allow them to remain part of their societies without compromising their adherence to Islamic code – considered a binding and comprehensive guide to life. Thus, new Islamic religious institutions have emerged in the West, such as the Islamic Society of North America (ISNA) and the European Council for Fatwa and Research (ECFR), founded in 1982 and 1997, respectively.[1] These institutions have contributed to creating a new category of Islamic law – the religious law of minorities (*fiqh al-aqalliyyat*) that aims at balancing traditional interpretations of Muslim law with the demands of everyday life in non-Muslim countries.[2]

[1] See the websites of these institutions, at www.isna.net; www.e-cfr.org/ar (last accessed October 15, 2010).
[2] More in Fishman, *Fiqh al-Aqalliyyat*; Shavit, "Should Muslims integrate into the West?"

Nevertheless, it seems that the strategies adopted by Muslims in the West, when dealing with their situations, are impractical for use by the Muslim minority in Israel. The current study found that the evolving Islamic legal theology (especially the religious law of minorities) in Israel is much less developed than that in the West; therefore, at present, one may not identify Islam in Israel as 'Israeli Islam,' as is the case with 'Euro-Islam' in Europe. Muslims in Israel still maintain strong ties with their Middle Eastern regional socio-cultural and religious space, with their peers in the Muslim Arab world. This fact is also manifested in the work and methods of the Israeli *ifta'* institutions that issue fatwas, such as ICIF, the CIS, and the SIM ad hoc committees, as well as in the public's search for and reliance on religious authorities and sources for rulings on mundane problems in daily life – these individuals and these institutions regularly solicit religio-legal opinions from the international Muslim world. Indeed, while they acknowledge the complex reality of Islam in Israel – similar to that in the West – they are hard pressed to balance the traditional interpretations of Islamic law with the demands of everyday life in the specific Israeli context. For this reason, they heavily rely on existing decisions made by international and Middle Eastern Islamic councils, such as the Fiqh Council of the Organization of the Islamic Conference and Islamic institutions in the West Bank and neighboring countries, such as al-Azhar in Egypt and Dar al-Ifta' in Saudi Arabia, as well as on prominent jurists, such as Shaykh Yusuf al-Qaradawi and others. The Muslims in Israel consider themselves to be an integral part both of the Arab Middle East and of the international Muslim community, having constant interaction with both.

The Muslim minority in Israel is distinct from its Western counterparts due to essential differences in various socio-cultural parameters, including nationality, language, culture, and ethnicity. In contrast to Western Muslim minorities, the issues troubling the scattered Muslim diaspora are mostly irrelevant to the Muslim Israeli minority – because it is indigenous, with its own collective historical narrative on the Holy Land, considered holy according to Muslim religious texts. Even the assimilation of the Muslim minority in Israel seems to be impractical, since it is in the interests of both the Jewish majority and the Muslim minority to preserve their distinct identities. This parallels the fundamental nature and intentions of the Islamic Movement in Israel, especially the NIM, whose highest priority is the enhancement of Muslim religious identity. Finally, the nationalist conflict between Arabs and Jews produces suspicion and hostility between the two closely related ethnic groups.

As for the relations between the Muslim minority in Israel and the Israeli establishment and Israeli society, it seems that they are also being impacted by the increasing religiosity and growing degree of observance among the Muslim population. These influences are reflected in the participants' responses regarding the Israeli establishment and its control of Islamic institutions; political participation in various local, regional, and national elections; the establishment of representational Islamic political parties; a preference for living under Islamic authority; and, finally, by the sense of alienation and feeling of dissatisfaction with the situation of Muslims in Israel.

However, the survey results also indicated a certain degree of ambivalence in the relations between the Muslim minority and the Israeli establishment. While the observant participants supported the idea of participating in various Israeli elections (i.e. joining the democratic establishment and, thus, gaining some amount of political control to improve their situation), at the same time they also claimed to prefer living in a state with an Islamic religious orientation. They see no conflict between Islamic law and participation in Israeli elections and, despite feeling like 'foreigners in their own homeland', they still want active involvement.

Moreover, while the respondents generally support the establishment of religious, social, cultural, economic, and political Islamic institutions, only a small percentage feel that this should be done by the Israeli government. These findings indicate a sweeping dissatisfaction with the existing official Islamic institutions, their funding, management, and performance. Nonetheless, most of the respondents are contented with the work of the existing IM's institutions, which they perceive to be more authentic, preferable alternatives to those provided by the Jewish state.

This study showed that the Muslim minority is generally open to the Jewish majority, as manifested by the frequent interaction between the survey participants and Jewish Israelis during their normal routines and by their mastery of Hebrew. More than 70 percent of the respondents claim that they either frequently or regularly meet with Jewish Israelis, and a vast majority (85.1 percent) of the participants have mastered the Hebrew language and are able to hold planned or random conversations (regardless of the topic being discussed) with Jewish Israeli acquaintances. These data indicate that Muslim employees tend to interact the most with Jewish Israelis, suggesting that the nature of these meetings is primarily functional, and also explaining why the large majority of those who often interact with Hebrew speakers are Muslim men (and not Muslim women).

Beyond the practical work interactions, it was found that a large percentage of the participants (63.9 percent) have Jewish friends, whom they have visited within the past two years (23.6 percent). That is, almost two-thirds of the Muslim respondents indicated that they have Jewish friends. This significantly reflects real life, rather than merely describing general, theoretical attitudes toward the Jews in Israel. Many interviewees indicated that they have Jewish friends, indicating an openness in the Muslim community toward their Jewish compatriots; this stands opposed to a common stereotypical perception in Israel regarding Muslim self-segregation and self-imposed social isolation. In fact, one-quarter of the respondents claimed that they visit their Jewish friends in their homes, again attesting to Muslim–Jewish social interaction.

Nonetheless, the Muslim minority seems to be aware of a certain amount of assimilation with the Israeli Jewish majority. Pearson tests found correlations between the extent to which the participants agreed that Muslims in Israel have values worth preserving and their attitudes toward political participation; living under an Islamic regime; and their sense of alienation. These tendencies are most obvious among those participants most committed to Shari'a practice, as evidenced by their more restricted interactions with the Jewish majority. Logic dictates that commitment to Islamic observance, the personal daily practice of Islam, may cause a greater degree of segregation and less integration, from fear of contact with non-Muslim influences (cultures and societies), especially that of the Jewish majority. Such avoidance of frequent contact is probably a natural form of self-protection from the influences of the modern 'secular' environment, perceived as a threat to Islamic values, a means of avoiding the process of assimilation.

Appendix A: English Questionnaire

Arab researchers from universities around the country are conducting a survey on Muslims in Israel, particularly focusing on identity, culture, religiosity, affiliations and tendencies. Your participation in this survey offers you a chance to express your opinions on these matters. Like the other participants in this research, your name was randomly chosen. Your answers will remain anonymous and will only be used for statistical purposes. We thank you in advance for your participation, which we consider vital for the success of this study.

Serial [| |] number:

Please respond to the various statements by **encircling** the most appropriate answer for you. If you are having trouble understanding a specific question, you can seek help from the interviewer.

I.   Islam and Religious Preference

1. I try to observe Islamic religious laws on a daily basis

1. To a very high degree
2. To a high degree
3. To a certain degree
4. Only to a certain degree
5. To a small degree
6. Not at all

2. I would also like the Muslims in Israel to practice Shari'a law

1. To a very great extent
2. To a great extent
3. To a certain extent
4. Only to a certain extent
5. To a small extent
6. Indifferent

154

3. **What is your *madhhab* affiliation?**

   1. Hanafi
   2. Maliki
   3. Shafiʻi
   4. Hanbali
   5. Other
   6. Unaffiliated

4. **What is your theological *madhhab*?**

   1. Ashaʻri
   2. Maturidi
   3. Ahl al-Hadith
   4. Other
   5. Unaffiliated

5. **To which of the current Islamic ideologies do you adhere?**

   1. Salafis
   2. Salafi Jihadists
   3. Moderates
   4. Liberals
   5. Other
   6. Unaffiliated

Do you agree/disagree with the following statements?

	I strongly agree	I agree	I agree to a certain extent	I disagree to a certain extent	I disagree	I strongly disagree
6. I have mastered the Islamic religious laws	1	2	3	4	5	6
7. I support the Sunnis, not the Shiʻis	1	2	3	4	5	6
8. Muslims in Israel have very important values and must preserve them	1	2	3	4	5	6
9. I am satisfied with Muslims' situation in the world	1	2	3	4	5	6
10. I am satisfied with the Muslims' situation in Israel	1	2	3	4	5	6

II.   Islamic Institutions in Israel

Do you agree/disagree with the following statements?

	I strongly agree	I agree	I agree to a certain extent	I disagree to a certain extent	I disagree	I strongly disagree
11. I rely on the official Islamic institutions in Israel, e.g., the Shari'a Courts	1	2	3	4	5	6
12. I rely on the Islamic institutions of the IM e.g., charity 'Zakah' institution	1	2	3	4	5	6
13. I support the ideological discourse of the IM	1	2	3	4	5	6
14. I support the ideological discourse of the NIM	1	2	3	4	5	6
15. I support the ideological discourse of the SIM	1	2	3	4	5	6

	State of Israel	Islamic Movement (NIM or SIM)	Regardless of whom	I do not support the establishment of Islamic institutions
16. I support the establishment of Islamic religious institutions by:	1	2	3	4
17. I support the establishment of Islamic cultural institutions by:	1	2	3	4
18. I support the establishment of Islamic social institutions by:	1	2	3	4
19. I support the establishment of Islamic economic institutions (e.g., banks) by:	1	2	3	4

III.   Attitudes towards State and Society

Do you agree/disagree with the following statements?

	I strongly agree	I agree	I agree to a certain extent	I disagree to a certain extent	I disagree	I strongly disagree
20. I support the political participation of Israeli Muslims in the local (municipal) elections	1	2	3	4	5	6
21. I support the political participation of Israeli Muslims in the national Knesset elections	1	2	3	4	5	6
22. I support the establishment of an Islamic party to participate in the Knesset elections	1	2	3	4	5	6
23. I prefer to live in a state with an Islamic religious orientation	1	2	3	4	5	6
24. I support Islamic political parties that rule in Arab countries	1	2	3	4	5	6
25. I reject Islamic party regimes, as in some 'Arab Spring' countries	1	2	3	4	5	6

Do you agree/disagree with the following statements?

	I strongly agree	I agree	I agree to a certain extent	I disagree to a certain extent	I disagree	I strongly disagree
26. The country between the Jordan River and the Mediterranean Ocean is a common homeland for Jews and Arabs						
27. I am willing to have Jewish friends						
28. I am willing to have Jewish neighbors						
29. Muslim Israelis act more like Jewish Israelis than like the Palestinians in the West Bank and Gaza Strip						
30. As a Muslim in Israel, I feel like a rejected stranger, an outsider						
31. I prefer to live in a village or town in which only Muslims reside						
32. There is a lot to learn from the West and very little from Arab/Islamic countries						
33. Palestine is an Islamic *waqf* land						
34. Palestine, between the Jordan River and the Mediterranean Ocean, is only for Muslims and Arabs						

35. I have mastered the Hebrew language and can discuss various issues with Jewish Israelis

1. I strongly agree
2. I agree
3. I agree to a certain extent
4. I disagree to a certain extent
5. I disagree
6. I strongly disagree

36. How often do you interact with Jewish Israelis?

1. Daily
2. Frequently
3. Infrequently
4. Seldom

37. **Do you have Jewish friends and have you visited them at home within the last two years?**

   1. I do not have Jewish friends
   2. I have Jewish friends, but I have not visited them at home in the last two years
   3. I have Jewish friends and I have visited them at home within the last two years

38. **When you evaluate your own social and economic achievements, with whom do you compare yourself?**

   1. With the Christians in Israel
   2. With the Jews in Israel
   3. With the Druze in Israel
   4. With Muslims in Arab countries
   5. With Muslim minorities in the West
   6. With modern societies
   7. Other

IV.   Identity

Do you agree/disagree with the following statements?

	I strongly agree	I agree	I agree to a certain extent	I disagree to a certain extent	I disagree	I strongly disagree
39. I support Muslim men only marrying Muslim women	1	2	3	4	5	6
40. I support Muslim women only marrying Muslim men	1	2	3	4	5	6
41. I support Muslims marrying according to traditional Islamic rituals	1	2	3	4	5	6
42. I support the gender separation of men and women at public events	1	2	3	4	5	6
43. I support the daily observance of Islamic religious laws	1	2	3	4	5	6
44. When choosing my friends, I stipulate that they must be observant	1	2	3	4	5	6
45. When choosing my life partner, I stipulate that he/she must be observant	1	2	3	4	5	6
46. I support Islamic preaching in Israel	1	2	3	4	5	6
47. I support men wearing Islamic religious attire ("Pakistani attire")	1	2	3	4	5	6
48. I support women wearing Islamic religious attire	1	2	3	4	5	6
49. I believe that Islamic religious attire mainly expresses Islamic identity	1	2	3	4	5	6
50. I support gender separation in the Arab schools in Israel	1	2	3	4	5	6

51. **I believe that Islam is more important than the state of Israel**

    1. I strongly agree
    2. I agree
    3. I agree to a certain extent
    4. I disagree to a certain extent
    5. I disagree
    6. I strongly disagree

52. **I believe that being Muslim is more important than being Israeli**

    1. I strongly agree
    2. I agree
    3. I agree to a certain extent
    4. I disagree to a certain extent
    5. I disagree
    6. I strongly disagree

53. **Which identity do you prefer?**

    1. Being an Israeli citizen
    2. Being a Muslim
    3. Being a Palestinian Arab

54. **How do you identify yourself, when asked to choose one of the following possibilities?**

    1. Arab
    2. Israeli Arab
    3. Palestinian Arab
    4. Palestinian in Israel
    5. Palestinian Arab in Israel

55. **From a religious belonging perspective, I consider myself as:**

    1. Sunni
    2. Shiʿi
    3. Other

56. **I consider myself to be:**

    1. Very religious
    2. Religious
    3. Somewhat religious
    4. Somewhat non-religious
    5. Not religious
    6. Not religious at all

Do you agree/disagree with the following statements?

	I strongly agree	I agree	I agree to a certain extent	I disagree to a certain extent	I disagree	I strongly disagree
57. I belong to a religious minority in Israel	1	2	3	4	5	6
58. I belong to a national minority in Israel	1	2	3	4	5	6
59. I support the idea of a caliphate ruling the Arab/Islamic world	1	2	3	4	5	6
60. I support the idea of a caliphate ruling the Muslims in Israel	1	2	3	4	5	6
61. I support the return of lapsed Israeli Muslims to their religious observance	1	2	3	4	5	6

V.   Shari'a vs. Local Customs, Norms, and Laws

62. **When local custom conflicts with Islamic religious law, I follow:**

   1. Local customs
   2. Islamic religious laws
   3. I try to combine both
   4. I reject both

63. **When Islamic religious law conflicts with the Israeli state law, I follow:**

   1. Israeli state laws
   2. Islamic religious laws (Shari'a)
   3. I try to combine both
   4. I reject both

64. **When the state imposes a law that clearly contradicts the Shari'a:**

   1. I reject the state law
   2. I reject the state law and bear the consequences
   3. I honor the state law
   4. I honor the state law for lack of a choice

65. For reliable religious authority, I turn to:

1. Local Islamic figures
2. Foreign Islamic figures
3. Islamic judges or courts
4. Personal study
5. Other

Do you participate in the following rituals and how frequently?

	Always	Very often	Fairly frequently	Infrequently	Quite infrequently	Never
66. 'Aqiqa (a birth ritual involving shaving of a child's head, distribution of money to the poor, animal sacrifice, and the naming of the child)	1	2	3	4	5	6
67. Halaqat al-dhikr (Islamic devotional and study circles, often practiced in the mosques)	1	2	3	4	5	6
68. The 'call to prayer' spoken into a child's right ear and the 'summons to prayer' in the left ear	1	2	3	4	5	6
69. Islamic marriage celebrations	1	2	3	4	5	6

VI.   The Muslim Woman

Do you agree/disagree with each one of the following statements?

	I strongly agree	I agree	I agree to a certain extent	I disagree to a certain extent	I disagree	I strongly disagree
70. Muslim women have the right to work within their settlements						
71. Muslim women have the right to work outside their settlements						
72. Muslim women have the right to full equality with Muslim men						
73. The basic role of the Muslim woman is to give birth and raise children at home						
74. Muslim women must be committed to Shari'a practice in all aspects of life						
75. In cases of personal status, Muslim women must appeal only to the Islamic courts						
76. In cases of conflict within the Muslim family, I only support following the Shari'a						
77. I support the state law forbidding the marriage of girls under 18 years of age						
78. I support the state law that forbids polygamy						

VII.   Personal Data

79: **Age:**

    1. 18–29
    2. 30–39
    3. 40–49
    4. 50–59
    5. 60 and above

80: **Gender:**

    1. Male
    2. Female

81. **Marital status:**

    1. Single
    2. Married
    3. Divorced/Separated
    4. Widow/Widower

82. **Place of residence:**

    1. Galilee
    2. Negev
    3. Mixed cities

83. **Your residential community** (where the interview was held) **is:**

    1. All Muslim
    2. Mostly Muslim
    3. Mostly Christian
    4. Mostly Druze

84. **Your educational level:**

    1. Literate
    2. Elementary education
    3. Secondary education
    4. BA
    5. MA
    6. Ph.D.

85. **Occupations:**

    1. Employee or clerk
    2. Self-employed

3. Unemployed, but seeking a job
4. Unemployed and not seeking a job
5. Retired
6. University student
7. Housewife

86. **The average net monthly income of an Arab family in Israel is 7,300 NIS. Compared with this income, your family income is:**

1. Much higher than average
2. A bit above average
3. Average
4. A bit below average
5. Much less than average

This Completes the Interview. Thank You for Your Cooperation.

87. **Please circle the name of your place of residence in the list below:**

1. Abu-Snan
2. Abu-Tlul
3. Ksayfeh
4. Umm el-Fahm
5. Iksal
6. Zymer-Marjeh
7. Beir el-Maksur
8. al-Tirah
9. Kufr Manda
10. A'ra'rah
11. Sha'b
12. El-Ramleh
13. Majd el-Krum
14. El-Na'urah
15. Nahf
16. Nazareth
17. Sakhneen
18. Acre ('Acca)
19. Rahat
20. Shfa-'Amr

Interviewer Declaration I hereby declare that I conducted the interview myself with a participant from the list of names in the sample, according to the directions I received. I know that a false declaration is a violation of the law of the State of Israel and breaks the disciplinary rules of the University, the Ministry of Education, etc.

Name of the interviewer:_____
Signature of the interviewer:_____

Appendix B: Arabic Questionnaire

استطلاع رأي حول المسلمين في اسرائيل

باحثون عرب من جامعات في البلاد يجرون استطلاع رأي حول المسلمين في إسرائيل لا سيما دينهم وثقافتهم وهويتهم وانتماءاتهم وميولهم. اشتراكك في الاستطلاع يمكنك من إبداء رأيك حول الموضوع. لقد اختير اسمك صدفة لغرض البحث. إجاباتك ستبقى سرية وتستعمل لأغراض إحصائية فقط. يجدر التنويه على انه تمت كتابة الاستطلاع بصيغة المذكر للاختصار فقط ولكنه موجه للجنسين. نحن نشكرك سلفا على اشتراكك الذي نعتبره ضروريا لإنجاح البحث.

الرقم التسلسلي: ☐ ☐ ☐

الرجاء الإجابة على الأسئلة عن طريق وضع **دائرة** على الخيار الأنسب إليك. في حالة الاستصعاب في فهم أي سؤال بإمكانك الاستعانة بالمقابل.

I. الدين والمرجعية الاسلامية

1. انا احتكم بسلوكياتي للشريعة الاسلامية:

1. الى حد كبير جدا   2. الى حد كبير   3. احتكم الى حد ما   4. لا احتكم إلى حد ما   5. الى حد قليل   6. لا احتكم بالمرة

2. او د ان يحتكم المسلمون في اسرائيل بسلوكياتهم للشريعة الاسلامية:

1. الى حد كبير جدا   2. الى حد كبير   3. يحتكموا الى حد ما   4. لا يحتكموا إلى حد ما   5. الى حد قليل
6. لا يحتكموا بالمرة

3. ما هو مذهبك الفقهي؟

1. الحنفي   2. المالكي   3. الشافعي   4. الحنبلي   5. مذهب اخر   6. لا ادري

4. ما هو مذهبك العقائدي؟

1. اشعري   2. ماتريدي   3. اهل الحديث (حنبلي)   4. مذهب اخر   5. لا ادري

5. الى أي من التيارات الفكرية الاسلامية المعاصرة انت تميل؟

1. سلفي   2. سلفي جهادي   3. وسطي   4. ليبرالي   5. اخر   6. مذهب اخر

هل انت موافق او غير موافق مع كل من المقولات الاتية:

غير موافق بشدة	غير موافق	غير موافق إلى حد ما	موافق الى حد ما	موافق	موافق بشدة	
6	5	4	3	2	1	6. انا ملم بالشريعة الاسلامية
6	5	4	3	2	1	7. في الصراع الدائر بين السنة والشيعة, انا اؤيد السنة بالكامل
6	5	4	3	2	1	8. للمسلمين بهذه البلاد قيم مهمة يجب الحفاظ عليها
6	5	4	3	2	1	9. انا راض عن وضع المسلمين بالعالم
6	5	4	3	2	1	10. انا راض عن وضع المسلمين في اسرائيل

II. المؤسسات الاسلامية في اسرائيل

هل انت موافق او غير موافق مع كل من المقولات الاتية:

غير موافق بشدة	غير موافق	غير موافق إلى حد ما	موافق الى حد ما	موافق	موافق بشدة	
6	5	4	3	2	1	11. انا اثق بالمؤسسات الاسلامية التي اقامتها اسرائيل (مثل المحاكم الشرعية)
6	5	4	3	2	1	12. انا اثق بالمؤسسات الاسلامية التي اقامتها الحركة الاسلامية (مثل مؤسسة الزكاه)
6	5	4	3	2	1	13. انا مؤيد للطرح الفكري للحركة الاسلامية
6	5	4	3	2	1	14. انا مؤيد للطرح الفكري للجناح الشمالي للحركة الإسلامية
6	5	4	3	2	1	15. انا مؤيد للطرح الفكري للجناح الجنوبي للحركة الإسلامية

III. العلاقة مع الدولة والمجتمع

لا اؤيد ذلك	لا يهم من يقيمها	الحركة الاسلامية (الشمالية او الجنوبية)	دولة اسرائيل	
4	3	2	1	16. انا اؤيد اقامة مؤسسات اسلامية دينية على يد
4	3	2	1	17. انا اؤيد اقامة مؤسسات اسلامية ثقافية على يد
4	3	2	1	18. انا اؤيد اقامة مؤسسات اسلامية اجتماعية على يد
4	3	2	1	19. انا اؤيد اقامة مؤسسات اسلامية اقتصادية (بنوك على سبيل المثال) على يد

هل انت موافق او غير موافق مع كل من المقولات الاتية:

غير موافق بشدة	غير موافق	غير موافق إلى حد ما	موافق الى حد ما	موافق	موافق بشدة	
6	5	4	3	2	1	20. انا اؤيد فكرة المشاركة السياسية في انتخابات الحكم المحلي (السلطات المحلية) للمسلمين في اسرائيل
6	5	4	3	2	1	21. انا اؤيد فكرة المشاركة السياسية في انتخابات الكنيست للمسلمين في اسرائيل
6	5	4	3	2	1	22. انا اؤيد فكرة اقامة حزب اسلامي يشترك في انتخابات الكنيست
6	5	4	3	2	1	23. افضل العيش في دولة ذات طابع ديني اسلامي
6	5	4	3	2	1	24. انا اؤيد وصول الاحزاب المتدينة الى الحكم في بعض الدول العربية
6	5	4	3	2	1	25. انا اؤيد ردود الفعل الرافضة لحكم الاحزاب المتدينة كما حدث في بعض دول الربيع العربي

هل انت موافق او غير موافق مع كل من المقولات الاتية:

غير موافق بشدة	غير موافق	غير موافق إلى حد ما	موافق الى حد ما	موافق	موافق بشدة	
6	5	4	3	2	1	26. البلاد من النهر الى البحر هي وطن مشترك لليهود والعرب
6	5	4	3	2	1	27. أنا مستعد أن يكون لي أصدقاء يهود
6	5	4	3	2	1	28. أنا مستعد أن يكون لي جار يهودي
6	5	4	3	2	1	29. المسلمون في اسرائيل يشبهون اليهود بطباعهم وبسلوكياتهم أكثر من الفلسطينيين في الضفة والقطاع
6	5	4	3	2	1	30. كمسلم أشعر غريبا ومرفوضا في إسرائيل
6	5	4	3	2	1	31. افضل العيش في قرية او مدينة يعيش بها مسلمون فقط
6	5	4	3	2	1	32. هناك الكثير لنتعلمه من الغرب وقليل فقط من الدول العربية والاسلامية
6	5	4	3	2	1	33. ارض فلسطين هي ارض وقف اسلامي
6	5	4	3	2	1	34. فلسطين من النهر للبحر هي للمسلمين والعرب فقط

35. انا متمكن من اللغة العبرية حيث يمكنني إجراء محادثة حول مواضيع مختلفة مع يهودي إسرائيلي

1. موافق بشدة   2. موافق   3. موافق الى حد ما   4. غير موافق إلى حد ما   5. غير موافق   6. غير موافق بشدة

36. بأي وتيرة تقابل يهود في حياتك اليومية؟

1. . كل يوم   2. على فترات متقاربة   3. على فترات متباعدة   4. تقريبا ولا مرة

37. هل لديك أصدقاء يهود وهل زرتهم في بيتهم خلال السنتين الأخيرتين؟

1. ليس لدي أصدقاء يهود

2. لدي أصدقاء يهود ولكني لم أزرهم في بيوتهم خلال السنتين الأخيرتين

3. لدي أصدقاء يهود وزرتهم في بيوتهم خلال السنتين الأخيرتين

38. عندما تقيم انجازاتك الاجتماعية والاقتصادية بمن تقارن نفسك:

1. بالمسيحيين في إسرائيل
2. باليهود في إسرائيل
3. بالدروز في إسرائيل
4. بالمسلمين في الدول العربية
5. بالأقليات المسلمة في الغرب
6. اخر - - - - -

IV. الهوية:

هل توافق او لا توافق مع كل من المقولات الآتية:

غير موافق بشدة	غير موافق	غير موافق إلى حد ما	موافق الى حد ما	موافق	موافق بشدة	
6	5	4	3	2	1	39. انا اؤيد ان يتزوج المسلمون فقط من مسلمات
6	5	4	3	2	1	40. انا اؤيد ان تتزوج المسلمات فقط من مسلمين
6	5	4	3	2	1	41. انا اؤيد ان يتزوج المسلمون حسب طقوس اسلامية
6	5	4	3	2	1	42. انا اؤيد ظاهرة الفصل بين الذكور والإناث في المناسبات العامة
6	5	4	3	2	1	43. انا اؤيد اتباع الشريعة الاسلامية كدستور لحياتي اليومية
6	5	4	3	2	1	44. في حال اختياري لأصدقائي اشترط بان يكونوا متدينين
6	5	4	3	2	1	45. في حال اختياري لشريك|ة حياتي اشترط بان ي|تكون متدين|ة
6	5	4	3	2	1	46. انا اؤيد العمل الاسلامي الدعوي في البلاد
6	5	4	3	2	1	47. انا اؤيد ظاهرة اللباس الديني الاسلامي للرجال (ما يعرف باللباس الباكستاني)
6	5	4	3	2	1	48. انا اؤيد ظاهرة اللباس الديني الاسلامي للنساء
6	5	4	3	2	1	49. اللباس الديني الاسلامي يعبر بالأساس عن الهوية الاسلامية

غير موافق بشدة	غير موافق	غير موافق الى حد ما	موافق الى حد ما	موافق	موافق بشدة	
6	5	4	3	2	1	50. انا اؤيد ظاهرة فصل الطلاب عن الطالبات بالتعليم العربي في اسرائيل

51. اعتقد ان هويتي الدينية الاسلامية اهم من هويتي القومية:

1. موافق بشدة 2. موافق 3. موافق الى حد ما 4. غير موافق الى حد ما 5. غير موافق 6. غير موافق بشدة

52. اعتقد ان هويتي الدينية الاسلامية اهم من هويتي الاسرائيلية:

1. موافق بشدة 2. موافق 3. موافق الى حد ما 4. غير موافق الى حد ما 5. غير موافق 6. غير موافق بشدة

53. أي من بين الهويات التالية هي الأهم بالنسبة لك؟

1. كونك مواطن إسرائيلي 2.كونك مسلم 3. كونك فلسطيني

54. كيف تعرف هويتك، لو طلب منك إختيار إحدى الإمكانيات التالية؟

1. عربي 2. عربي إسرائيلي 3. عربي فلسطيني 4. فلسطيني في إسرائيل 5. عربي فلسطيني في إسرائيل

55. من ناحية الانتماء الديني, انا اعتبر نفسي:

1. سني 2. شيعي 3. اخر

56. من ناحية الدين انا اعتبر نفسي:

1. متدين جدا 2. متدين 3. متدين نوعا ما 4. غير متدين نوعا ما 5. غير متدين 6. غير متدين بالمره

هل توافق او لا توافق مع كل من المقولات الاتية:

غير موافق بشدة	غير موافق	غير موافق إلى حد ما	موافق الى حد ما	موافق	موافق بشدة	
6	5	4	3	2	1	57. اعتبر نفسي جزء من اقلية دينية في البلاد
6	5	4	3	2	1	58. اعتبر نفسي جزء من اقلية قومية في البلاد
6	5	4	3	2	1	59. اؤيد فكرة حكم الخلافة في العالم العربي والإسلامي
6	5	4	3	2	1	60. اؤيد فكرة حكم الخلافة على المسلمين في اسرائيل
6	5	4	3	2	1	61. هنالك ظاهرة رجوع الى الدين عند المسلمين في اسرائيل وانا اؤيد مثل هذه الظاهرة

V. الشريعة والعرف والطقوس

62. في حال التناقض بين العادات والتقاليد من ناحية والشرع الاسلامي من ناحية اخرى، انا افضل:

1. العادات والتقاليد   2. الشرع الاسلامي   3. احاول الدمج بينهما   4. ارفض كليهما

63. في حال التناقض بين قانون الدولة مع الشرع الاسلامي (القطعيات: العقائد القاطعة التى يجب الإيمان بها مثل اركان الايمان وأركان الاسلام) اي منهما تفضل:

1. قانون الدولة   2. الشرع الاسلامي   3. احاول الدمج بينهما   4. ارفض كليهما

64. في حال فرضت الدولة قانون يناقض الشرع الاسلامي بشكل صريح (القطعيات):

1. ارفض القانون   2. ارفض القانون واتحمل المسؤولية   3. احترم القانون   4. احترم القانون للضرورة

65. في حال اردت معرفة حكم شرعي معين:

1. استعين بمواقع\اشخصيات اسلامية محلية   2. استعين بمواقع \اشخصيات اسلامية خارجية   3. الجأ الى الفضائيات الاسلامية   4. اجتهد بنفسي   5. اخر

هل اشتركت في اي من الطقوس الدينية التالية والى أي مدى:

	دائما	كثير جدا	كثير الى حد ما	قليل الى حد ما	قليل جدا	بالمره لا
66. العقيقة	1	2	3	4	5	6
67. حلقات الذكر الدينية	1	2	3	4	5	6
68. الاذان في اذن الطفل	1	2	3	4	5	6
69. زواج حسب الفرق الدينية	1	2	3	4	5	6

VI. المرأة المسلمة

هل انت لوافق او لا توافق مع كل من الامور ۷، ۲، الآتيه

	موافق بشدة	موافق	موافق الى حد ما	غير موافق إلى حد ما	غير موافق	غير موافق بشدة
70. من حق المرأة المسلمة الخروج للعمل في بلدتها اذا رغبت بذلك	1	2	3	4	5	6
71. من حق المرأة المسلمة الخروج للعمل خارج بلدتها اذا رغبت بذلك	1	2	3	4	5	6

غير موافق بشدة	غير موافق	غير موافق إلى حد ما	موافق الى حد ما	موافق	موافق بشدة	
6	5	4	3	2	1	72. من حق المرأة المسلمة المساواة الكاملة مع الرجل المسلم
6	5	4	3	2	1	73. الدور الأساسي للمرأة المسلمة هو الانجاب ورعاية الاطفال والمنزل
6	5	4	3	2	1	74. على المرأة المسلمة الالتزام بالشريعة الاسلامية في شتى مناحي الحياة
6	5	4	3	2	1	75. في قضايا الاحوال الشخصية على المرأة المسلمة ان تحتكم للمحاكم الشرعيه فقط
6	5	4	3	2	1	76. في حال وقعت خلافات داخل العائلة المسلمة, اؤيد الاحتكام لشرع الله فقط
6	5	4	3	2	1	77. اؤيد القانون الذي يمنع زواج الفتاة تحت سن 18
6	5	4	3	2	1	78. اؤيد القانون الذي يمنع تعدد الزوجات

VII. أسئلة شخصية:

79. الجيل:
1. 18–29 2. 30–39 3. 40–49 4. 50–59 5. 60 وما فوق

80. جنس:
1. ذكر 2. أنثى

81. الوضع الاجتماعي:
1. أعزب 2. متزوج 3. مطلق/منفصل 4. أرمل

82. **الموقع الجغرافي او مكان السكن:** 1.. الجليل 2. المثلث 3. النقب 4. **المدن المختلطة**

83. من ناحية التجانس الديني, البلدة التي تجري بها البحث:
1. كلها مسلمة 2. غالبيتها مسلمة 3. غالبيتها مسيحية 4. غالبيتها درزية

84. التعليم:
1. لم أتعلم 2. أنهيت تعليمي الابتدائي 3. أنهيت تعليمي الثانوي 4. حاصل على لقب ب.أ 5. حاصل على لقب م.أ 6. حاصل على لقب الدكتوراه

85. العمل:

1. عامل أجير او موظف   2. مستقل   3. لا أعمل ولكن أبحث عن عمل   4. لا أعمل ولا أبحث عن عمل

5. متقاعد   6. طالب جامعي   7. ربة بيت

86. معدل الدخل الشهري الصافي للعائلة العربية في إسرائيل هو 7300 ش.ج. بالمقارنة مع هذا الدخل، هل دخل عائلتك:

1. أعلى بكثير من المعدل
2. أعلى بقليل من المعدل
3. مثل المعدل
4. أقل بقليل من المعدل
5. أقل بكثير من المعدل

بهذا انتهى البحث. شكراً على تعاونك

87. الرجاء وضع اشارة دائرة حول اسم مكان السكن من القائمة التالية:

1. أبو سنان 2. أبو تلول 3. كسيفة 4. أم الفحم 5. إكسال 6. زيمر مرجه 7. بئر المكسور 8. الطيرة 9. كفر مندا 10. عرعره 11. شعب 12. الرملة 13. مجد الكروم 14. الناعورة 15. نحف 16. الناصرة 17. سخنين 18. عكا 19. رهط 20. شفاعمرو

88. للاستعمال المكتبي، مراقبة على الاستمارة: 1. صودق عليها   2. لم يصادق عليها

تصريح المقابِل

أصرح بهذا أنني أجريت بنفسي المقابلة من قائمة الأسماء في العينة حسب التوجيهات التي حصلت عليها، وأعلم ان تصريحاً كاذباً هو مخالفة لقانون الدولة ومخالفة للأنظمة التأديبية (الجامعة، وزارة المعارف وغير ذلك).

اسم المقابِل _____   توقيع المقابِل _____

Glossary of Arabic Terms[1]

ahl al-hall wa-'l-'aqd   those qualified to elect or depose a caliph on behalf of the Muslim community.

ahl al-kitab   'People of the Book': Christians and Jews.

'aqd nikah   marriage contract.

'aqiqa   a birth ritual involving the shaving of a child's head, distribution of money to the poor, animal sacrifice, and the naming of the child. The 'call to prayer' is spoken into the child's right ear and the 'summons to prayer' into the left ear.

Dar al-Ifta'   religious establishment for issuing fatwas. See *ifta'*, *fatwa*, *mufti*.

dar' al-mafasid yataqaddam 'ala jalb al-masalih   the prevention of damage is preferable to the promotion of benefit.

darura   necessity.

al-darurat tubihal-mahzurat   necessity overcoming a prohibition.

da'wa   the call for Islam, Islamic dissemination.

fatwa   (pl. *fatawa*) an advisory opinion by a qualified scholar on a religious or legal matter.

fiqh   'understanding': the science of Shari'a, Islamic jurisprudence.

fiqh al-aqalliyyat   Islamic religious law of minorities.

fitna   temptation, discord.

ghadd al-basar   lowering the gaze.

Hadith   the report of a saying, action, or acquiescence by the Prophet Muhammad.

hajj   pilgrimage.

hakimiyya   sovereignty.

halal   licit, lawful, permissible.

halaqat al-dhikr   Islamic devotional and study circles, are often practiced in the mosques.

haram   illicit, unlawful, prohibited.

hay'a   board, council.

---

[1] Translation of some of these terms rely on Esposito (ed.), *The Oxford Dictionary of Islam*.

hukm   (pl. *ahkam*) Allah's ruling, rule, judgment, moral value.

'ibada   service to God, the foremost religious and civic duty of a Muslim.

ifta'   the issuing of fatwas. See Dar al-Ifta'.

ijma'   consensus, one of the *usul al-fiqh*.

ijtihad   independent legal reasoning to resolve new legal problems.

ikhtilat   intermingling of men and women.

al-Ikhwan al-Muslimun   Muslim Brotherhood

'ilm   knowledge, science.

imam   'leader': leader of prayer, caliph; commonly used to refer to a religious leader.

istidlal   inference, a distinct legal method for deriving rules; see also *turuq al-istidlal*.

istihsan   juristic 'approval', a discretionary opinion.

istikhlaf   vice-regency.

jihad   'exertion', 'striving': struggling for the sake of Allah, whether in self-purification, against oppression and injustice or in a just war.

khalwa   'privacy'; often referring to the sequestering of potential marriage partners according to Islamic law.

khalwa shar'iyya or sahiha   licit *khalwa*, permissible for married couples or unmarriageable kin.

Khawarij or Kharijis   early group in Islam, neither Sunni nor Shi'i. The group survives today, known as the Ibadis, with fewer than a million adherents.

khilafa   'caliphate': a form of Islamic government.

lajna   committee, board.

Laylat al-Mi'raj   the Prophet's ascent to heaven.

madhhab   (pl. *madhahib*) Islamic school of thought.

mahram   husband or close male relative of a woman to whom marriage is prohibited by Islamic law (e.g. father, grandfather, brother, son, uncle, nephew).

Majallat Dirasat Islamiyya   Magazine of Islamic Studies.

majma'   council.

majma' 'ilmi Islami   scientific council of 'ulama'.

malahi   leisure and entertainment.

maqasid al-shari'a   intentions of the Shari'a.

masdar tashri'i tab'i   ancillary legislative source.

maslaha   interest, well-being, welfare.

al-maslaha al-'amma   public interest.

mu'azins or muezzin   a male Muslim who issues an *adhan* (call to prayer).

mufti   a specialist in Islamic law who issues fatwas.

qadi   judge.

qiyas   analogical reasoning.

riba   usury, interest.

sadaqah   charity.

sahih   authentic, correct, sound.

sahwa   Islamic resurgence.

salaf   forebears, ancestors.

al-salaf al-salih   the Righteous Forebears.

Shari'a   'a path', 'a way': Allah's law, Islamic theology and law.

shaykh   'old man': a term of respect often used for religious scholars.

siyasa   policy, governance, administration.

siyasa shar'iyya   *siyasa* within the limits assigned to it by Shar'ia.

Sunna   (pl. *sunan*) normative custom; legally binding precedents set by
the Prophet as represented in Hadith tradition.

takaful   mutual responsibility.

Tariqat al-Qasimi al-Khalwatiyya al-Jami'a   Khalawati Sufi order in
Israel

tarjih   choosing the preponderant opinion.

turuq al-istidlal   methods of argumentation.

'ulama'   (sing. *'alim*) 'those who possess *'ilm*'; religious scholars.

umara'   (sing. *amir*) commanders, rulers, princes.

'urf   custom or customary.

usul   (sing. *asl*) roots, sources, origins.

usul al-fiqh   roots or sources of *fiqh*, science of legal reasoning and
derivation.

al-wala' wa'l-bara'   loyalty and enmity.

waqf   Islamic religious endowment.

wasatiyya   'moderation' or 'the median path'.

wu'az   (sing. *wa'iz*) preachers.

wulat al-amr   (sing. *wali al-amr*) authority-holders.

zakat   alms tax.

Bibliography

INTERNET SITES

www.alifta.net/default.aspx
www.alforkan.org
www.alqasimy.com/afta.php
www.dar-alifta.org/default.aspx?LangID&Home=1&LangID=2.
www.egatha.org/eportal
http://e-cfr.org/new/
www.eshraka.com/web/pages/Details.aspx?Id=1299
http://fatwa.islamweb.net/mainpage/index.php
www.fatawah.com
http://fatawa.qsm.ac.il/index.htm
www.islamweb.net
www.islamonline.net
www.isna.net
www.pls48.net
www.palscholars.com/index.php?option=com_content&view=section&layout=
   blog&id=11&Itemid=62.
www.qsm.ac.il

NEWSPAPERS AND MAGAZINES

Abaa wa-Abnaa [Arabic]
Davar [Hebrew]
Ha'aretz [Hebrew]
Ishraqa [Arabic]
Ma'ariv [Hebrew]
al-Mithaq [Arabic]
Sawt al-Haqq wa'l-Huriyya [Arabic]

PRINTED SOURCES

'Abd al-Qadir, Khalid. *Fiqh al-qalliyyat al-muslima.* [Jurisprudence of Muslim
   minorities] Tripoli [Lebanon]: Dar al-Iman, 1998 [Arabic].
Abou El Fadl, Khaled. *And God Knows the Soldiers: The Authoritative and Author-*
   itarian in Islamic Discourses. Lanham, Md.: University Press of America,
   2001.

Islam and the challenge of democratic commitment, *Fordham International Law Journal* 27(1) (2003): 4–71.

Islamic law and Muslim minorities: the juristic discourse on Muslim minorities from the second/eighth to the eleventh/seventeenth centuries, *Islamic Law and Society* 1(2) (1994): 141–187.

Legal debates on Muslim minorities: between rejection and accommodation, *Journal of Religious Ethics* 22(1) (1994): 127–162.

Speaking in God's Name. Oxford: Oneworld Press, 2001.

Abou Ramadan, Musa. Judicial activism of the Shari'ah Appeals Court in Israel (1994–2001): rise and crisis, *Fordham International Law Journal* 27 (1) (2003): 254–298.

Notes on the anomaly of the Shari'a field in Israel, *Islamic Law and Society* 15 (2008): 84–111.

Abu Freih, Farraj. Islam in the Negev: Conflict and Agreement between the 'Urf and the Shari'a amid the Arab Muslim Community in the Negev. MA thesis. Beer-Sheva: Ben-Gurion University of the Negev, 2014 [Hebrew].

Abu-Lughod, Lila. Orientalism and Middle East feminist studies, *Feminist Studies* 27(1) (2001): 101–113.

Abu-Manneh, Butrus. The Husaynis: the rise of a notable family in 18th century Palestine. In David Kushner (ed.), *Palestine in the Late Ottoman Period: Political, Social and Economic Transformation* (93–108). London: E. J. Brill, 1986.

Abu Zahra, Muhammad. *'Usul al-fiqh.* [Islamic legal theories] Cairo: Dar al-Fikr al-'Arabi, 1957 [Arabic].

Aburaiya, 'Issam. The 1996 split of the Islamic Movement in Israel: between the holy text and Israeli–Palestinian context, *International Journal of Politics, Culture, and Society* 17(3) (2004): 439–455.

Concrete religiosity versus abstract religiosity: the case of the division of the Islamic Movement in Israel, *Megamot* 43(4) (2005): 682–698 [Hebrew].

Developmental Leadership: The Case of the Islamic Movement in Umm al-Fahm, Israel. MA thesis. Worcester, Mass.: Clark University, 1989.

Agbaria, Ayman K., and Muhanad Mustafa. The case of Palestinian civil society in Israel: Islam, civil society and educational activism, *Critical Studies in Education* 55(1) (2014): 44–57.

Two states for three peoples: the "Palestinian Israeli" in the future vision documents of the Palestinians in Israel, *Ethnic and Racial Studies* 35(4) (2005): 718–736.

'Ali, 'Abdullah Yusuf. *The Holy Qur'an.* Brentwood, Md.: Amana Corporation, 1989.

'Ali, Nohad. *Between 'Ovadia and 'Abdallah: Islamic Fundamentalism and Jewish Fundamentalism in Israel.* Tel Aviv: Resling Press, 2013 [Hebrew].

Changes in the identity and attitudes of the supporters and opponents of the Islamic Movement in Israel. In Rassem Khamaissa (ed.), *Arab Society in Israel: Population, Society, Economy* III (304–324). Jerusalem: Van Leer Institute, 2009 [Hebrew].

Islamic Movement and the challenge of minority status: the independent community as a case study. In Meir Hatina and Muhammad al-Atawneh (eds.),

Muslims in the Jewish State. Tel Aviv: Hakibbutz Hameuchad, forthcoming [Hebrew].

The Islamic Movement in Israel between religion, nationalism and modernity. In Y. Yonah and Y. Goodman (eds.), *Maelstrom of Identities: A Critical Look at Religion and Secularity in Israel* (132–164). Jerusalem: Van Leer Institute, 2004 [Hebrew].

The notion of "el-mogtama' el-aisami" of the Islamic Movement. In Elie Rekhess (ed.), *The Arab Minority in Israel and the 17th Knesset Elections* (100–111). Tel Aviv: Moshe Dayan Center for Middle East and Africa Studies, 2007 [Hebrew].

Political Islam in an ethnic Jewish state: its historical evolution, contemporary challenges and future prospects, *Holy Land Studies* 3(1) (2004): 69–92.

Religious Fundamentalism as an Ideology and a Practice: A Comparative Study of Jews' Shas and the Islamic Movement in Israel. Ph.D. thesis. Haifa: Haifa University, 2006 [Hebrew].

'Alwani, Taha Jaber. *Towards a Fiqh of Minorities: Some Basic Reflections.* Herndon, Va.: International Institute of Islamic Thought, 2003.

Amara, Muhammad. The collective identity of the Arabs in Israel in an era of peace, *Israel Affairs* 9 (2003): 249–262.

The nature of Islamic fundamentalism in Israel, *Terrorism and Political Violence* 8(2) (1996): 155–170.

Amara, Muhammad, and Izhak Schnell. Identity repertoire among Arabs in Israel, *Journal of Ethnic and Migration Studies* 30 (2003): 175–194.

Amaratunga, Dilanthi, David Baldry, Sarshar Marjan, and Rita Newton. Quantitative and qualitative research in the built environment: application of mixed research approach, *Work Study* 51 (2002): 17–31.

Asaliyya, Ziyad. Athar al-qawanin al-isra'iliyya fi al-qada' al-shar'i fi Isra'il [The impact of Israeli law on the Islamic judiciary in Israel]. MA thesis. Hebron: Hebron University, 2003 [Arabic].

Ashraf, 'Abd al-'Ati. *Fiqh al-aqalliyat al-muslima bayna al-nazariyya wal-tatbiq* [Jurisprudence of Muslim minorities between theory and practice]. Bethlehem: Dar al-Kalima, 2008 [Arabic].

al-'Asqalani, Ibn Hajar. *Fath al-bari bi sharh sahih al-bukhari* [Victory of the creator in al-Bukhari's *Sahih*]. Beirut: Dar al-Fikr, 1993 [Arabic].

al-Atawneh, Muhammad. Leisure and entertainment (*malahi*) in contemporary Islamic legal thought: music and the audio-visual media, *Islamic Law and Society* 19(4): 397–415.

Wahhabi Islam Facing the Challenges of Modernity: Dar al-Ifta in Modern Saudi Arabia. Leiden: E. J. Brill, 2010.

'Atiyya, Muhammad Jamal al-Din. *Nahwa fiqh jadid li'l-aqalliyyat* [Towards a new jurisprudence of minorities]. Cairo: Dar al-Salam, 2003 [Arabic].

al-Banna, Hasan. *Mudhakkarat al-da'wa wa'l-da'iya* [The diary of preaching and a preacher]. Kuwait: Maktabat Afaq, 2012 [Arabic].

Beckford, James. Religious movements and globalization. In R. Cohen and S. Rai (eds.), *Global Social Movements* (165–183). London: Athlone Press, 2000.

Binder, Leonard. *Islamic Liberalism: A Critique of Development Ideologies*. Chicago: University of Chicago Press, 1988.

Browers, Michaelle. *Political Ideology in the Arab World: Accommodation and Transformation*. Cambridge: Cambridge University Press, 2009.

Brown, Peter. *Authority and the Sacred Aspects of the Christianisation of the Roman World*. Cambridge: Cambridge University Press, 1995.

The Cult of the Saints: Its Rise and Function in Latin Christianity. Chicago: University of Chicago Press, 1981.

Brubacker, Rogers. *Grounds for Difference*. Cambridge, Mass.: Harvard University Press, 2015.

Bukay, David (ed.). *Muhammad's Monsters: A Comprehensive Guide to Radical Islam for Western Audiences*. Green Forest, Ark.: Balfour Books, 2004.

Büssow, Johann. *Hamidian Palestine Politics and Society in the District of Jerusalem, 1872–1908*. Leiden: E. J. Brill, 2011.

Cacioppo, John T., G. R. Semin, and G. G. Berntson. Realism, instrumentalism, and scientific symbiosis: psychological theory as a search for truth and the discovery of solutions, *American Psychologist* 59 (2004): 214–223.

Caeiro, Alexandre. The power of European fatwas: the minority *fiqh* project and the making of an Islamic counterpublic, *International Journal of Middle East Studies* 42(3) (2010): 435–449.

Crecelius, Daniel. al-Azhar in the revolution, *Middle East Journal* 20 (1966): 31–49.

Dakwar, Jamil. The Islamic movement inside Israel: an interview with Shaykh Ra'id Salah, *Journal of Palestine Studies* 36(2) (2007): 66–76.

Dar al-Ifta' al-Masriyyah. *Fatawa dar al-ifta'* [Dar al-Ifta''s legal opinions]. Retrieved from www.dar-alifta.org/default.aspx?LangID&Home=1& LangID=2 [Arabic].

Darwish, 'Abd Allah Nimr. *Akhi al-'aqil ijlis bina nufakkir sa'a* [My rational brother: let us sit for a while and think]. A series of letters. Kufr Qasim: Mitba'at Kufr Qasim, 1994 [Arabic].

al-Hall al-muqtarah wa'l-salam al-manshud [The proposed resolution and the desired peace]. *al-Mithaq* (24 August 2001) [Arabic].

al-Islam huwa al-hall [Islam is the solution]. Unpublished booklet (2005) [Arabic].

Mashru'ana al-hadari bayna al-intilaq wa'l-inghilaq [Our civilizing project: between openness and seclusion]. Unpublished book. 1999 [Arabic].

al-Dawish, Ahmad. *Fatawa al-lajna al da'ima li'l-buhuth al-'ilmiyya wa'l-ifta' wa'l-da'wa wa'l-irshad* [The legal opinions of the Permanent Committee for Scientific Research and Legal Opinions], 23 vols. Riyadh: Maktabat al-'Ibikan, 2000 [Arabic].

Dawud, Ahmad Muhammad 'Ali. *al-Qararat al-isti'nafiyya fi'al ahwal al-shakhsiyya* [Extraordinary decisions on personal status]. 'Amman: Maktabat Dar al-Thaqafa li'l Nashr wa'l Tawzi', 1999 [Arabic].

de Jong, Frederick. The Sufi orders in nineteenth and twentieth century Palestine, *Studia Islamica* 58 (1983): 148–180.

Denzin, Norman, and Yvonna Lincoln (eds.). *Handbook of Qualitative Research*. 2nd edn. Thousand Oaks, Calif.: Sage Publications, 2000.

Dessouki, Ali E. Hillal. The Islamic resurgence: sources, dynamics, and implications. In Ali E. Hillal Dessouki (ed.), *Islamic Resurgence in the Arab World* (3–31). New York: Praeger, 1982.

Douglas, Mary. *Purity and Danger: An Analysis of the Concepts of Pollution and Taboo.* London: Routledge, 1966.

Dumper, Michael. *Islam and Israel: Muslim Religious Endowments and the Jewish State.* Washington, D.C.: Institute for Palestine Studies, 1994.

Eisenman, Robert. *Islamic Law in Palestine and Israel.* Leiden: E. J. Brill, 1978.

Eisenstadt, Shmuel. The resurgence of religious movements in processes of globalization: beyond end of history or clash of civilisations, *International Journal on Multicultural Societies* 2(1) (2000): 4–15.

Esposito, John L. (ed.). *The Oxford Dictionary of Islam.* Oxford: Oxford University Press, 2003.

Esposito, John, and Dalia Mugahid. *Who Speaks for Islam? What a Billion Muslims Really Think.* New York: Gallup Press, 2007.

Fishman, Shammai. *Fiqh al-Aqalliyyat: A Legal Theory for Muslim Minorities.* Washington, D.C: Hudson Institute, 2006.

Freas, Erik. Hajj Amin al-Husayni and the Haram al-Sharif: a pan-Islamic or Palestinian nationalist cause? *British Journal of Middle Eastern Studies* 39(1) (2012): 19–51.

Friedman, Richard B. On the concept of authority in political philosophy. In Richard Flathman (ed.), *Concepts in Social and Political Philosophy* (121–145). New York: Macmillan, 1973.

Ganem, Hunaida, Nohad 'Ali, and Ghadah Abu Jabir-Najm. *Attitudes towards the Status and Rights of Palestinian Women in Israel.* Nazareth: Women Against Violence, 2005.

Geaves, Ron, Markus Dressler, and Gritt Klinkhammer (eds.). *Sufis in Western Society: Global Networking and Locality.* London: Routledge, 2009.

Geertz, Clifford. "Ethnic conflict": three alternative terms, *Common Knowledge* 2(3): 54–65.

The Interpretation of Cultures. New York: Basic Books, 1973.

Islam Observed: Religious Development in Morocco and Indonesia. Chicago: University of Chicago Press, 1968.

Ghanem, As'ad. *The Palestinian Arab Minority in Israel, 1948–2000: A Political Study.* New York: State University of New York Press, 2001.

The perception by the Islamic Movement in Israel of the regional peace process. In Ilan Pappe (ed.), *Islam and Peace: Islamic Attitudes toward Peace in the Contemporary Arab World* (83–99). Givat Haviva: Institute for Peace Research, 1992 [Hebrew].

Gharrah, Ramsees (ed.). *Arab Society in Israel: Population, Society, Economy VII.* Jerusalem: Van Leer Institute, 2015 [Hebrew]. Retrieved from www.vanleer.org.il/sites/files

Hadawi, Sami. *Bitter Harvest: A Modern History of Palestine.* London: Scorpion Publishing, 1989.

Haddad, Yvonne. Islamists and the "problem of Israel": the 1967 awakening, *Middle East Journal* 46 (2) (1992): 266–285.

Haidar, Aziz, Henry Rosenfeld, and Reuven Kahane (eds.). *Arab Society in Israel: A Reader.* Jerusalem: Hebrew University of Jerusalem, 2003 [Hebrew].

al-Haj, Majid. The Arab internal refugees in Israel: the emergence of a minority within the minority, *Immigration and Minorities* 7(2) (1988): 149–165.

Higher education among the Arabs in Israel: formal policy between empowerment and control, *Journal of Higher Education Policy* 16 (2003): 351–368.

The sociopolitical structure of the Arabs in Israel: external vs. internal orientation. In John E. Hofman (ed.), *Arab–Jewish Relations in Israel: A Quest in Human Understanding* (92–123). Bristol, Ind.: Wyndham Hall, 1988.

Hallaq, Wael. *Authority, Continuity and Change in Islamic Law.* Cambridge: Cambridge University Press, 2001.

Shari'a: Theory, Practice, Transformation. Cambridge: Cambridge University Press, 2009.

Takhrij and the construction of juristic authority. In Bernard Weiss (ed.), *Studies in Islamic Legal Theory* (317–335). Leiden: E. J. Brill, 2002.

Harder, Hans. *Sufism and Saint Veneration in Contemporary Bangladesh: The Maijbhandaris of Chittagong.* London: Routledge, 2011.

Hashem, Mazen. Contemporary Islamic activism: the shades of praxis, *Sociology of Religion* 67(1) (2006): 23–41.

Hatina, Meir, and Muhammad al-Atawneh (eds.). *Muslims in the Jewish State.* Tel Aviv: Hakibbutz Hameuchad, forthcoming [Hebrew].

Hay'at 'Ulama' Filistin fi al-Kharij. *Fatawa hay'at 'ulama' filistin fi al-kharij* [Legal opinions of the Board of Religious Scholars in Palestine and abroad]. Retrieved from www.palscholars.com/index.php?option=com_content&view=section&layout=blog&id=11&Itemid=62.

Hourani, Muhammad. The *tawba*: repentance among Israeli Moslem Arabs, *Bamikhlalah* 2 (1991): 102–110 [Hebrew].

al-Hut, Bayan. *al-Qiyadat wa'l-mu'assasat al-siyasiyya fi filistin, 1917–1948* [The political leaders and institutions in Palestine, 1917–1948]. Beirut: Mu'assasat al-Dirasat al-Filistiniyya, 1986 [Arabic].

Ibn Bayyah, 'Abd Allah. *Sina'at al-fatwa wa-fiqh al-aqalliyyat* [The making of legal opinions and minority jurisprudence]. Jeddah/Beirut: Dar al-Minhaj, 2007 [Arabic].

Ibn Baz, Abdul-Aziz, and Salih Ibn Uthaymeen. *Muslim Minorities: Fatawa Regarding Muslims Living as Minorities.* Hounslow: Message of Islam, 1998.

Israel, Central Bureau of Statistics. *Statistical Abstract of Israel*, no. 61, 2010.

Israeli, Raphael. The impact of Islamic fundamentalism on the Arab–Israeli conflict, *Jerusalem Viewpoints* (Jerusalem Center for Public Affairs, 1988): 1–6.

Muslim Fundamentalism in Israel. London: Brassey's, 1993.

Muslim fundamentalists as social revolutionaries: the case of Israel, *Terrorism and Political Violence* 6(4) (1994): 462–475.

Jamal, Amal. The political ethos of Palestinian citizens of Israel: critical reading in the future vision documents, *Israeli Studies Forum* 23(2) (2008): 3–28.

al-Jaziri, 'Abd al-Rahman. *al-Fiqh 'ala al-madhahib al-arba'a* [Islamic jurisprudence according to the four orthodox schools]. Beirut: Dar al-Arqam, 1999 [Arabic].

Kaufman, Ilana. Escalation in the demands of the minority: the "future vision" documents of the Arab Palestinians in Israel, *State and Society* 7(1) (2010): 11–35 [Hebrew].

Kedar, Mordechai. Our children are in danger: education as viewed by the Islamic Movement in Israel. In Ami Ayalon and David J. Wasserstein (eds.), *Madrasa: Education, Religion and State in the Middle East: Studies in Honor of Michael Winter* (353–381). Tel Aviv: Tel Aviv University, 2004 [Hebrew].

Kemp, Adriana. From politics of location to politics of signification: the construction of political territory in Israel's first years, *Journal of Area Studies* 6(12) (1998): 74–96.

Kepel, Gilles. *Allah in the West: Islamic Movements in America and Europe.* Cambridge: Polity Press, 1997.

Klein, Claude. *Israel as a Nation-State and the Problem of the Arab Minority in Search of a Status.* Tel Aviv: International Center for Peace in the Middle East, 1987.

Krämer, Gunder, and Sabine Schmidtke (eds.). *Speaking for Islam: Religious Authorities in Muslim Societies.* Leiden: E. J. Brill, 2006.

Kramer, Martin. *Islam Assembled: The Advent of the Muslim Congresses.* New York: Columbia University Press, 1986.

Kupferschmidt, Uri M. *The Supreme Muslim Council: Islam under the British Mandate for Palestine.* Leiden: E. J. Brill, 1987.

Kurzman, Charles (ed.). *Liberal Islam: A Sourcebook.* New York: Oxford University Press, 1998.

Kushner, David. The district of Jerusalem in the eyes of three Ottoman governors at the end of the Hamidian period, *Middle Eastern Studies* 35(2) (1999): 61–82.

Lambton, Ann K. S. *State and Government in Medieval Islam: An Introduction to the Study of Islamic Political Theory.* Oxford: Oxford University Press, 1981.

Layish, Aharon. The adaptation of religious law to modern times in a strange ambiance: *Shari'a* in Israel, *Divre ha-Akademiyah ha-Le'umit ha-Yisre'elit le-Mada'im* 9(2) (2005): 13–51 [Hebrew].

The heritage of Ottoman rule in the Israeli legal system: the concept of *umma* and *millet.* In Peri J. Bearman, Wolfhart Heinrichs, and Bernard G. Weiss (eds.), *The Law Applied: Contextualizing the Islamic Shari'a* (128–149). London: I. B. Tauris, 2007.

Legal Documents from the Judean Desert: The Impact of the Shari'a on Bedouin Customary Law. Leiden/Boston: E. J. Brill, 2011.

Lewis, Bernard. *Islam and the West.* Oxford: Oxford University Press, 1993.

The Political Language of Islam. Chicago: University of Chicago Press, 1988.

Politics and war. In Joseph Schacht and C. E. Bosworth (eds.), *The Legacy of Islam* (156–209). Oxford: Clarendon Press, 1974.

Lewis, Philip. The Bradford Council for Mosques and the search for Muslim unity. In S. Vertovec and C. Peach (eds.), *Islam in Europe: The Politics of Religion and Community* (103–128). London: Macmillan, 1997.

Louër, Laurence. *To Be an Arab in Israel.* London: Hurst, 2007.

Lustick, Ian. *Arabs in the Jewish State: Israel's Control of a National Minority.* Austin: University of Texas Press, 1980.

Luz, Nimrod. The Islamic Movement and the seduction of sanctified landscapes: using sacred sites to conduct the struggle for the land. In Elie Rekhess and

Arik Rudnitzky (eds.), *Muslim Minorities in Non-Muslim Majority Countries: The Islamic Movement in Israel as a Test Case* (75–84). Tel Aviv: Moshe Dayan Center, 2013.

Mahmud, Khalid. The ethical behavior of the Sufi disciple with his sheikh in the Khalwati order. In *In the Footsteps of Sufism: History, Trends and Praxis: The First International Conference at al-Qasemi Academy* (Baqa al-Gharbiyya: al-Qasemi College, 2001), 23–24.

al-Majlis al-Islami li'l-Ifta'. *Fatawa al-Majlis al-Islami li'l-Ifta'* [The legal opinions of the Majlis al-Islami li'l-Ifta']. Umm al-Fahm: Mu'assasat al-Risala li'l Nashr wa'l I'lam, 2012 [Arabic].

Fatawa al-mar'a al-muslima [Legal opinions on the Muslim woman]. Umm al-Fahm: Mu'assasat al-Risala li'l-Nashr wa'l-I'lam, 2015 [Arabic].

al-Majlis al-'Urubbi li'l-Ifta' wa'l-Buhuth, *Qararat wa-fatawa al-majlis al-'urubbi li'l-ifta' wa'l-buhuth* [The decisions and legal opinions of the al-Majlis al-Aurubbi li'l-Ifta']. Cairo: Dar al-Tawjih wa'l-Nashr al-Islamiyya, 2002 [Arabic].

Malik, Ibrahim. *The Islamic Movement in Israel: Between Fundamentalism and Pragmatism*. Givat Haviva: Arabic Studies Institute, 1990 [Hebrew].

March, Andrew. Liberal citizenship and the search for an overlapping consensus: the case of Muslim minorities, *Philosophy and Public Affairs* 34(4) (2006): 373–421.

Sources of moral obligation to non-Muslims in the "jurisprudence of Muslim minorities" (*fiqh al-aqalliyyat*) discourse, *Islamic Law and Society* 16 (2009): 34–94.

Masud, Muhammad K. Islamic law and Muslim minorities, *ISIM Newsletter* 11 (2002).

Masud, Muhammad K., Brinkley Messick, and David S. Powers (eds.). *Islamic Legal Interpretation: Muftis and their Fatwas*. Cambridge, Mass.: Harvard University Press, 1996.

Mawdudi, Abu al-A'la. *The Islamic Law and Constitution*. Lahore: Islamic Publications, 1969.

Mayer, Thomas. *The Awakening of the Muslims in Israel*. Givat Haviva: Arabic Studies Institute, 1988 [Hebrew].

Islamic Resurgence among the Arabs in Israel. Givat Haviva: Arabic Studies Institute, 1986.

The "Muslim Youth" in Israel, *ha-Mizrah he-Hadash* 32 (1989): 10–21 [Hebrew].

Melucci, Alberto. The symbolic challenge of contemporary movements, *Social Research* 52 (1985): 790–816.

Mi'ari, Mahmoud. al-Haraka al-islamiyya fi Isra'il [The Islamic Movement in Israel], *Shu'un Filastiniya* 215–216 (1991): 3–15 [Arabic].

Moussalli, Ahmad. Hasan al-Turabi's Islamist discourse on democracy and shura, *International Journal of Middle East Studies* 30 (1994): 52–63.

Mudzhar, Muhammad Atho, Fatwas of the Council of Indonesian 'Ulama': A Study of Islamic Legal Thought in Indonesia, 1975–1988. Ph.D. thesis. Los Angeles: University of California, 1990.

Mustafa, Muhanad. Political participation of the Islamic Movement in Israel. In Elie Rekhess and Arik Rudnitzky (eds.), *Muslim Minorities in Non-Muslim*

Majority Countries: The Islamic Movement in Israel as a Test Case (95–113). Tel Aviv: Moshe Dayan Center, 2013.

al-Najjar, 'Abd al-Majid, *Ma'alat al-af'al wa-atharaha fi fiqh al-aqalliyyat* [Practical outcomes and their impact on *fiqh al-aqalliyyat*]. Paris: al-Majlis al-'Urubbi li'l-Ifta'wa'l-Buhuth, 2002 [Arabic].

Neuberger, Binyamin. The Arab minority in Israeli politics, 1948–1992: from marginality to influence, *Asian and African Studies* 27(1–2) (1993): 149–170.

Paz, Reuven. The Islamic Movement in Israel and the municipal elections of 1989, *Jerusalem Quarterly* 53 (1990): 3–26.

Peres, Yochanan. Modernization and nationalism in the identity of the Israeli Arabs, *Middle East Journal* 24(4) (1970): 479–492.

Peres, Yochanan, and N. Yuval-Davis. Some observations on the national identity of the Israeli Arabs, *Human Relations* 22(3) (1969): 219–233.

Polka, Sagi. The centrist stream in Egypt and its role in the public discourse surrounding the shaping of the country's cultural identity, *Middle Eastern Studies* 39 (2003): 39–64.

al-Qaradawi, Yusuf. *Fi fiqh al-aqalliyyat al-muslima* [On Muslim *fiqh al-aqalliyyat*]. Cairo: Dar al-Shuruq, 2007 [Arabic].

al-Ijtihad al-mu'asir bayna al-indibat wa'l-infirat [Contemporary *ijtihad* between discipline and dissolution]. Beirut: al-Maktab al-Islami, 1998 [Arabic].

Qutb, Sayyid. *Milestones*. New Delhi: Islamic Book Service, 2008.

Rabinowitz, Dan. Umm al-Fahm: dilemmas of change, *ha-Mizrah he-Hadash* 37 (1995): 169–179 [Hebrew].

Ramadan, Tariq. *Western Muslims and the Future of Islam*. Oxford: Oxford University Press, 2004.

Raudvere, Catharina, and Leif Stenberg (eds.). *Sufism Today: Heritage and Tradition in the Global Community*. London: I. B. Tauris, 2009.

Reiter, Yitzhak. *National Minority, Regional Majority: Palestinian Arabs versus Jews in Israel*. Syracuse: Syracuse University Press, 2009.

Qadis and the implementation of Islamic law in present-day Israel. In R. Gleave and E. Kermeli (eds.) *Islamic Law: Theory and Practice* (205–231). London: I. B. Tauris, 1997.

Rekhess, Elie Fundamentalist Islam among Israeli Arabs. In Kitty Cohen (ed.), *Perspectives in Israeli Pluralism* (34–44). New York: Israeli Colloquium, 1991.

The Islamic movement in Israel: the internal debate over representation in the Knesset, *Data and Analysis* 2 (Tel Aviv: Moshe Dayan Center, 1996): 1–5.

Islamization of Arab identity: the Islamic Movement, 1972–1996. In Elie Rekhess and Arik Rudnitzky (eds.), *Muslim Minorities in Non-Muslim Majority Countries: The Islamic Movement in Israel as a Test Case* (63–74). Tel Aviv: Moshe Dayan Center, 2013.

Israeli Arabs and the Arabs of the West Bank and Gaza: political affinity and national solidarity, *Asian and African Studies* 23(2–3) (1989): 119–154.

Political Islam in Israel and its connection to the Islamic Movement in the territories. In Elie Rekhess (ed.), *The Arabs in Israeli Politics: Dilemmas of Identity* (73–84). Tel Aviv: Tel Aviv University, 1998 [Hebrew].

The politicization of Israel's Arabs. In Alouph Hareven (ed.), *Every Sixth Israeli: Relations between the Jewish Majority and the Arab Minority in Israel* (135–142). Jerusalem: Van Leer Foundation, 1983.

Resurgent Islam in Israel, *Asian and African Studies* 27 (1–2) (1993): 189–206.

Rekhess, Elie (ed.). *The Arabs in Israeli Politics: Dilemmas of Identity.* Tel Aviv: Moshe Dayan Center, 1998.

Rekhess, Elie, and Rudnitzky, Arik (eds.). *Muslim Minorities in Non-Muslim Majority Countries: The Islamic Movement in Israel as a Test Case.* Tel Aviv: Moshe Dayan Center, 2013.

Rogan, Eugene. *Frontiers of the Late Ottoman Empire: Transjordan, 1850–1921.* Cambridge: Cambridge University Press, 1999.

Rosmer, Tilde. The Islamic movement in the Jewish state. In Khaled Hroub (ed.), *Political Islam: Context versus Ideology* (182–209). London: Saqi Books/London Middle East Institute, 2010.

Raising the green banner: Islamist student politics in Israel, *Journal of Palestine Studies* 45(1) (2015): 24–42.

Rouhana, Nadim. Accentuated identities in protracted conflicts: the collective identity of the Palestinian citizens in Israel, *Asian and African Studies* 27 (1993): 97–12.

Palestinian Citizens in an Ethnic Jewish State: Identities in Conflict. New Haven: Yale University Press, 1997.

Rouhana, Nadim, and As'ad Ghanem. The crisis of minorities in an ethnic state: the case of the Palestinian citizens in Israel, *International Journal of Middle East Studies* 30(3) (1998): 321–346.

Roy, Olivier. EuroIslam: The *jihad* within, *The National Interest* 71 (2003): 63–73.

The Failure of Political Islam. Cambridge, Mass.: Harvard University Press, 1994.

Rubin-Peled, Alisa. *Debating Islam in the Jewish State: The Development of Policy toward Islamic Institutions in Israel.* Albany: State University of New York Press, 2001.

Towards autonomy? The Islamist Movement's quest for control of Islamic institutions in Israel, *Middle East Journal* 55(3) (2001): 378–398.

Rudnitzky, Arik. *The Arab Minority in Israel and the "Jewish State" Discourse.* Jerusalem: Israel Democracy Institute, 2015 [Hebrew].

al-Salim, Farid. *Palestine and the Decline of the Ottoman Empire: Modernization and the Path to Palestinian Statehood.* London: I. B. Tauris, 2015.

Salla, Michael. Political Islam and the West: a new "cold war" or convergence? *Third World Quarterly* 18(4) (1997): 729–742.

Sayigh, Rosemary. *Palestinians: From Peasants to Revolutionaries.* London: Zed Press, 1979.

Sela, Avraham. Palestinian society and institutions during the Mandate: changes, lack of mobility and downfall. In Avi Bareli and Nahum Karlinsky (eds.), *Economy and Society in Mandatory Palestine, 1918–1948* (291–348). Beer-sheba: Merkaz le-Moreshet Ben-Guryon, 2003.

Semyonov, Moshe, Noah Lewin-Epstein, and Iris Braham. Changing labour force participation and occupational status: Arab women in the Israeli labour force, *Work, Employment and Society* 13(1) (1999): 117–131.

Shafir, Gershon, and Yoav Peled. *Being Israeli: The Dynamics of Multiple Citizenship*. Cambridge: Cambridge University Press, 2002.

Shahar, Ido. *Legal Pluralism in the Holy City: Competing Courts, Forum Shopping, and Institutional Dynamics in Jerusalem*. Farnham: Ashgate, 2015.

Shahin, Emad Eldin. *Political Ascent: Contemporary Islamic Movements in North Africa*. Boulder: Westview Press, 1997.

al-Shatibi, Abu Ishaq. *al-Muwafaqat fi usul al-ahkam* [Reconciliation of the fundamentals of Islamic law]. Cairo: Maktabat Muhammad ʿAli Sbih, 1969 [Arabic].

Shavit, Uriya. Should Muslims integrate into the West? *Middle East Quarterly* 17(4) (2007): 13–21.

al-Shawadifi, Safwat. *Fatawa hayʾat kibar al-ʿulamaʾ biʾl-mamlaka al-ʿarabiyya al-saʿudiyya* [Legal opinions of the Board of Senior ʿUlamaʾ in Saudi Arabia]. Cairo: Maktabat al-Sunna, 1991 [Arabic].

al-Shawkani, Muhammad. *Nayl al-awtar sharh muntaqa al-akhbar* [The attainment of the objectives]. Cairo: Dar al-Hadith, [1938] [Arabic].

Shepherd, Naomi. *Ploughing Sand: British Rule in Palestine, 1917–1948*. London: John Murray, 1999.

Sindawi, Khaled. The Shiite community in Israel: past and present. In Meir Hatina and Muhammad al-Atawneh (eds.), *Muslims in the Jewish State*. Tel Aviv: Hakibbutz Hameuchad, forthcoming [Hebrew].

Sivan, Emmanuel. The enclave culture. In Martin E. Marty and R. Scott Appleby (eds.), *Fundamentalisms Comprehended* (11–63). Chicago: University of Chicago Press, 1995.

Skovgaard-Petersen, Jakob. *Defining Islam for the Egyptian State: Muftis and Fatwas of the Dar al-Iftaʾ*. Leiden: E. J. Brill, 1997.

Smooha, Sammy. The Arab minority in Israel: radicalization or politicization? *Studies in Contemporary Jewry* 5 (1989): 1–21.

Are the Palestinian Arabs in Israel radicalizing? *Bitterlemons International* 24(2) (2004): 221–226.

The implication of transition to peace for Israeli society, *Annals of the American Academy of Political and Social Science* 555 (1988): 23–45.

Is Israel Western? In Eliezer Ben-Rafael and Yitzhak Sternberg (eds.), *Comparing Modernities: Pluralism versus Homogeneity: Essays in Homage to Shmuel N. Eisenstadt* (413–442). Leiden: Brill, 2005.

Jews and Arabs in Israel. Boulder and London: Westview Press, 1992.

Minority responses in a plural society: a typology of the Arabs in Israel, *Sociology and Social Research* 67(4) (1983): 436–456.

Still Playing by the Rules: Index of Arab-Jewish Relations in Israel, 2012: Findings and Conclusions. Haifa: University of Haifa/Israel Democracy Institute, 2013.

Smooha, Sammy, and Asʿad Ghanem. *Ethnic, Religious and Political Islam among the Arabs in Israel*. Haifa: University of Haifa, 1998.

Political Islam among the Arabs in Israel, in Theodor Hanf (ed.), *Dealing with Difference: Religion, Ethnicity and Politics – Comparing Cases and Concepts* (143–173). Baden-Baden: Nomos Verlagsgesellschaft, 1999.

Soffer, Arnon. Jewish and Islamic fundamentalism in Israel: reasons, processes and results, *Geographia Religionum* 13 (1989): 155–174.

al-Taji, Maha. Arab Local Authorities in Israel: Hamulas, Nationalism and Dilemmas of Social Change. Ph.D. thesis. Seattle: University of Washington, 2008.

Tal, Inbal. *Spreading the Movement's Message: Women's Activism in the Islamic Movement in Israel*. Tel Aviv: Moshe Dayan Center, 2015 [Hebrew].

Women's Activism in the Islamic Movement in Israel, 1983–2007: Influences, Characteristics and Implications. Ph.D. thesis. Haifa: Haifa University, 2011 [Hebrew].

Taylor, Charles. *Multiculturalism and the Politics of Recognition*. Princeton: Princeton University Press, 1992.

Tibi, Bassam. *Arab Nationalism: A Critical Enquiry*. New York: St. Martin's Press, 1990.

al-Tirmidhi, Muhammad b. ʿIssa. *Sunan al-Tirmidhi* [Completion]. Cairo: Matbaʿat Mustafa al-Babi al-Halabi, 1975–1978 [Arabic].

Tubulyak, Sulayman Muhammad. *al-Ahkam al-siyasiyya li'l-aqalliyyat al-muslima fi'l fiqh al-Islami* [Political provisions for Muslim minorities in Islamic jurisprudence]. Beirut: Dar al-Nafaʾis, 1997 [Arabic].

Tuck, Richard. Why is authority such a problem? In P. Laslett, W. Runciman, and Q. Skinner (eds.), *Philosophy, Politics and Society* (194–207). 4th series. Oxford: Blackwell, 1972.

Turner, Victor. *Ritual Process: Structure and Anti-Structure*. Piscataway, NJ: Transaction Publishers, 1995.

al-ʿUthaymin, ʿAbd Allah. *Ibn ʿAbd al-Wahhab: hayatuhu wa-fikruhu* [Ibn ʿAbd al-Wahhab: his life and thought]. Riyadh: Dar al-ʿUlum, 1987 [Arabic].

van Bruinessen, Martin, and Julia Day Howell (eds.), *Sufism and the "Modern" in Islam*. London: I. B. Tauris, 2007.

Voll, John. *Islam: Continuity and Change in the Modern World*. Boulder: Westview Press, 1982.

Wasserstein, Bernard. *The British in Palestine: The Mandatory Government and the Arab–Jewish Conflict, 1917–1929*. Oxford: Basil Blackwell, 1991.

Watt, Montgomery. *Islamic Political Thought: The Basic Concepts*. Edinburgh: Edinburgh University Press, 1968.

Waxman, Dov, and Ilan Peleg. Neither ethnocracy nor bi-nationalism: in search of the middle ground, *Israel Studies Forum* 23(2) (2008): 55–73.

Weismann, Itzchak. Sufi brotherhoods in Syria and Israel: a contemporary overview, *History of Religions* 43 (2004): 303–318.

Weiss, Bernard. Interpretation in Islamic law: the theory of *ijtihad, American Journal of Comparative Law* 26 (1978): 199–212.

The Search for God's Law: Islamic Jurisprudence in the Writings of Sayf al-Din al-Amidi. Salt Lake City: University of Utah Press, 1992.

Wuthnow, Robert. World order and religious movements. In A. Bergson (ed.), *Studies of the Modern World System* (57–75). New York: Academic Press, 1980.

Zahalka, Iyad. The development of Islamic law in Israel. In Meir Hatina and Muhammad al-Atawneh (eds.), *Muslims in the Jewish State* (Tel Aviv: Hakibbutz Hameuchad, forthcoming) [Hebrew].

The development of local Islamic jurisprudence in Israel, *Bayan* 1 (2014):
4–8.
al-Murshid fi al-qada al-shar'i [Guidance for the Islamic judiciary]. Tel Aviv:
Israel Bar Publishing House, 2008 [Arabic]
Zu'bi, 'Abd al-Rahman. The Khalawati Sufi Order in Palestine and Israel. MA
thesis. Haifa: Haifa University, 2003 [Hebrew].

Index